NARRATIVES
OF
ECSTASY

James Rolleston

NARRATIVES OF ECSTASY

ROMANTIC TEMPORALITY in MODERN GERMAN POETRY

Wayne State University Press   Detroit 1987

Library of Congress Cataloging-in-Publication Data

Rolleston, James, 1939–
    Narratives of ecstasy.

    Bibliography: p.
    Includes index.
    1. German poetry—19th century—History and criticism.
2. German poetry—20th century—History and criticism.
3. Romanticism—Germany.   4. Poetry.   I. Title.
PT547.R65   1987   831'.009'145   87-2020
ISBN 0–8143–1841–X

The following publishers have generously granted
permission to quote poems in full: Arche Verlag, Zürich,
for "Abschied" by Gottfried Benn; S. Fischer Verlag,
Frankfurt, for "Die Silbe Schmerz" by Paul Celan;
Suhrkamp Verlag, Frankfurt, for "Spur der Zukunft" by
Hans Magnus Enzensberger, "Im Frühling" by Jürgen
Becker, and "Nebenwirkung" by Karin Kiwus; Verlag
Klaus Wagenbach, Berlin, for "Harmlose Begegnung" and
"Lautlos" by Erich Fried; and Verlag Eremiten-Presse,
Düsseldorf, for "Epoche" by Christoph Meckel.

For Christopher and Victoria

CONTENTS

Contents

ACKNOWLEDGMENTS

The first draft of this study was written under a generous grant from the American Council of Learned Societies. Many people have helped me with advice and criticism at the various stages of its conception, notably Frank Borchardt, Peter Demetz, Jay Geller, Donna Hoffmeister, Wolfgang Leppmann, and Walter Sokel. Most important of all has been Stanley Corngold, whose detailed probing and exhortations to be both ambitious and lucid have amounted to the imperative: close reader, read thyself. If I have still not always succeeded in capturing what Novalis calls the "individual coloration of the universal," it is surely not the fault of these loyal friends. Loyalty, as well as the necessary serenity, has similarly marked the excellent secretarial work of Lisa Dellwo, Chris Michaelides, and Norma Dockery.

This is also the place to mention the indispensable, loving support of Rosalind Coleman, who has had to live with the book almost as long as I have.

9

INTRODUCTION

Romanticism and Narrative Poetics

This study of the modern German poetic tradition consists of close readings of fifteen texts, guided by an exploration of Romantic thinking about time, history, and the function of literature. The project rests on several premises, the most important of which is the claim that in the fragments of Novalis and Friedrich Schlegel is to be found an encyclopedia, a comprehensive language of possibilities for thinking and feeling in the modern age. This claim is to be distinguished from the accepted view of the Romantics as an intellectual ancestry, a set of motivic source books for later writers.

The title of a book documenting echoes and invocations of Romanticism in subsequent literature, *Das Nachleben der Romantik*,[1] suggests the distinction I want to establish. In this version of literary history, Romanticism has died yet enjoys an afterlife. My argument, however, is that Romanticism did not die, that its theoreticians ignited a single conflagration of the mind, which has both consumed and sustained human beings compelled to live within the parameters of the historical imagination. Poetry lives on the edge of that fire, forcing surface continuities to disintegrate, extremes of vision and destruction to meet. To the poet, as to the original Romantics, the fire involves no "other" world; it is the synchronized reality of a specific historical moment, perceived suddenly as a chaos—and as a text latent with hidden, fragmented, and potential meanings. Only through the energy of the chaotic moment do the hieroglyphs become legible, the meanings rescuable. From this double gesture a narrative poetics is born; the very act of rupturing everyday time requires the telling of a new story, a story that must link the entirety of the past to the entirety of the future. The moment of rupture cannot enter language, cannot be experienced, without a before and an after; yet the truth of history onto which it opens is not easily endured. The characteristic assault of modern German poetry is launched against the seductions of melancholy and controlled emotion, against the loss of its own truth.

Romanticism generated a metaphysical vocabulary that quickly passed into accepted usage, but lost much of its resonance in the process. For example, "tendency," as it is now used, hardly conveys what Friedrich Schlegel meant when he said that the French Revolution, Fichte's *Science of Knowledge* (*Wissenschaftslehre*), and Goethe's novel *Wilhelm Meister's Apprenticeship* were the greatest "Tendenzen" of the age. In the two areas this study is primarily concerned with, poetry and time, the Romantics sought to develop a flexible, "in-between" vocabulary that would set rusted intellectual machinery in motion, the kind of motion they saw everywhere in the political and scientific life of their time. Thus "Poesie," as they use it, is certainly a much broader concept than "lyric poetry"; yet it does foreground such elements as linguistic compression, momentary vision, and harmonious energy, which we associate with "the lyrical." And like the ancient biblical writers, the Romantics found it essential to deploy visual terms like "chaos" and "burning up" ("Verbrennen") in order to express the theoretical consequences of thinking historically. For the terminology for evoking the productive rhythms of the human collectivity, "history," was simply lacking. Individual creativity was describable, as was plain chronology; but the newly conceptualized presence of the past, the need to dissolve the lifelessly general into the potently particular, the sense that the successivity of events had little to do with their power source—all this called for a language tracking the breaks in time, rather than its illusory continuities.

The vocabulary of temporal breaks, central to Romantic thinking, has been familiarized through the tradition of the avant-garde.

12

But the avant-garde insistence on disruption as an end in itself, a call to permanent novelty, would have been anathema to the Romantics. The genealogical links established by Werner Vordtriede and Hugo Friedrich[2] between the Romantics and the French Symbolist avant-garde, although a valuable corrective to the passive image of Romanticism as mere repertoire, tell only part of the story. If the Romantics, particularly Novalis, wrote fragments in which they speculated on the emancipation of language from meaning, they also imagined new syntheses between the languages of poetry, science, music, religion, philosophy, dream, and everyday living. And this focus on multiple possibilities signifies neither inconsistency nor open-ended, nonbinding speculativeness. For the Romantics historicized, uprooted, every single category of knowledge and experience in order to establish the perspective of modernity. In this perspective the energized present moment opens onto the entirety of the past; but the resultant vision of sovereignty and intellectual coherence is in drastic tension with a sense of the present as exiled, unfree, provisional. Heuristically, the Romantics diagnosed this modern experience in terms of an "Absolute" imaginable and imagined as fullness—yet experienced only as withdrawn, indeed as precipitately receding, from the world. What are the implications of this absence? Is not the experience of absence necessarily also an experience of presence, however momentary? And does not any such experience carry with it the responsibility to "translate" (a favorite verb of the Romantics) visionary truth into the life of intelligible, usable narrative?

To suggest the ways in which such questioning conditions the parameters and available terminology of modern thought, I have assembled a composite "fragment" from Friedrich Schlegel:

> In the novel the religion of human beings, in poetry that of humanity. . . . Every person has all humanity, all history in himself; otherwise he could not become aware of history at all. The primary document, the monument are only aids to invention. . . . God produced the world in order to portray himself. . . . The individual is infinite, because its task is to portray the infinite. . . . In the highest perspective on humans there operates the concept, to which everything must be referred, the concept of culture (Bildung). . . . In Christianity God becomes human; in the new religion the human being is to become God through Bildung. . . .

13

God is a subjectivity that has raised itself to an infinitely higher power.[3]

There is much important work on Schlegel that sorts and classifies the specific resonances of the major terms in these sentences within the overall spectrum of his thought.[4] My purpose in juxtaposing such disparate utterances is, rather, to suggest how each conceptualizing act implies the next one quoted (or an assertion of comparable scope) in a chain of insights that delineates both the ground and the imaginative limits of the modern mental landscape.

The challenge of the lyric, Schlegel's texts tell us, is to compel meditation on the notion of humanity as such; to think about humanity is to think about change, relationships between past and future, inside and outside, as encoded in the word "Bildung." To attempt a definition of "Bildung" is to confront its implicitly open-ended quality, the impossibility, indeed undesirability, of placing limits on the potentiality of change. But to refuse limits is not to collapse into shapelessness but, on the contrary, to accept the challenge of what Schlegel calls "portraying the infinite," to crystallize every minute possibility suggested by the past into a newly imagined whole, in short to construct history. And to decide what constitutes history is to be impelled toward sketching an encyclopedia of mankind's various pasts, the self-inventions that have installed themselves and established historical priorities embodied in the theory and tradition of Christianity. But to move from encyclopedia to imaginative program, from contemplation to action, requires the spark, the intuitive and reckless heightening ("Potenzierung") generally called lyrical.

What can thus be articulated as a chain, an intellectual circle, is in practice conditioned by time at every point. To imagine an encyclopedia of historical possibilities is itself a process, an entry into time modifying the very possibilities being imagined. To make any kind of claim for a lyrical intuition is to provoke an interrogation of the past, a selection and immediate justification, however compressed, of the remembered elements that are to be reactivated.

We have arrived at the central category of my study: narrative. In order to render the experience of temporal rupture communicable, poets must reproduce it as narrative from a before to an after; but in order to root this narrative of uprooting in an intelligible discourse, the poem's details must incarnate the possibility of historical meaning which, though singular and specific, is always latent in the repertoire

14

of modern experience. To this meaning, to this larger story there can be no direct access, since the "continuities" of history are intelligible only as the sum of moments of rupture. Yet the dream of this ultimate story conditions the structuring of the lyric. The modern poem is produced by two narratives simultaneously in process. The first of these, which I call the contingent narrative, is the sequencing of the experiential details to constitute an unchallengeable textual event. "The poet worships chance," said Novalis in a fragment establishing a crucial distinction between the modern poem and its lyrical predecessors.[5] The authenticity of "chance" is indispensable to this poetics; the value that baroque and neoclassical theory placed on "representative" experience has become a recipe for failure. For in the modern perspective only the singular, unrepeatable moment can unlock the fullness of history. And the reason is not that "subjectivity" is itself now an absolute, but that only through the rupture of conventional time, the unprotected opening into "chaos," can a given experience encounter, appropriate, and assign meaning to the history that has produced it.

To think in these terms is to abandon forever the middle ground where cultivated balance, representative experience, is possible. And the modern poet cannot unthink this transformation of the world. Hence, the poem must speak its events as if they are happening unpredictably, one time only, their meaning as opaque as is the case with any event occurring suddenly in lived time. For it is only in such a sequencing, a narrative of contingency "as if" the events are unfolding outside the speaker's control, that what Novalis terms "the individual coloration of the universal" can be projected into language.

But of course the goal of poetry is to reintegrate the moment of rupture with a linguistic before and after, to produce a temporality in which the fullness of the past and the specificity of the contingent coalesce into a legible text. This is achieved by staging a second narrative simultaneously with the first and in radical tension with it, a narrative of interpretation. Again a simulacrum of coherent subjectivity is reconstituted in this language, as the speaker struggles to interpret the contingent sequence in its eruptive force. In a sense the interpretive narrative has priority: the reader "knows" that the persona who speaks in the first line has a theoretical continuity, as the poem's "maker," after the last line dies away. Through this persona's interpretation the events have been reorganized as viable language.

But in another sense the interpretive process is drowned in the

15

stream of contingency, which in this poetics has the unassailable privilege of chance ("Zufall"). The poem's speaker will conclude the text with an act of interpretation, a sealing in of the contingent narrative. But the logic of modern poetics insists that this interpretation *not* be read as final or binding. The interpretive narrative is an indispensable scaffolding, an unstable structuring enabling the translation of the moment of rupture into a readable text. But interpretation cannot ultimately contain or codify that moment: the poem's conclusion embodies the gathering of momentum by the contingent sequence, with which the interpretive narrative sometimes merges, from which at other times it seems alienated, uncomprehending. Disturbed by this instability, readers have perennially been tempted to anchor the poem outside itself, in the text of the poet's documented subjectivity. But the "outside" of the poem, in which it does indeed culminate, is not the author's life, which the interpretive narrative, a language of rupture, precisely transcends. The text's destination is history: not the passivity of history-as-becoming (the tautological context so ruthlessly castigated by Nietzsche),[6] but the performative imagining of historical change as sketched in Schlegel's fragments.

The poem's implicit invocation of history, the overflow of its contingent narrative into a text that cannot yet exist, certifies the presence of a third story weaving in and out of the first two: the historical narrative. The spontaneity of the contingent is never, in a modern poem, achieved through naive recounting. These texts are "encyclopedic" in that they are always aware of the sources of their tropes, both the traditions of poetry past and the current voguish gestures (for example, the earnest listening-to-nature staged half seriously, half ironically by Eichendorff, Mörike, and Droste-Hülshoff). The preeminence of the concept of "Bildung" in Romantic poetics derives from its power to anchor the moment of rupture. "Bildung" designates the achievement of the lyrical moment, its installation into culture. It suggests the insistent presence of the cultural repertoire in any contingent narrative. And, finally, it points to the "shaping" ("bilden") activity of the critical consciousness as it strives to ironize and dissolve the sequences of past historical narration; the process of rupture conditions each move in the interpretive series, since the production of history necessarily pulverizes the continuities of "history."

What are the criteria for deciding which poems best achieve this translation of the contingent into history? The hermeneutic circle is inescapable here; if the poem's "outside," the goal of its interpretive

16

sequence, is the synthesis of its two overt narratives through intensification ("Potenzierung") as singular history, then the reader's critical presence is implicit in the solitary scenarios characteristic of modern poems. The historical narrative can be articulated only by the reader-critic; indispensable to the individual poem, this "divinatory criticism" ("divinatorische Kritik," in Schlegel's phrase) necessarily involves the whole weave of existing poems, the encyclopedia that is to be remobilized as history. But in crafting such a synthesis, the critic is offering only a potential fulfillment of the text's own narrative ambition. For the installation of criticism and the possibility of history within the poem ensures that the textual narratives remain open-ended, even when, as in Keller's "Still Moment," a concluding "moral" is drawn. To juxtapose sentences from Schlegel once again: "Every work of art, indeed every poem, is only an attempt at synthesizing consciousness. . . . Poetry is an infinite rhetoric and a logical spiritual music."[7]

My aim here is to project a single historical narrative through the poems selected, with the understanding that the very act of selection is the first step of the narration. My critical method is to match, to reenact as precisely as possible, the three narrative processes already functioning within the text itself. The critical reenactment of the contingent narrative is close reading as such, a careful mapping of how the particular sequencing of events coalesces into a temporal paradigm. The interpretive narrative, the persona's analytical presence, finds its critical equivalent in the correlation of a given text with others closely allied in tone, both by the same poet and by contemporaries. This is a quest, not for conventions or standard postures, but rather for the historical moment as it speaks through, is spoken by, multiple voices.

[margin note: Author's reenactment of the process in his book]

And finally, the articulation of the historical narrative, to which the book as a whole lays claim, is shaped by the interplay between these poems and the encyclopedia of modernity sketched in the fragments of Novalis and Friedrich Schlegel. This critical weaving is a movement both backward and forward. My hypothesis is that these fragments potentially voice all the subsequent moments of the modern historical narrative, but the emphasis is on the word "potentially." The poems actualize a thought that could not become fully resonant without them. They delve into the Romantic encyclopedia and touch its fragments into life, through the double contact with the poems' own historical horizons and with the imagining of historical change in which their narratives culminate.

17

These fragments are themselves definable as moments in a ceaseless struggle to write the meta-narrative of modern temporal possibilities. For in the decade after the French Revolution every kind of time-structure could be used to organize experience, from the momentum of revolution itself to magical royalism, from systematic philology to Bohemian wandering. The word "history" expresses rather than shapes this multiplicity. Hence the Absolute, indispensable to Romantic thinking, is drawn out of its theological otherness, its stasis, and interpreted as an image of history fulfilled, a "regulative idea" without which humanity cannot master its new vision of history proliferating. As Manfred Frank shows in his exhaustive study *Das Problem "Zeit" in der deutschen Romantik,*[8] the initial provocation, for both Friedrich Schlegel and Novalis, was the problematic absence in Johann Gottlieb Fichte's *Science of Knowledge* (*Wissenschaftslehre*, 1794) of a satisfactory connection between the absolute Self (outside time) and the continuously temporal self, projecting the world inside time.[9]

Once all temporal models, the religious fullness of the Absolute as well as the multiplying intellectual and political versions of history, are seen to be inseparable from the individual moments of rupture which give access to them, then temporality as such has to be reconceptualized. For the Absolute, as the heuristic structure of temporal yearning, is produced by the acts of revolt, the refusals of limits that characterize modern experience as such; in this perspective time is not an emptiness to be offset by heavenly fullness, but neither is it a serene succession of equal moments. Rather, it imposes on the singular individual a struggle to synthesize three "ecstasies" ("Ekstasen"), three totalizations of time—past, present, and future—which are articulated quasi-spatially, defined through separation.

The initial act in this struggle, the act that enables poetic speaking, is the disruption of the illusion that life is placidly continuous. This illusion is not just an epistemological mistake; it is deathliness, the suffocation of "dead presentness" ("tote Gegenwart," in Schlegel's phrase), the tightly textured surface that masks the "chaos" into which consciousness must plunge. Only in chaos does the relationship between the beginning and end of time, the totalities of past and future, become intelligible; indeed the relationship imposes itself absolutely, for it is the "truth" linking individual subjectivity to the ground of being. Yet it is a truth devoid of empirical use value, an "order" glimpsed only from the heart of disorder. In a sense no "progress" beyond this moment of disruption is possible, even though it opens onto every

18

imaginable transformation. In the moment of chaos/fullness everything changes—but only for the moment. The three poetic narratives
weave the discovering glimpse into the countertexture of loss.

For the poets discussed in my first chapter—Eichendorff,
Mörike, and Droste-Hülshoff—this storytelling is intrinsic and explicit: the quadrilateral of before and after, self and world, is organized around an identifiable moment of rupture and near collapse. The
poems maintain a precarious momentum, which establishes its own
role as a relational instrument between self and world: this relationality underpins a culture of "Bildung," a vision of identity between personal and historical time zones.

In the texts of the second chapter the narration is more systematic, the temporal quest more urgent; yet a decisive shift has taken place,
the shift toward the privileged moment as an end in itself. It is no paradox that Storm, Keller, and Meyer are very concerned with their reader-
ship, with self-confirming definitions of the lyrical; for to structure all interpretation around the intimate narrative of contingency, to imagine
history as a mosaic of ineffable yet discrete glimpses—such a project presupposes a set of communicative conventions, an audience schooled in
this ecstatic language.

This poetry is linked by dialectical reversal to the Expressionist vision. The language for communicating privileged moments sickens,
wears down, becomes culturally unavailable. Yet its failure opens no
way back to a viable historical narrative: the stagnation of history
merely becomes visible in horrifying intimacy. The Expressionists confront images of the world that mirror each other precisely: either the
rupturing of the present is continuous, the struggle for privileged vision yielding its own nightmares; or all rupture has become impossible, all private experience irrelevant, all poetic speaking a matter of
grotesquerie and satire. Theirs is a paralyzed apocalypse. Either their
narrations stay trapped in the concrete, reiterating visual intensities until they become hallucinatory; or they weave multiple myths into a
story that tells only of disintegration. The suddenly spatial vision of
temporality as a completed entity, the omnipresence of a sickened absolute stifles all possibilities of contingent narrative.

The shift from this style to that of the poets in my fourth chapter
is above all a shift in the status of language. Expressionism is already a
poetry of completion, a repertoire of modern possibilities and impossibilities. But it is also a radically vulnerable poetry, speaking incessantly
of the grotesque congealing of privileged moments into deathly pres-

ent. In the subsequent "high modernist" style, however, language produces both momentary intensities and allegories of history from within its own folds. These texts prowl around the abysses of modern temporal collapse protected, as it were, by the invisible cloak of linguistic self-confidence. Benn's theme is the aridity of nominally individual living, and Celan recapitulates the stagnation of history; but the shape of the interpretive narrative is similar, postulating a sudden release from historical patterning into words that are simultaneously exhilarating, abstruse, and somehow provisional, even contingent. This aesthetic is able to incorporate political and social concreteness on the same terms as the most arcane alchemical learning.

Because of this expansiveness the contemporary writers of my final chapter are nourished dialectically by their predecessors. The new style is one of contraction and renewed vulnerability, stripped of modernism's protective cloak. But its concreteness, its political aggressiveness, is both practiced and oblique, its version of history emancipated from the obsessive oscillation between stagnation and apocalypse. Today's poets renew the Romantic image of the deathly present in a most literal sense: the contemporary consumer machine is undead rather than dead, a languid yet ferocious processing of experience that cancels the authenticity of all distinctions, all moments, all images of history. These poems become quests for the micromovements of marginalized contingency, suspicious inspections of the concrete, refusals of expansive language, probings for that weak point in the machinery that might permit a prizing open of inauthentic experience, a provocation once again of authentic rupture.

This book tells a particular story of modern German poetry, not the whole story. Both the method of close reading and the specific selection of texts are called into existence by this story, the struggle for a narrative poetics, and would not necessarily be appropriate for other versions of modern literary history (e.g., studies of motifs, of the relations between poetic and other kinds of language, or of the social attitudes encoded in poetry). But to project a history of ecstatic narratives is simply to carry forward the poems' own interpretive enterprise. The story told here sets familiar and less familiar texts in often unexpected conversations with each other. Moreover, I would argue that major poets such as Heine, Brecht, and Eich, although not discussed in detail here, work within the narrative poetics of their historical moment, enriching its productive power as they press against its limits. Thus, Heine's irony is always fueled by an imperative of

"Bildung," which never quite becomes lifeless for him; and Brecht's political discourse is imbued with the "modernist" vision of a symbiosis between experimental yet self-referential texts and quasi-utopian restructuring of social time—a vision that complicates his reception by a younger generation lacking his confidence in language. And for this generation it is this very slippage in the viability of the narrative imagination that imposes their agenda. A mocking caricature of history both licenses and contaminates an immense repertoire of temporal myth making. No longer intelligibly linear, history is a machine producing endless, nonbinding interpretive texts—and pulverizing the very conception of "Zufall," of binding singularity. In this apparently post-post-Romantic universe contemporary poets have reached back again into the Romantic encyclopedia and resolutely set about reimagining the contingent.

CHAPTER ONE

"Bildung" and the Possibility of History: Eichendorff, Mörike, Droste-Hülshoff

The importance of "Bildung" as an ecstatic narrative structure for both the Romantics and the generation succeeding them cannot be overestimated. Manfred Frank evokes the many dimensions of the term in Friedrich Schlegel's vocabulary:

> "Bildung" is undoubtedly a central concept of his thinking. "Bildung," Schlegel notes, "is antithetical synthesis and totalization to the point of irony." As the "approximation to God's image" it is "the highest good for this life and for the other," namely the methodical totalizing of all indifferent particularities; a distinction it shares with irony. Bildung is the purpose of life, whose striving becomes meaningful solely through directedness toward the infinite. . . . Bildung is at the same time applied historiography. . . . In the concept of Bildung history is revealed as a failed unification with God.[1]

"Bildung" shapes human time by linking momentary ecstasies both to each other and to the entirety of history as it is glimpsed in the instant

23

of rupture. Yet such shaping knows its own failure, is drenched with irony. The synthesis of consciousness and time is neither harmonious nor organic in the Goethean sense. Precisely because the historical macrocosm can only be intuited through rupture and radical discontinuity, the aspiration of the productive self toward the stabilizing image of "Bildung" must undercut itself. The poems to be discussed in this chapter embody this critical moment precisely. In the very act of translating a sensitive self-projection into a continuous temporality, the poetic persona commits hubris. The interpretive recovery which the texts achieve, their authentic moment of "Bildung," is predicated on radical loss of control, involuntary chaos.

"Bildung" is thus both more and less than translations such as "development" or "education" suggest: it is more, in that the self embarked on an ecstatic narrative cannot accept the language of half-measures involving stages or balance, but must always struggle for direct access to the coherence of history through the demolition of illusory continuities. And "Bildung" is also less than "development" in that such Promethean strivings are certain to fail, since the linkage between history's beginning and end is always already completed; the empirical temporality in which we are immersed can never be assigned teleological meaning. To live the moment fully is to be impelled toward rupture.

We are accustomed to thinking of the Romantics as launching modernity through the double "discovery" of self and history—which is indeed the case. But the paradox is that these powerful notions are defined from the outset as lacking viability, a lack inherent in the very intellectual process that gave birth to them. The complexities of this moment of birth are present, like echoes from the creation of the universe, in all subsequent attempts to imagine temporal coherence. And they are of controlling importance, if often consciously repressed, in the major texts of the early nineteenth century. Thus Eichendorff, in his 1846 study of Romanticism, calls the movement "a magnificent rocket . . . which, aloft, disintegrated without trace into a thousand colorful stars."[2] The image of the rocket could hardly be more appropriate. The ideas of Romanticism exist in a state of momentum, repeatedly actualizing their own claims to validity through acts of linguistic intensification. Yet the adverbial phrase "without trace" expresses an impossible claim by Eichendorff to distance from this source. For "traces" are everywhere in the post-Romantic landscape, magnetic fragments drawing language into temporal projects, like Hegel's,[3] which will somehow include all the particularities of social experience.

Yet the totalizing claims of these projects are ultimately destabilizing. The more "history" neglects the rupturing detail, rising toward a "higher" zone of continuity, the more the actual production of history stagnates. Post-Romantic poems disrupt this sameness, open their language to collapse, in order to rescue the dream of "Bildung" from its seemingly inevitable exhaustion. These texts realize fully Novalis's program of "worshipping chance": the details of experience gain their threatening authenticity through the very process of being magnetized into the poem's own continuum.

Although "Bildung" is the key structuring concept of this metaphysics, and although Goethe's *Wilhelm Meisters Lehrjahre* is the text authorizing its conceptualization, there is nothing steadying or organic about Romantic definitions of the term. To be sure, Friedrich Schlegel describes it at one point as "development of autonomy."[4] But the intensely philological consciousness of the Romantics puts all such abstractions in question, not by sceptical reduction but by the very fertility of their speculations. "Autonomy" (literally self-standing) is thus circular: what is this "self" and where is it to "stand"? Despite the organic overtones of "development" (literally unfolding), Friedrich Schlegel's definitions of "Bildung" suggest that such "unfolding" is restlessly disruptive, the opposite of gradual, almost a decentering. Even as the self projects its own continuity as "Bildung," the energy of its irony drives it to consume such self-projections; and indeed Schlegel speaks of the "mystical intention of self-destruction in Bildung."[5]

The basis of this rhythm of violence, this impossibility of development in the conventional sense, is that the goals yearned for every day are by definition other than the human achievements actually certified by history; the dynamism and striving of human existence is only intelligible against a background of inaccessible stasis: "What is right already exists and does not need to be realized. . . . Bildung is in one perspective completely present, unmoving."[6] With this last sentence Schlegel seems to distance "Bildung" as far as possible from "development of autonomy," yet he is only altering perspective, using the Janus-faced concept of "Bildung" to link the individual's sense of incessant subjective change ("development") to the a priori stasis of the historical whole. "Bildung" is a time zone adequate to the new suspension of all fixities, the dissolution of boundaries between inside and outside, self and world.

Schlegel's strategy, particularly in the fragments, is to redefine self and world simultaneously, to apply the categories of the one to the other. Thus it is an illusion to insist on the uniqueness of the individual: "Tone, coloration, life, individuality are characteristic only of mythology, physics, history."[7] But conversely, the world we see "outside" ourselves only seems to be placid and unchanging; in fact it is subject to the same laws of intense and drastic change, of yearning and incompletion, which we sense within ourselves: "The thesis that the world is incomplete derives from the thesis that the world is an individual; space and time are the first individuals, produced organically."[8]

The disruption of the inside-outside distinction permits Schlegel to use categories such as "organic" again, albeit heuristically, without the Goethean analogy between human life and natural rhythms. Such an analogy rests on the obsolete (for Schlegel) assumption that subject and object coexist within their own stable spheres of activity.

But the demolition of Goethe's morphological assumptions does not lead to chaos—or rather, the Romantics accept and coopt the notion of chaos, by rendering it philosophically essential. Schlegel is in quest of laws for organizing the new pluralism; and "Bildung" is the word he uses to describe this quest, a quest that is both open-ended (the entire empirical world is to be retheorized) and self-limiting (the empirical cannot be transcended): "Bildung is the striving for a law and the law of striving."[9] Schlegel uses "Bildung" to evoke a process of endlessly experimental construction; unlike the Fichtean "fantasy," "Bildung" claims no ontological priority, merely a refusal of all preassigned categories: "The essence of Bildung consists of making something into nature (why not also into the world?) and at the same time into a human entity. Bildung consists in the relationality between nature and humanity. This concept also has the greatest affinity with God."[10] An "affinity with God" by no means implies that "Bildung" opens the way to some permanent higher realm. God certainly denotes the absolute, but it is an absolute accessible only in historically circumscribed glimpses yielded by ceaseless imaginative pressure against the limits of the empirical.

Criticism, irony, "Bildung": all these concepts signify the demolition of continuities, including those produced by one's own imaginative projects. For empirical sequences simply bear no relation to the story of history. Only through the isolation and intensely skeptical interpretation of "unmotivated" contingent events is an approximation of that story even conceivable. "Striving for a law": this "law" is neither something given, to be uncovered, nor a mystical vehicle of escape from the empirical. It is the law of discourse, the structuring of the

26

world both produced and reproduced, established and canceled, by human narrative projects. Such projects necessarily disrupt, hence "transcend" the empirical, but transcendence is strategically valid only if it is fueled, not by vague longings, but by an act of totalization, an allegorization within a contingent narrative of the entire human story: "Constitution of humanity as a counterweight against empiricism and economic reasoning, precisely because it is these modes of thinking that perpetually dismember humanity."[11] The abstraction "humanity," like every other dream generated by acts of temporal rupture long past, is never reducible to a quality, to something possessed. Or rather, it has become legible in the text of history as a whole, history potentially synonymous with "Bildung." Schlegel cautiously sketches a model of history that is made, not given: "Humanity must be constituted; for its very essence lies in such structuring. Thus the notion of reason must make progress, otherwise it is not reason."[12] It is typical of the care with which Schlegel deploys his speculative categories that the inherited ideas of humanity and progress are readmitted and reconceptualized: no allegory of the whole can exclude them. It is the human imaginative powers themselves that require both a describable totality ("history") and the conviction that specific actions or insights stand in a direct relationship to that totality. To narrate a series of contingencies is to invoke these assumptions—but simultaneously to put them in question, to force them into the "chaos" that drains such terms of all conventional meaning. Narration does not reproduce the empirical, it confronts it through temporal disruption and restaging— and the resultant pointing of every detail toward a beginning and an end. Schlegel's term for this narrative act is "charakterisieren": "To 'characterize' something is clearly both a critical and a prophetic undertaking, and the only one adequate to the approximation of the 'universe.' "[13] With the word "universe" ("Universum") we have reached the key concept through which the whole process of "Bildung" becomes tangible, quantifiable. For Schlegel uses "Universum" as the image for the complex set of relations between self, society, nature, and history projected as meaningful in a given time and place; far from being a mere reflection of a given society's collective viewpoint, the immanent universe is produced, constituted by the ceaseless human thrusting against the limits of experience, which are established as well as dismantled by the imagination. The "universe" is always shifting, not in a random flux but through a "progressive" building and subverting of imaginative structures. A universe may define decades, even centuries, of conventional time, while amounting to a mere instance in the story of time as an entirety: "The universe is perhaps only a historical concept, which embraces world, humanity, reason, nature."[14]

Once Schlegel's logic permits him to articulate the "Universum" as a totalization subject to describable change, hence accessible to narrative projects, the conception of "Bildung," which integrates the various temporalities of self, society, and nature, is greatly strengthened. For the philosophical landscape that contained only the striving imagination and withdrawn absolute is changed: the "universe" is a mediating concept, linking one moment of striving to the next, magnetizing the imagination's acts of disruption into a "higher" continuity. The "universe" as "historical concept" justifies the activity of writing history, the dream of approximating microcosm to macrocosm. In effect the "universe" is a "supreme fiction," to borrow Wallace Stevens' phrase; it is a purely provisional structure of coherence between the elements mentioned by Schlegel in his definitional notation: the time of public events ("world"), of the rational consciousness of any given individual life ("reason"), of natural sequences ("nature"), and of collective dreams ("humanity").

The ceaseless human projection of the "universe" gradually etches the outline of a definable "object," which Schlegel calls the "epoch," and enables the individual imagination to articulate the limits of its world even as it struggles to breach them: "The epoch is the universe-as-object, both inciting to change and assigning limits—the true universe is internal."[15] Clearly the "universe" is both result and condition of "Bildung" defined as "striving for a law"; and this "Bildung" is possible because of its own inherited energy, the accumulated projections of earlier and contemporary strivings, which at a given moment constitute the "law"-giving universe. And ultimately, Schlegel implies, such laws are overcome; the universe-as-object is canceled not by destruction, but by gradual yet decisive shifts in the perceived relations between its elements. The process is that of generation by mirrors, the "infinite series of mirrors" of the programmatic *Athenäumsfragment*.[16] And the distinction between the philosophical and the aesthetic imagination necessarily collapses. Philosophy cannot but acknowledge its createdness, while poetry cannot hold back from the task of articulating the whole: "The highest godlike poetry must also be a portrayal of the universe; this, then, is no longer either poetry or philosophy but both at once."[17]

The historical ambition for poetry as "portrayal of the universe" suggests a definition of "portrayal" remote from its normal spatial connotations. The totality of the "universe" exists strictly in time; its "portrayal" is therefore the imagination's seizure of history in its momentary self-manifestation. The projects of individual subjects, even of whole schools of thought, are necessarily flawed in their claims to totality, but they accumulate through the historical process of reflection and criticism. The initial lack, the absence of the longed-for totality, can never be transcended, but it can be infinitely intensified ("potenziert"), so that the very failure of striving, the shape of ironic withdrawal, receives an even more ironic affirmation as the shape of the "epoch" itself.

Our difficulty with the term "epoch" arises from the common misunderstanding of it as a vaguely determining force, something in the air that prescribes behavior, like fashion. For Schlegel, however, it is not an impersonal given but a collective imaginative creation, an aesthetic-philosophical enterprise: "the universe as object." And it can come into existence only through an initial act of human revolt against a merely passive destiny, namely the uncompromising rejection of "the present," understood as an inert sequence of neutral time units. Time in the guise of an infinitely divisible, calculable present (digital time is today's version) denies the original encoding of temporality as a central expression of human longing for wholeness. If time is released from theological bondage only to become empty, sequential presentness, then the human mind has generated a mere mirage in a desert. For the Romantics temporality is produced by conscious disruption of the illusory present into the ecstasies of past and future, which are latent (repressed) within it. "Total presentness would be death," says Schlegel.[18] And Novalis characterizes his own program as "Annihilation of the now."[19]

Friedrich Schlegel and Novalis are in explicit agreement about the need for radical rupture of "continuous" present time. But a difference of emphasis is detectable in their phrasing: for Schlegel presentness is a sterile trap, to be opened outward by the critical imagination; for Novalis it is an illusion to be "annihilated." And this difference of emphasis is symptomatic of a vivid polar tension between the two men's time theories, a tension that has a decisive impact on the poetics of the entire modern period. Their views are close to coinciding concerning the initial act of rupture, and the same is true when they speak of time's teleology, the paradox that its thrust is toward its own already completed state within the entirety of history. Schlegel writes:

29

"Only in the whole is the real contained; there must therefore be a moment when the truth of the whole becomes visible, even if one has arrived at the whole through assembling the various parts."[20] And a comparable passage in Novalis reads: "Only the whole is real. Only that
thing would be absolutely real which would not return to being a component part. The whole quivers in stasis—like the people in a game
who sit down without chairs, the one on the next person's knee, in a
shifting circle."[21]

Schlegel's version of the whole is imagined through induction: it
remains other, but only theoretically so, in that a moment of time is
also imaginable in which the totality of the real could be reassembled
and synthesized. The word "contained" is significant: there is no difference in texture between experience in the world and reality "contained
within" the whole; but the relationship between the parts and the
whole can never be stablized within ordinary experience, for that relationship is produced by ceaseless destroying, propelling into "chaos,"
as well as by structuring. Schlegel's whole is both unitary and pluralis-
tic, a refusal of mere particularity yet also an open vessel that "contains" the accumulated fruits of human striving.

Novalis, on the other hand, speaks not of containing, but only of
"being." The otherness of history conditions all his thinking. It is not
that there is *no* relationship between the whole and the empirical, but
that any such relationship involves a transformation in kind. The
"thing" that might enter the reality of the whole would lose the possibility of reentering the empirical, of becoming again a "component
part"; in other words, it would cease to be a thing. Wholeness, temporal completion, is identical with the world—but a world in which particularity is abolished, in which all entities, human and natural, are in-
tertwined in a quivering yet stable unity. This means that all human
projects, indeed the intentional self as such, are significant, not in themselves but only insofar as they make possible the unmediated glimpses
of history, that a transformed texture provides.

Schlegel's key words, as we have seen, are "Bildung" and
"Universum." The thrust of the imagination and the critical consciousness produce a residue that gives meaning to conventional, horizontal
time in its narrative compression as history. Sequential time must be
disrupted but can regain meaning dialectically, as "the epoch";
Schlegel is able to use the word "progress." For Novalis, by contrast,
the central terms are "spirit" ("Geist") and "perfection" ("Vollkom-
menheit"); immanent in history as a whole, these qualities enter the

30

world only through mysterious simultaneities, symbolic collapses of horizontal time. The successivity of time is the very condition of humanness; Manfred Frank shows convincingly that Novalis had no use for any style of thinking that implied timelessness could be realized. The "golden age" is strictly a regulative concept, an imaginative strategy.[22] And the impossibility of transcending time means that our empirical selves are permanently trapped within the sterile present. Each successive moment plunges to extinction in a vortex, and the only imaginable progress is a progress of consciousness, a graduate purification of the empirical self into its role as vehicle of history.

Paradoxically, however, Novalis's clear dissociation between human intentionality and the strictly contingent unfolding of the whole has far from restrictive results. Mysticism is domesticated as the possibilities of heightened perception proliferate. Subtle changes in the macrocosm become always and everywhere imaginable:

> When speaking of fact or action one normally thinks of something occurring or having occurred in time. The fact we are speaking of here, however, must simply be thought of as purely spiritual, not isolated yet also not in a temporal chain—as a moment, so to speak, that embraces the eternal universe, includes it within itself, wherein we live, move, and have our being: an infinite fact that occurs in every moment as an entirety, a creative principle forever identically at work, manifest as subjectivity.[23]

Novalis's temporal vision is insistently vertical ("mystical" is an entirely appropriate adjective, as is "magical"); every dimension of the whole is always potentially present in any given moment, and thus any significant change in consciousness changes the remote yet immanent unfolding of history. The process of purification leading to such change means that there is no direct relation, such as Schlegel's critical consciousness maintains, between intentional act and epochal result. But the "apprenticeships" that dominate Novalis's fictions suggest that purification can be initiated within the intentional mind, through study and self-abnegation; indeed that such a mind, ultimately purified, could conceivably write the "history of nature." If the particularities of the empirical are viewed as filled with the possibility of a "higher" existence, then all the critical terminology, the vocabulary of art, science, and history, becomes usable on a heuristic basis. For these energies of consciousness dislocate presentness and rearticulate human and natural temporality as a single, potentially legible text. They provoke a momentary fusion with the spiritual world as the free individual transcends his or her own projects, overcomes the empirical self as such, and enables a provisional narration, guaranteed by the moment's authenticity, of the "Bildung" of the whole:

> The nobility of the self consists in free transcendence of itself—consequently the self can never, in a certain sense, be absolutely transcendent, for otherwise its effectiveness, its pleasure, its achievement, in short the self as such, would cease to be. Virtue is a posture of ever-intensifying delight, a feeling of power, independence from the incidental.[24]

This freedom from randomness, this focusing of experience, is simultaneously a delight in detail in a different sense, an awareness that the freedom of self and the perfection of "Geist" can blend at any time in any place. "The poet worships chance," says Novalis,[25] and his thinking insists on a continuous interaction, open to all "magical" possibilities, between the infinite particularity of the world's details, and the strict homogeneity, the oneness of history: "The more a poem is personal, local, time-bound, and idiosyncratic, the closer it stands to the center of poetry."[26] There is no accumulation, no temporal collectivity of human achievement like Schlegel's "epoch." Rather, history must be seen as centrifugal, a rushing away without any residue except the ashes of human events, purified moments resonating as music of the temporal spheres: "The process of history is a burning up. Mathematical nature consumes infinite nature."[27] The destiny of the empirical is certainly terrifying, devoid of hope or meaning. Yet Novalis's fiction is populated by characters who accept this destiny, who have learned to devote their entire energies to study and critical reflection, to the quest for the temporality of history, latent yet disguised by the almost impenetrable code of nature. Decoding is possible only through rhythmic alignment of the observer's subjective time with that of the world; such a symbiosis opens onto the ultimate relationality of combining and dissolving: "The world is a thought under constraint. When something is consolidated, thoughts become free. When something dissolves, thoughts become bound."[28] As these processes are repeated, the macrocosmic change is literally measurable: "Ultimately there will be no more nature. Gradually it will be transformed into a spiritual world."[29]

32

Clearly "nature" is part of Novalis's continuum, as subject to history and change ("consolidation" and "dissolution") as are all phenomena in space and time. (For Schlegel, by contrast, nature retains its otherness, its neoclassical function as a set of ideally operating laws.) Less clear is the meaning of the word "gradually" in the last quotation. Gradualness would seem to presuppose the kind of sequenced time that the imagery of fire and vortex precludes. The problem lies in the limitation of available words. Novalis seems to be thinking of a series of still pictures, moments of clarity that fuse a jumble of dreams, strivings, and failures into a single image: to "consolidate" history into a series of such pictures (as Novalis does in "Die Christenheit oder Europa") is to perceive not so much an accumulation as a thinning out, a gradual reduction of time's negativity. The final picture (imaginable but not realizable) would be a reemergence of the initial "spiritual worlds" of pure music, pure thought. Once presentness is disrupted, all time images become usable in heightened form, and Novalis can rephrase "gradualness" as its apparent opposite: "Nature is transformed in sudden shifts."[30]

Schlegel's critical, generative concept of humanity ("Humanity must be constituted") underlies the radical difference between his "Bildung" and that of Novalis, from which teleology is never absent; human time is ultimately the phased emergence of cosmic landscape: "The human being is a historically shaped individual in receipt of its own history. Gradually emergent humanity. When humanity has reached its highest stage, then whatever is higher will be revealed and unfold of its own accord."[31] "Gradually emergent humanity" evokes the "gradual" spiritualization of nature. The fragment makes very clear that "the higher," while defining the human essence, is not directly accessible to the consciousness constrained, as it must be, by empirical projects; it is genuinely magical, present in all the "chances" that surround us, but precisely not in our intentionality.

Indeed, Novalis shows himself aware of a contrast between himself and the Schlegel brothers in this very context; the more emancipated the human mind appears to be in its creative self-expression, the more important it is to understand such emancipation as a moment of self-conscious synthesis comprising "art," "nature," and progressive "spirit": "The Schlegels, when they speak of the purposiveness and artifice of Shakespeare's works, overlook the fact that art belongs to nature, is, as it were, nature in the act of contemplating, replicating, and shaping itself. To be sure, the art emerging in a highly developed nature is infinitely removed from the artificiality of the ratio, the exclusively rational spirit."[32] Novalis's antianthropomorphism, his alignment of "Bildung" with a purified consciousness of historicized nature, rests on the premise that it is the self-centeredness, the time-bound intentionality of the human mind, that consigns spiritual truth to "chance" and the margins of consciousness.

The autobiographies we construct for ourselves, our sagas of development, draw us ever further from the single world-story that is always in progress, yet needs us for its telling. For every element that comes to the fore in a narration of the world's time is already imbued with forgotten meanings. The temporality of "spirit" is a dissolution, compression, and unification of everyday time: "Our life is imperfect, because it has phases. There should be only one phase, then it would be infinite. The process of relating the phases is the substantive one. Where increased fullness is bound up with compression, there life prevails."[33] The compression of which Novalis speaks implies a poetics: the transformational moment is made, not from a shaping or criticizing of the present, but from an act of rupture blossoming into an ecstatic narrative, a projection of a wholly porous "future" saturated with the textural changes wrought by past moments that have "burned," plunged into the vortex: "Through the life of the future one can rescue and ennoble the life of the past."[34] Indeed it is this capacity of human beings to recapture images of the past that certifies their significance and central function as agents of "spirit." For human consciousness can perceive, in the apparent disaster of ceaseless surface decay and loss, the indispensable instrument of a purified temporality: "Immediate nature is not the whole of nature. What existed once, lives on, just not in immediate nature."[35]

We have seen that on one imaginative level, Novalis conceives nature as "gradually" evolving in a spiritual direction; on an empirical level, however, nature clearly operates according to its own cyclical laws. Nature's repetitions can be seen as a kind of eternity, the world's negative self-perpetuation through inertia ("Trägheit"). However, the residue of "what existed once" marks any landscape as historical; the human observer is confronted by fragments of an uncompleted story, masked by the inertia of presentness and natural repetition. The task of the imagination is always to start from the random moment (which, once chosen, ceases to be random) and to postulate the completion of its narrative significance. Such a commitment diverts crucial human energies away from intentional projects and toward the half-hidden

34

points of juncture between the empirical and the spiritual. Man, the time creature, is uniquely equipped for this task: "The eternal is a property of all things. Mortality and mutability are precisely the qualities of higher natures. Eternity is a mark of spiritless beings. Eternity is to be synthesized with temporality."[36]

With this distinction between "eternity" (nature's static repetitions) and temporality (the zone inhabited by humans aware of their mortality), Novalis makes explicit the aesthetic framework of his thinking. It is the mind's drive to refigure experience as narrative that provides an intelligible model for the transformations bringing humanity gradually closer to "the higher." For art emerges from the crucible of temporality into a special kind of eternity, one that is not constituted by repetition. Neither Novalis nor Schlegel assign to art a privileged position above the other productions of the human spirit, such as philosophy. However, Novalis's ontology is more clearly "aesthetic" in its ultimate allegiance to concepts of harmony and unity. Schlegel's aesthetics revel in the play of consciousness, the discords of criticism, irony, whim ("Willkür"), the multiplying mirrors of the programmatic *Athenäumsfragment;* Novalis's insistence on the world's unitary narrative leads him to a view of art rooted in the universal polarity between centered spiritual evolution and the proliferating randomness of the incidental. The poet's freedom, his compression and distension of the moment into an ecstatic narrative, is analogous to the creative principle of the universe, which blends a cyclical ending into every spontaneous beginning. The poet's privilege derives solely from his fidelity to the principle of wholeness, his vision of history as ultimately a unity that can be intuited (though not directly perceived) as such because of its beginning and ending in the purity of "spirit":

> Let the poet's realm be the world, compressed into the perspective of his time. . . . He can use anything, he needs only to blend it with spirit, he must make a whole from it. He must portray both the general and the particular—all portrayal consists in the fusion of opposites, and the poet's freedom in relating phenomena emancipates him from subjective limitations. All "poetic nature" belongs to nature as such.[37]

Novalis's ideal art is music, with its autonomous time scale. At the same time this is an immanent music, a music of the earth not the spheres, in which the sheer randomness of the particular is not only retained but heightened: "The book is nature encoded into symbols (like music) and completed."[38] Modernist criticism has taken a wrong turn in interpreting a statement like this to mean that Novalis favors an abstract, self-contained art. The whole importance of art in his unitary thinking derives from its ability, as a model of distillation and compression, to illuminate the not otherwise perceivable unity of all history, all cosmic time. A key word here is dissolution ("Auflösung"); art projects the narrative compression of time *and* its collapse back into mere linearity—and Novalis finds the appropriate musical image: "The more man develops his sense for living rhythm, the more he is interested also by discord—because of the process of dissolution."[39]

This ability of art in general, and poetry in particular, to dissolve itself, to include the transitions to and from its own transformed worlds, gives it a different imaginative role from that of philosophy. Philosophy's goal is transformation also, but always in the direction of linguistically guaranteed coherence; poetry, by contrast, deploys a chameleonlike language with a color spectrum ranging from purity to banality, a language that unifies yet continually contextualizes its unity: "If the philosopher orders, defines, everything, the poet dissolves all bonds. His words are not general signs but sounds, incantations that cause groups of beautiful words to revolve around them. . . . For the poet language is never too poor, but always too general."[40] Poetic language is the "play" of the world unlocking the coherence present within the random: "To play is to experiment with chance."[41]

Both Schlegel and Novalis place great stress on the word "freedom"; but whereas for Schlegel the term connotes the activity of the imagination as such, its power of combination ("Kombinatorik"), its irony *and* its responsibility toward the "universe," for Novalis it is a quality always present in the narrative of "spirit." Freedom is released *through* the imagination, emanating from and then forever mirroring the initial imaginative act, namely, the disruption and transformation of inert time into ecstatic temporality. Manfred Frank summarizes:

> From out of time's congealing into pastness freedom always emerges victorious. . . . This victorious "transcendence" constitutes the opening to futurity and is the cosmic "self-touching" of the imagination itself. This reflective self-discovery, which unlocks futurity, must, however, take place *within* the present (as the act of reflection); its product will be a "hovering" synthesis that, itself without substance, gazes as it were with one

36

face into the past, with the other into the future. The present is Janus-faced.[42]

The notion of "hovering," of a Janus-faced productive moment,
can be adapted as a description of the poetics of the post-Romantic
generation. Although Romantic theory embodies the full range of possibilities of a modern poetics, these poets established their historical
moment ("Universum") by viewing Romanticism as a phenomenon
both singular and past (much Romantic speculation remained unpub-
lished). Yet the polarity I have outlined reverberates through the rich
ambivalence of their language, their precarious fusion of energy and
melancholy. These poets subscribe instinctively to the vigorous theory
of "Bildung" in Schlegel: the possibility of transforming contingency
through interpretive and historical narration is the most powerful and
immediate Romantic legacy. At the same time, Novalis's disruption of
time into moments and chance occurrences, privileged or otherwise,
appears ever more attractive as a program for the disoriented post-
Napoleonic world. Can the idea of productive "Bildung" be adapted
to a discontinuous, collapsing version of time? Can the narrative of
"Bildung" include, even culminate in, psychological failure without di-
minishing the transformational role of ecstatic consciousness?

There is a comparable ambivalence in post-Romantic images of
nature, which for Schlegel functions as a model system: "In Bildung
nature dominates."[43] "Art's purpose is Bildung toward nature."[44]
Novalis's relocation of nature within history, on the other hand, permits a greater openness toward nature's hostile face and toward the
chaos of its particularity. Can an allegiance to nature's organic beauty
be reconciled with the risk-taking view of it as an illusory stability, a
concealed and ever-threatening vortex?

Finally, the post-Romantic view of language itself hovers tensely
between the polar views of the two thinkers. Schlegel's liberated,
ironic view of language, his concept of productivity through linguistic
mirrors and frames, is in vivid tension with Novalis's musical ideal, his
notion of a language aspiring toward pure sound, pure meaning detached from the network of purpose and intention. Can an analytical,
energetic poetic presence be synthesized with a language that would
free itself from intentionality, would narrate the hidden story of the
world itself? The poets, of course, sought to answer all these questions
in the affirmative, at least in their major poems. "We are summoned to
undertake the Bildung of the earth," wrote Novalis,[45] and this broad-

est imaginable use of the word "Bildung" underpins the texture of the next generation's poetry. Friedrich Sengle demonstrates the open, experimental consciousness that accompanies the melancholy of the years 1815–48;[46] no contradiction seems unmanageable, no idea or emotion needs to be excluded from a poetic text.

The synthesizing ambitions of "Bildung" are well exemplified in the work of Joseph von Eichendorff, whose ironic distance from romanticism as a "movement" is inseparable from the fact that his poems perfectly embody the ecstatic structure of Romantic temporality.

Vergebner Ärger
Joseph von Eichendorff

Im alten Hause steh' ich in Gedanken;
Es ist das Haus nicht mehr, der Wind mit Schauern
Geht durch das Gras im Hof, und Eulen lauern
In leeren Fenstern, die schon halb versanken.

Mich ärgern nur die jungen, kecken Ranken,
Die wie zum Spott noch schmücken Tor und Mauern,
Die grünen Birken, die mit falschem Trauern
Leicht überm Grabe meiner Lieben schwanken.

So, Nachteul' selber, auf dem öden Gipfel
Sass ich in meines Jugendglücks Ruinen,
Dumpfbrütend über unerhörten Sorgen;

Da blitzten Frühlingslichter durch die Wipfel,
Die leuchtend unter mir das Land beschienen,
Und nichts nach Eulen fragt der junge Morgen.[47]

(1839)

Vain Annoyance

Wrapped in thought I stand in the old house;
It is the house no longer, the shuddering wind
Ruffles the courtyard grass, and owls are lurking
In empty windows, already crumbling away.

Only the young, bold vines annoy me,
Adorning gate and walls as if in mockery,
The green birches, swaying in false mourning
Lightly above the grave of my loved ones.

Thus, myself a night owl under the desolate eaves,
I sat amid the ruins of my youthful hopes,
Glumly pondering unheard-of cares;

38

When streaks of spring light blazed through the treetops,
Uncovering the luminous land beneath me,
And the young morning arrives with no concern for owls.

In another sonnet from *Sängerleben* Eichendorff opens with a quatrain that amounts to a poetic program:

Nicht Träume sind's und leere Wahngesichte,
Was von dem Volk den Dichter unterscheidet.
Was er inbrünstig bildet, liebt und leidet,
Es ist des Lebens wahrhafte Geschichte.[48]

It is not dreams nor empty visions,
Which mark the line between poet and people.
What fervently he shapes, loves, and suffers,
Is the authentic history of life.

It seems fair to stress the presence of "shape" ("bilden") and "history" ("Geschichte") in this formulation: the poet's mission is to articulate the "true" shape of human time. At the same time, he does not do this through the special quality of his experience or the vividness of imagery; his "dreams" and "visions" lay no claim to privileged status. The alternative to the deathly abstraction of linear time is not the empty timelessness of "Wahngesichte," but the ruthlessly disruptive moment, through which alone "Bildung" becomes imaginable. Eichendorff's images are deliberately unstable, oscillating ceaselessly between an almost naive claim to contingent immediacy and an erosion of that claim through a skeptical interpretive narrative. As Theodor Adorno puts it: "None of Eichendorff's images is merely what it denotes, yet none can be assimilated to a stable classifying principle. . . . In his poetry images are really pure elements, destined to dissolve within the poem itself."[49]

One obvious difficulty with this program is that the images can become too lifeless, too much a series of *topoi*, if the poem's structure fails to bind them into a firm and manifest relationality. Thus the contingent sequence of "Vergebner Ärger"—brooding night thoughts dispelled by the energetic natural dawn—is so omnipresent in Eichendorff that it is always in danger of becoming mechanical, trivial. The theme of the entry into nature can only be validated by a language that "becomes" nature; and this becoming will not be achieved by mere rhythmic adaptation. Only through an insistence on human otherness, the opening into a confused, alienating "chaos" of perception,

39

can Eichendorff propel the poem into a natural-historical domain energized by "Bildung." To quote Adorno again: "The act of turning man into language, letting the flesh become word, endows language with the expressivity of nature and again transfigures the movement of language into life."[50]

Adorno's phrase "the act of turning man into language" is especially felicitous, in that it draws attention to one of the most striking aspects of "Vergebner Ärger," the fact that we don't really know, or care, what the speaker's "thoughts" are. They seem devoid of content, and the more their weightiness is stressed ("unheard of cares"), the less "weight" they carry in the poem. The text confronts two versions of an empty present tense, the pretentious emptiness inhabited by the consciousness and the proliferating emptiness of uninhibited nature; from the almost sculptural blending of these spheres (the weaving of the vines in line 5 characterizes the poem as a whole) a new possibility of time, "a world out of nothing" in Novalis's phrase,[51] is brought into being. But the initial staging of the confrontation between subjectivity and nature intensifies only the dimension of sterility and deathliness. The painful distension of the indifferent continuum of present time, the apparent resistance of all contingency to the narrative will, evokes a vision of paralysis.

Eichendorff's strategy of situating the self on the edge of the world is well known: the self always has to some degree the role of observer. The corollary to this quasi-detachment is that the detachment is by definition incomplete: the consciousness is always already inside the world, a world that functions without it in a perpetual present. To become functional, the consciousness must put itself at risk, disrupting the indifference of the present, entering the "chaos" that dissolves all reassuring identities.

The first line of "Vergebner Ärger" expresses a controlled version of this risk taking. The speaker is "standing," symbolically interrupting time's flow, in a house certified as specific (by the definite article) and as old; through the oldness of the house, the consciousness is claiming its prerogative as the dispenser of time values, asserting the validity of its private time sequence, the rooting of its present moment in a lived and knowable past. This nostalgic claim is presumably the content of the "thoughts"; but there is no echo of such a claim in the world. This private time scale is without resonance, its significance derived exclusively from the urge for significance.

The compressed, tense opening line is systematically devastated

40

by the remaining images of the quatrain. "Es ist das Haus nicht mehr"—the very phrasing undermines everything the first line has asserted. The verb precedes the noun: the presentness of indifferent "being" takes precedence over the house's nominalistic claim to be; and the "no longer" cancels the "old" of line 1. The house cannot stand as a symbol of time continuity since it has succumbed to the presentness that resists narration. The other images then disseminate the indifferent present like a wave, oscillating just far enough into the dimensions of past and future to render them impotent. There is something ghostly about the wind: the grass *could* be invoked as an organic image, an emblem of future, but the disorderly "Schauern" of the wind turns it into mere random growth. The indifferent present is, precisely, this ceaseless mutual cancellation of past and future, a "chaos" only now perceptible as such. The sequence is then repeated, as the owl's empty alertness implies the possibility of a future event; but the windows open onto the past of mere decay, the past that is not a past but an accumulation of directionless present moments. The decay is incomplete, negating the windows' identity without permitting a poetry of ruins. The decisive adjective "leer" sums up the death-in-life of the scene: in one sense the windows are not "empty," they are occupied by owls; but their function in the contingent sequence is to express the radical blockage of the narrative, the accumulation of details resisting interpretive freedom. The self, having "entered" a house that is neither inside nor outside the presentness of nature, finds itself in a drastic exile, marginal without prospect of change.

The poem's title suggests comic opera, so lightly does it sound. But the situating of the verb "annoy" ("ärgern"), in the center of seven lines of corroding nature images, has an effect that is anything but light: the self seems desperately insistent on its presence in the indifferent scene, slashing verbally at the vine's tendrils. Nature taunts the self, proliferating effortlessly into parodies of the shapes of consciousness. However, Eichendorff's dialectic is also coming into play; there are four significant tonal shifts in this quatrain vis-à-vis the first one, suggesting a realignment of temporal possibilities. First, the oscillation of the present into past and future is widening: the tendrils are energetic, purposeful in their mockery, and in their "youth" designating the season as springtime; and the past regains a footing in the poem through death, the graves being no less authentic for being overgrown and subject to parody. Second, the adjectives—"bold," "green," "false"—evoke life and emotion, however negatively: the very grotesquerie of nature's performance readmits the possibility of value and narrative movement. A third shift is expressive of the speaker's broadening field of vision: whereas in the first quatrain he is, as it were, pinioned by nature in the disintegrating house, now he is actively observing, moving aggressively through the undergrowth like a surveyor. And what he discerns is *shape,* the physical shape of the crumbling walls, as well as the metaphysical shape of the trees in relation to the grave; the very act of perceiving nature's bitter parodies reinstates a structured temporality, for no matter how "false" the mourning, mourning as such is human, permitting a version of the past to reenter the contingent narrative. Finally, the horizontal, downward-pressing imagery of the first quatrain is replaced by a lightness, a vertical elan. The gaze rises through the walls to the tree-tops before arching down again to the specificity of the grave: the patterning of the vowels—"jungen," "schmücken," "grünen," "überm"—reinforces a sense of gracefulness, an authentically Romantic marriage of parody with arabesque.

A decisive shift marks the center of the text, from lightness to heaviness, exterior to interior, evening to night. The second quatrain, with its lightening of texture, has made it possible for the self to reenter the poem: it now does so, but as a paradox. It is both absolutely other, cut off in its internal brooding, and a "night owl," a part of the decaying scene, without claim to separate identity. The shift in posture, from standing to sitting, underlines this abandonment of intentionality. The self accepts the collapse of its initial attempt to impose its continuity on the world, indeed it joins in the mockery of that project. Despite the strikingly new tonality of this tercet, nothing new is added; instead, the earlier images are gathered and recapitulated as abstractions. The doubleness of the consciousness—as brooding ego and as extension of indifferent nature—is mirrored in the doubleness of the imagery. The ruins are both the decaying house and the disintegrated past; the "Gipfel" is both the upper floor of the house and the vantage point from which the consciousness can survey its life as a whole.

This ascent of the self is a confirmation in literal terms of the vertical movement at work in the second quatrain. Precisely because the self has abandoned its continuities of memory, because it accepts the destructive power of the present, it is borne upward on the energy of the world itself. The tercet seems totally static, without energy: but the movement of the text is being coiled up into it like a spring. The contingent narrative is energized by the very language of interpretive failure.

42

This is apparent also in the shift of the tense into the past. At the same time as the self is becoming a "night owl," dismantling its separateness, it is also moving in the opposite direction, ironizing its pretensions as past, distending the temporal frame into a continuum ripe for rupture. At the dark point of this meditative sequence, a point of tension and incompletion, the events are suddenly viewed from a distance. This narrative complexity is at the heart of the text's production of "Bildung," representing that transcendence of the collapsing present, which makes a fuller temporality suddenly imaginable, without any breach in the world's empirical conditions.

The coincidence of the moment of rupture with a "generative" natural moment is guaranteed by a release, in these final lines, of linguistic tensions latent throughout the poem. In line 3 "Eulen lauern," with the stressed *l* + diphthong combination, evokes a static balefulness. In line 9 "So, Nachteul' selber" is a phrase with no short syllables, halting the movement of the text in a nighttime of abstract introversion. But in the last line, in "nichts nach Eulen," there seems to be no long syllable, and the *l* of "Eulen," instead of resisting forward motion, merges fluidly with all the other *l*'s of this last tercet. It is hard to believe that the same word can be used to such different effect.

The exuberant rejection of the owl image signifies the abandonment of the struggle for a controlled, subjective continuity with the past. At the same time the ascent of the self to the desolate peak ("öden Gipfel") of the preceding tercet is suddenly of central importance. Eichendorff fills these last lines with light imagery, to the point of blithe redundance ("leuchtend . . . beschienen"): the self is nothing but an observer—yet the quasi-divine implication of its physical location is maintained ("unter mir"). It is as if the self, on its Novalis-like inward journey, has in fact been journeying outward and become the agent of a transformed external world. The very negation in the last line reinforces this effect: this is indeed a "world out of nothing," an ordinary dawn allegorized as rupture, as a moment of incessant, universal beginning. If the shift to the past tense in line 10 installed a storytelling, framing consciousness at the text's center, the return to the present tense with "fragt" breaks through all frames, opening the "Bildung" of the poem into the "Bildung" of the world. At the same time, the verb "fragt" maintains the connection to the struggles of consciousness even as it transcends them: the morning's nonquestioning is the answer to the agonizing questions about time unfolded in the text.

Although the movement of the text is dialectical, this answer is *not* a synthesis. Synthesis is the poem's starting point, the desire of consciousness to project an illusion of ordered time linking self and nature through the mediating artifact of the house and its "history." Nature will have none of it. Its indifferent continuity drives the persona, with its will to a narration of dominance, to paralysis, and self-mockery. Only at the moment of reduction of self to "nothing" does the narration of a "world out of nothing" become actual. And the regaining of a central role by the self is predicated on its abandonment of all synthesizing projects—except the project of the poem itself.

The poem, then, constitutes the world's "Bildung," its "authentic history," through its very refusal of the fictions of progress. In one sense the self declines steadily, from "steh' ich" to "nichts"; in another sense it rises, literally in fact, to the point where it joyously affirms the otherness of the morning. Far from overcoming the alienation of self and world, the poem insists on it: the strangulation of the past by weeds in section 1, the mockery of death in section 2, the introverted gloom of section 3—none of these is canceled by the exuberance of the final lines. The only "progress" is textural, in the sense outlined by Novalis: a gradual temporal refinement, made up of distinct and separate moments that, instead of accumulating within a subjectivity, actually lighten the world, allow its youth to reemerge as "future."

Gerhard Möbus has described the proximity of Eichendorff's poetics to those of Novalis, and notes a close verbal parallelism relevant here. Novalis writes: "Among modes of knowledge poetry is youth."[52] And Eichendorff both echoes and refocuses the fragment: "Youth is the poetry of life."[53] Poetry is integral to "Bildung," to temporality as such. In poetic narrative the enigmatic uniformity of time is dissolved, the ecstasies of past and future, mourning and youth, meet in rupture. The move of the universe toward the spirit is not a move toward maturity or conceptual wisdom but a lightening, a gradual dissolution of conventional time. "Youth," then, is the point of intersection between a humanity that cannot help growing older, accumulating the ruins of past projects, and a world that is gradually transforming those ruins into the purity of original being, of "the young morning." The "inertia" of cyclical nature mocks the past, but the moment of youth absorbs it, purifies it into new life.

If the fundamental meaning of "Vergebner Ärger" is thus in close accord with the temporal poetics of Novalis, a counterrhythm closer to the pole of Schlegel's ideas lends it much of its energy. The organic proliferation of nature is essential to the impact of the quatrains: the reader must *feel* the physical encroachment of the weeds on the old stones. Similarly, the final tercet gains its power from a sudden reassembling of images of a purposeful, dynamic nature long accumulated in Western poetic memory. This organic motif remains an unmanageable presence, deployed as a playful refusal of the self's will to control his world and his time zone.

Playfulness, in fact, is the text's constant link to Schlegel's poetics, beginning with the title: the comic-opera lightness of the title is both belied by the seriousness of the poem's concerns and recovered by the purified momentum of the final line. Schlegel's play of mirrors and irony provides a second reading, as it were, of the schematic precision of the self's movements in this poem. In the first quatrain the self can be seen as a kind of sorcerer's apprentice, a buffoon unable to keep his existential props under control; in the first tercet he resembles the same buffoon in a sulk, crawling into a corner where nature cannot get at his "unheard of cares." This comic subtext, this distancing from the self, merges completely with the poem's "elevated" tone in the final lines. The contingent narrative yields itself to translucent interpretation at the precise moment when the will to interpretive control simply dissolves into the otherness of the morning.

In the pigeon-holing language of literary histories Eduard Mörike is sometimes labeled a "realist," because the "nature" of his poems is felt to be more empirically observed and locally rooted than that of the early Romantic texts. But to juxtapose his "Im Frühling" with Eichendorff's poem is to be reminded of Schlegel's dictum that "idealism includes realism": for the longing to allegorize the ecstatic moment is explicit throughout Mörike's text, whose intense intimacy is produced by that longing.

Im Frühling
Eduard Mörike

Hier lieg' ich auf dem Frühlingshügel:
Die Wolke wird mein Flügel,
Ein Vogel fliegt mir voraus.
Ach, sag' mir, alleinzige Liebe,
Wo du bleibst, dass ich bei dir bliebe!
Doch du und die Lüfte, ihr habt kein Haus.

Der Sonnenblume gleich steht mein Gemüte offen,
Sehnend,
Sich dehnend
In Lieben und Hoffen.

Frühling, was bist du gewillt?
Wann werd' ich gestillt?

Die Wolke seh' ich wandeln und den Fluss,
Es dringt der Sonne goldner Kuss
Mir tief ins Geblüt hinein;
Die Augen, wunderbar berauschet,
Tun, als schliefen sie ein,
Nur noch das Ohr dem Ton der Biene lauschet.
Ich denke dies und denke das,
Ich sehne mich und weiss nicht recht, nach was:
Halb ist es Lust, halb ist es Klage;
Mein Herz, o sage,
Was webst du für Erinnerung
In golden grüner Zweige Dämmerung?
—Alte unnennbare Tage![54]
(1828)

In Springtime

I lie here on the springtime hill:
The cloud lifts me like a wing,
A bird flies ahead of me.
O tell me, supreme and unique love,
Where you dwell, that I might dwell with you!
But you and the winds, you have no home.

Like the sunflower my consciousness stands open,
Longing
Stretching out
In loving and hoping.
Springtime, what is your wish?
When will my yearning be stilled?

I see the cloud move, and the river,
The golden kiss of the sun penetrates
Deep into the flow of my blood;
The eyes, strangely intoxicated,
Act as if they were falling asleep,
Only the ear listens still to the bee's hum.
I think of this and that.
I yearn, yet for what I don't really know:
I feel partly pleasure, partly a painful lack;
Tell me, my heart,
What memories are you weaving

46

Into the twilight of golden green twigs?
—Old unnameable days!

This famous but elusive poem has proved resistant to coherent interpretation. Its combination of stylized, almost allegorical language with intimate detailing, of improvisatory musing with teleological urgency, makes it a complex text even by Mörike's standards. If the poem's situation—a speaker in search of meaning for his life through the experience of spring—is understood too literally, the temptation is to read it as a psychodrama, complete with climaxes and turning points. Thus, both Renate von Heydebrand and Christiaan Hart Nibbrig agree that the beginning of the third section marks a decisive turning away from "outer" to "inner" worlds, but disagree as to exactly when this happens. Von Heydebrand argues that with the phrase "the golden kiss of the sun": "Inner feeling already again drenches external phenomena."[55] Hart Nibbrig, however, sees the first three lines of the section as constituting together "a final image of the world's happiness"; the subsequent inevitable slippage, he says, leads the speaker to adopt a strategy of emotional compensation: "As a substitute for the lost world and the immediate experience of it, the 'heart' summons up new experiential content from the past."[56]

The fact that the two critics pick different points in the poem to connote a decisive "shift" suggests that the very idea of the shift is dubious. Although the poem is full of little quickenings of the pulse followed by almost static musings, it carefully avoids a tone of dramatic intensity. Indeed, although it opens with an external image and closes with an internal one, it seems to play with the opposition of outer and inner worlds, to maintain a porous texture, which permits the two to mingle and blurs the transitions from one to the other. The shaping consciousness takes absolute priority over *all* experience, preventing the reader from singling out some images as more intensely felt, more directly observed, or conversely, more psychologically distanced than others. Both of the critics mentioned are aware of this, but place their awareness at the end of their readings, as if it were possible to explore the *topoi* of the poetic experience "before" turning to the constitutive role of rupture and the quest for narrative in producing that experience. Thus von Heydebrand observes: "The poem is a model example of the type of the solitary lyric, monologic reflection, since it has as its very theme the special features of the type."[57] And Hart Nibbrig concludes his discussion with the insight that the end of the poem signifies the kind of creative ferment that produces its beginning: "The immediate, present experiential fullness, which in the first part of the poem seems to be a given, is in fact already at that point a poetic re-creation."[58]

These perceptions entail a decisive modification in our reading of the poem's "subjective" gestures. They explain why the text will not permit the reader to assign priority to any one theme (say, love, nature, or memory) over the others, and why the self, despite the intensity of its sensations, remains anonymous, nonspecific in its emotions. Whereas Eichendorff's self-absorption culminates in rupture, Mörike's text stages an initial disruption that causes the contingent narrative to be drenched in interpretation from the outset. And it is the very failure of interpretation, the cumulative indeterminacy, that bonds the two poems; both are historical narratives of "Bildung" through a release from controlled subjectivity.

Through the exceptionally stylized opening section, with its reminiscence of Goethe's "Ganymed," Mörike alerts us to the way he is using language. He is interweaving images of immediacy with phrases that recapitulate the history of spring poems, in order to articulate the dependence of all perception, all ecstasy, all memory on a series of linguistic Chinese boxes. A simple mimetic phrase releases another phrase freighted with cultural associations, which in turn open up the time zones of myth. The very perception of a natural phenomenon becomes immediately a cultural event, and what the poem shows us is the dialectical interplay of this process with the human longing to shed its cultural burdens and recapture the immediacy encoded in the rituals of spring.

Mörike is no skeptic; his use of language not only insists on the ceaseless intervention of associative chains, but also possesses the concision and power of the sacred. It is this sacred concision, this reverent simplicity, that gives the illusion that language can convey physical perception spontaneously and immediately. The reality, of course, is that such language achieves its impact through the utmost refinement and closure. In its gestures of stumbling, faltering, yearning for a nonlinguistic immediacy, the poem colonizes new, explicitly linguistic territory. The posture of uncertainty, of tentativeness, enhances the productivity of "Bildung" by generating even more intimate Chinese boxes at the center of the text. By simultaneously blurring the line between self and nature and enticing the reader to wonder about the poetic persona's "real" experience, Mörike fashions new images of

"Bildung," of productive fusion between contingent and interpretive narration.

"Im Frühling" evolves through a series of negations: love is inaccessible, longing is never satisfied, intense experience dissolves, the will to feeling is distracted, the past is "unnameable." And yet the text in no way conveys a rhythm of hope and disillusionment. These feelings are invoked but immediately subsumed within a larger temporal scheme, in which the self's desires are already embedded. That is not to say that Mörike is giving us a generalized or representative self; nothing could be more intimate and precise than its moments of intensity. Rather, the self is viewed heuristically, as if it were both familiar and strange, close to and remote from the writing consciousness: we feel we can predict its characteristics, yet such conformity to familiar patterns in no way detracts from the uniqueness of the narrative.

As the self oscillates between dream and negation, it compresses all the possibilities of a human life into the nonevents of a spring day. Just as there is no space in which the intimate disappointments of the self could isolate themselves as significant in their own right, so, conversely, the commonplace of nature's indifference to man cannot establish a foothold in the fluidity of this language. These negative truths are everywhere yet nowhere. The poem's ambition is nothing less than the articulation of Romantic "Bildung" through a seamless language, a narrative intertwining the contingent and the interpretive so fully that its claim to the authenticity of history cannot be withstood. The distance between human and natural time is stated and restated; but through the saying of it, through the accumulated negations, such distance is simply, irresistibly overcome. The poem is, in itself, Schlegel's "universe as object": that is, it shapes the historical moment known as Biedermeier, makes it recognizable, by risking the utter destruction of the "comfortable," self-exploring Biedermeier persona.

In "Im Frühling," as in "Vergebner Ärger," we witness a complex interplay between the passive and the self-organizing self, between the Romantic poles of depersonalized refinement and intensification ("Potenzierung") through distancing consciousness. Both poems begin with the speaker situating himself in a location from which insight is anticipated. But Mörike's persona is passive, lying down, receptive solely to external nature, whereas Eichendorff's is full of intentionality, standing, absorbed in the interior of house and self. Moreover, the speaker of "Im Frühling" begins atop a hill; Eichendorff's speaker ends in an equivalent high spot, with its symbolism of mystical wholeness and control.

In "Vergebner Ärger" the dismantling of the intentional self leads finally to a pure, observing joyousness, a release from interior time. Mörike's speaker is also dismantled, but to precisely the opposite effect: as his physical passivity becomes intensified to the point of rigidity, the fluidity of the interpretive narrative isolates and intensifies the tiniest contingency. Passing through a phase of irritation, apparent superfluity, the odyssey of the conscious self culminates in a flood of interior time and creative intentionality ("What are you weaving"). The complexities of Eichendorff's texture are to be found in the quatrains; the poem moves toward ever greater transparency, with a noticeable refusal to deploy the self's "thoughts" as a basis for continuity. Mörike, by contrast, gives the sections of his poem the appearance of petering out, as if the consciousness were incapable of sustaining complexity and found itself forced to start again from scratch; but in fact the motifs of each section are carried forward and recombined with ever greater complexity in the latter part of the poem. Whereas Eichendorff thins out the distressing present moment to the point where it is ruptured by the singularity of the dawn, Mörike intensifies the mesmerized self-reflections of his persona until the uniquely human quality, memory, submerges all interpretation in an "interior" fullness that reweaves all externalities into a narrative of "Bildung."

The first section is dominated by the single self: the "ich" is referred to explicitly in each of the first five lines. And this singular self conditions every perception of the world. Hill, cloud, wing, bird—all are singular, as is, most important, the concept of love, which the speaker invokes as both essence and event, a unifying moment toward which the world's individualities are always striving. Producing this singleness is a rigidly self-organizing consciousness. On the one hand, the self registers the world with total passivity; on the other, it translates its sensations immediately into quasi-mythical constructs. Each item in the world is, as it were, filtered into a stylized landscape that incorporates the inherited images of spring as the emblem of expansiveness, lofty aspiration, and love. This consciousness is religious in the sense that it refuses to accept the validity of the world's surfaces and outlines; it is always thrusting through appearances, singling out a chance movement in nature and freezing it into a symbolic event: "A bird flies ahead of me." Moreover, this network of selective significance is unified around the anticipated redemptive power of love, and the poem's crucial first negation, the failing repetition of "dwell" ("bleiben,") suggests the breakdown of the mythical-religious consciousness. For the movement "behind" the world's surfaces must have shape, there must be a Logos, a source from which the patterning of the mythical mind derives its authority. But for Mörike the patterns dissolve, myth shaping fails.

The poem's first plural word occurs in line 6: "the winds." What the winds, ancient symbols of the spirit, do is to return the consciousness along the way it has come, back from the closure of the depth illusion to the openness of surface. The "house" that does not exist can readily be understood as the house of religious culture, the conceptual structure that formerly held sensory perceptions in place. There is no danger to the text in suggesting such an allegory. For Mörike's poem neither opposes one allegorical principle to another nor refutes allegory as such. Rather, allegory plays here the same role as sense perceptions: it blurs boundaries, renders the self uncertain whether its experience is actual, willed, remembered, or merely quoted. To operate in this way, allegory must be first invoked and then dissolved; its singleness cannot be sustained, but the moment of its dissolution becomes structurally central to the narrative. "Supreme and unique love" ("Alleinzige Liebe") is a necessary illusion, a gesture toward an impossible historical unity that continues to reverberate through the interpretive narrative.

"Love" becomes "loving" in the second section, marking a shift from allegory to process. In a sense the language becomes more, not less, abstract; the section is really devoid of concrete imagery (as Renate von Heydebrand points out, the sunflower, being out of season, is strictly for purposes of analogy).[59] But this intensified abstraction connotes a necessary split, a loosening, in the highly organized yet rhetorically frustrated consciousness of the opening section. On the one hand, a barely noticeable detachment has entered the language: the self is not identical with its "consciousness" ("Gemüte") but is registering, charting, its new openness. And on the other hand, the consciousness is no longer passive: with the shift from "lie" to "stands," the self declares its willed entry into the organic sequences of spring. It gives up its unified self-image and its preestablished teleology, opening itself to spring's unpredictability.

The poem's perspective oscillates ceaselessly, however, and even as the language moves urgently to a climax on the word "Frühling" the consequences of this willed process become clear. The self begs to "know" what spring has in store: as the analyzing, questioning intellect detaches itself from the newly open, sensuous consciousness the activity of the self becomes double, experiencing and observing with equal intensity. The final rhetorical question appears at first to retreat to the longing for shelter of the first section: the self can still only imagine fulfillment as closure, as the satisfaction of already defined desires. Yet the openness of language suggests that these initial interpretive gestures are already becoming contingent events within a larger narrative only now perceptible. Certainly the mechanisms of longing that drive the self remain intact; the "universe" would remain unrealized if the text claimed easy transformation. But the question "wann" seems not to demand an answer, but rather to insist on itself as a pure temporal question, the act of an intellect no longer willing the control of perceptions. The self tacitly acknowledges that the stilling of desire is as impossible as the cessation of springtime growth. Instead the very activity of analytical consciousness, the ceaseless observation of human longing, is interwoven with the longing itself. These two questions addressed to the spring echo and extend the self's longings in the very same words with which they frame and analyze them.

The apparently simple change from "The cloud lifts me like a wing" to "I see the cloud move" encodes the transformed perspective at the poem's center. The cloud is no longer either allegorized or possessed. Instead, the text oscillates between extreme readings of the same experience and only gains in coherence thereby. Thus, the static positioning of the self resonates anew through the perceptual shift toward change and movement ("wandeln"). As the speaker stops insisting on his own presence in the world, suddenly far more of the world becomes accessible to him. Although the first section had located the self in a posture of elevated comfort, paradoxically the atmosphere had been confined, cloud and bird artificially close. Now the perspective is open to all the extremes of distance and proximity; cloud and river are contained in a single visual sweep. Moreover, the verb "see," successor to the comparably situated "lie" and "stands," acknowledges the final establishment of a purely observing consciousness. The self lets go of its own sensations, relaxes; and the result, evoked in the next two lines, is a plunge from the fascinated stasis of the observer into a flood of oneness, intimacy, fusion with the world.

Now that the self has become open to the extremes of stillness and movement, near and far, detachment and relaxed acceptance, the world comes to meet it with a hitherto unimagined repertoire of sensuous blending and activation of the unconscious. The verb is extraordinarily intensified—"dringt . . . tief . . . hinein"—and the tension between the still stylized image of "the golden kiss of the sun" and the quasi-scientific "blood flow" suggests the way in which the growing intricacy of the interpretive narrative has generated new and irresistible contingencies. The allegorical time of the opening section is preserved in the sun's kiss and simultaneously submerged in the anonymous, circular time of the blood.

Mörike's continuities are grounded in extreme contrast. Even though we are becoming aware that the story of the text is its refusal of all "stories," all central threads or master categories, it is still astonishing to witness the shift from the dynamism of sun and blood to the static microcosm of the eyes and ears. This poem refuses its own climaxes, evoking the intensity of the sun's impact and then immediately tracing the intimate detailing of its aftermath. For the notion that experience precedes analysis is utterly abolished in this language; the key to the momentum of an ever more integrated narrative is the persistence of interpretation at the microcosmic level, the vibration of consciousness in the interstices of pure sensation. Thus the eyes are simultaneously ecstatic, "intoxicated," and manipulative ("Act as if . . ."). At the very moment of sensual immediacy it becomes clear that the detached consciousness is being transmuted into an irreducible presence which narrates the springtime world, yet is also part of it.

The poem's opening section shows language as constraining, prematurely coding experience; this third section allows language to reemerge as the elemental stuff of sensory life. This ecstasy on the edge of silence is embedded in the heart of narrative, a moment precipitated by a before and already expanding into an after. The body becomes almost inert under the sun's impact; but the consciousness spins words that capture that inertness, spreading the sun's intensity out from the mementary into a time zone that simply, passively persists. It is surely not too fanciful to view the hum of the bee, the sound image that survives the inertia of all other manifestations of life, as representing the "chaos" of a rupture so subtle that the self is unaware either of the danger of silence or of the latent presence of a fulfilled narrative. At this moment of stasis the sound of the world, both within and without the observing mind, dissolves into the shapeless "music" of an infinitely distended point of time. But the potentiality of words, even or especially at the moment of their submergence in the bee's hum, is central to this narrative, here threatening to fall below a threshold into the

53

nonverbal. This is one of the most striking of the poem's "negatives": in order to exist authentically it must risk falling silent, must open its language to oblivion. For in this risk taking lies the possibility of metamorphosis: as the detached consciousness has become the pure hum of language without a goal, so now the blankness of passive sensation becomes a space to be filled by memory.

The continuity from "listens" to "I think of this and that" is again one of contrast. From intense alertness the texture shifts to disconnectedness. Refusal of intentionality becomes, by a subtle modulation, aimlessness. The informal groping of these lines, astonishing if one contrasts them with the opening allegorical ambitiousness, illuminates how completely the moment of rupture has been actualized. No organizational allegories, no motivations of sense are any longer in force, neither a before nor an after is imaginable from the perspective of this moment. Certainly, principles of development are at work: the day is passing, an organic intimacy between self and nature is in process. But Schlegel's conception of "self-destruction" remains central. The poem, seamless as its continuities appear to be, grinds to a seemingly definitive halt. If the self is to fulfill its role as giver of time to the poem-as-"universe," the possibility that "chaos" may produce only silence and impotence must first be actualized. The experience of ecstasy, so fully evoked, is musically dissolved (the "Auflösung" of Novalis's poetics) by the collapse into the mediocrity of "partly . . . partly." The continuity of consciousness, which guarantees a minimal interpretive narrative, is always also a continuity of loss. The words "Only . . . still" ("Nur noch") signify temporal decay at the heart of a concentrated moment: as one first reads them, they indicate a focusing of consciousness on a single pure perception; in the light of the following lines they also presage the disintegration of that final perception into the certainty of its loss. But it is precisely the narrative moment of loss that opens the text to its marvelous conclusion. For memory is the affirmation of loss, an ecstatic disruption of the present moment, which Mörike articulates as the only possible fulfillment of that moment. It is not individual nostalgia, not the content of the memories that counts, but the act of remembering itself.

Hart Nibbrig has demonstrated the central role of remembering in Mörike's poetics,[60] and the verb "weaving," with its creative aura, is all the more striking because a self-consciously passive persona is released into symbolic action for the first time. The poem's final negation, the "unnameable days," suggests that these remote yet tangible, "weavable" days constitute a temporality produced entirely by the text, a past that is not past, time become porous, fluidly transferrable into the always present moment of the poem. The time opening into the poem is not "possessed" by the speaker, but at once opens out into the world, energizing a universal "Bildung." Again, a multiplicity of time sequences is involved. In one sense the self instigates a definitive momentum into the interior, analogous to the day passing into the night. But the imagery of weaving and dusk, the closeness of the "twigs" and the organic vividness of their coloration at a moment when colors nominally fade—all this curves self and world back toward each other in a new unity grounded in the very process of loss. Memory activates a narrative, linking the moment of rupture to the unconsciously shaped ecstasy of the past. Eluding conscious distinctions between true and false, memory imposes the uncensorable "truth" of history. And the validity of this transforming act is inseparable from the transformation that the world has already wrought on the hitherto passive self; only through the experience of ecstasy and loss can memory, the realm of the lost, be entered.

The poem puts in question each of its own movements toward vision: but this questioning has the impact of an ironic intensification, subtly uprooting the world ever more completely, not only from presentness but also from the persona's self protective expectations of poetry as such. If the visionary experiences are not maintained, so also the failures do not fail, the negations do not negate. Each motif is lived and relived until finally the language enters a time zone where the past of memory, the present of sensory intensity, and the future of historical possibility are imagined as ecstatic simultaneity; and the words of this imagining, now beyond all interpretation, constitute a model of what I have termed historical narrative. In Novalis's terms, they "undertake the 'Bildung' of the earth."

It is pointless to try to sort out which elements in Mörike's text are closer to Schlegel's poetics, which to Novalis's, so consummate is the fusion of the two. Hart Nibbrig formulates Mörike's temporal conception in terms strongly reminiscent of Novalis: "Time is the principle of evolution, the condition of possibility for unifying the contingent."[61] The even tone of "Im Frühling," its refusal of drama, its gradual, textural change, its intent focus on the magical properties of detail—all this is consonant with the poetics of Novalis. Indeed, a fragment of Novalis conveys fully the way in which to reach back is to reach forward, to remember is to transform the past into the porousness of potential future history: "All remembering is present. In the more purified world all re-membering will appear to us as an essential preliminary to poetry."[62] More in Schlegel's spirit are the continuous central self, its attempts at transcendence and perilous relapses toward the banal, and the negation and metamorphosis of motifs into an ever more complex, self-mirroring version of the "universe as object." A unique text results, fueled by a confidence that none of the failures of consciousness or dispersions of experience are definitive: the certainty of loss is used to overcome, through the intensification ("Potenzierung") of the poem's own time, the uncertainty and withdrawal of every other insight.

To move from Mörike's landscape to that of Annette von Droste-Hülshoff is in many respects to stay in the same place. The transformation of the moment of rupture into a continuity of "Bildung" is the overt preoccupation of both poets, and a faith in the structuring power of poetic language, in both its formality and its intimacy, characterizes their historical narrative.

Im Moose
Annette von Droste-Hülshoff

Als jüngst die Nacht dem sonnenmüden Land
Der Dämmrung leise Boten hat gesandt,
Da lag ich einsam noch in Waldes Moose.
Die dunklen Zweige nickten so vertraut,
An meiner Wange flüsterte das Kraut,
Unsichtbar duftete die Heiderose.

Und flimmern sah ich durch der Linde Raum
Ein mattes Licht, das im Gezweig der Baum
Gleich einem mächt'gen Glühwurm schien zu tragen,
Es sah so dämmernd wie ein Traumgesicht,
Doch wusste ich, es war der Heimat Licht,
In meiner eignen Kammer angeschlagen.

Ringsum so still, dass ich vernahm im Laub
Der Raupe Nagen, und wie grüner Staub
Mich leise wirbelnd Blätterflöckchen trafen.
Ich lag und dachte, ach, so manchem nach,
Ich hörte meines eignen Herzens Schlag,
Fast war es mir, als sei ich schon entschlafen.

Gedanken tauchten aus Gedanken auf,
Das Kinderspiel, der frischen Jahre Lauf,
Gesichter, die mir lange fremd geworden;

Vergessne Töne summten um mein Ohr,
Und endlich trat die Gegenwart hervor,
Da stand die Welle, wie an Ufers Borden.

Dann, gleich dem Bronnen, der verrinnt im Schlund
Und drüben wieder sprudelt aus dem Grund,
So stand ich plötzlich in der Zukunft Lande;
Ich sah mich selber, gar gebückt und klein,
Geschwächten Auges, am ererbten Schrein
Sorgfältig ordnen staub'ge Liebespfande.

Die Bilder meiner Lieben sah ich klar,
In einer Tracht, die jetzt veraltet war,
Mich sorgsam lösen aus verblichnen Hüllen,
Löckchen, vermorscht, zu Staub zerfallen schier,
Sah über die gefurchte Wange mir
Langsam herab die karge Träne quillen.

Und wieder an des Friedhofs Monument,
Dran Namen standen, die mein Lieben kennt,
Da lag ich betend, mit gebrochnen Knieen,
Und—horch, die Wachtel schlug! kühl strich der Hauch—
Und noch zuletzt sah, gleich einem Rauch,
Mich leise in der Erde Poren ziehen.

Ich fuhr empor und schüttelte mich dann,
Wie einer, der dem Scheintod erst entrann,
Und taumelte entlang die dunklen Hage,
Noch immer zweifelnd, ob der Stern am Rain
Sei wirklich meiner Schlummerlampe Schein
Oder das ew'ge Licht am Sarkophage.[63]

(1842)

In the Moss

When recently the night to the sun-tired land
Sent subtle messengers of evening,
I lay alone still in the forest moss.
The dark twigs nodded confidingly,
The leaves whispered at my cheek,
Invisible the wild rose exuded fragrance.

And through the linden's space I saw
A pale, flickering light that seemed to hover
Like a powerful glowworm amid the tree's branches
Luminescent as a face in a dream,

57

"Bildung" and the Possibility of History

And yet I knew it was the light of home,
Steadily burning in my own chamber.

All around so still that I could sense
The caterpillar nibbling on the leaf, and the green dust
Of tiny particles gently striking me in showers.
I lay and pondered, oh, such varied things,
I heard the beating of my own heart,
I almost felt as if I were aleady asleep.

Thoughts arose out of other thoughts,
Games of childhood, rhythm of years in a fresh world,
Faces long ago become strange to me;
Forgotten sounds resounded in my ear,
And finally the present time emerged,
The wave sweeping erect, poised as if about to land.

Then, like the spring vanishing into the ground
And bubbling up again some distance away,
Suddenly I was standing in the land of the future;
I saw myself, reduced, bent over,
By the family reliquary with weakened eyesight
Arranging dusty love pledges with care.

Vividly I saw my loved one's images,
In a costume now long out of fashion,
Saw myself intently extract, from faded cases,
Locks of hair, rotten, almost dissolved to dust,
Saw, across my deeply furrowed cheek,
The meager tear flowing slowing down.

And again, by the cemetery gravestone
Where names were carved familiar to my love,
I lay in prayer, with broken knees,
And—listen, the quail cried, the cool breeze brushed me—
And finally I saw myself, like a puff of smoke,
Drawn down into the pores of the earth.

I jerked awake and shook myself at that,
Like one who has barely escaped suspended animation,
And staggered away, past the dark bushes,
Doubting still whether the star at the world's edge
Was in truth my bedside lamp at home
Or the eternal light by the sarcophagus.

One of the most striking lines in Mörike's poem is "I think of this and that," and it has an analogue in the third stanza of "Im Moose": "I lay and pondered, oh, such varied things." These informal lines, embedded in a context of considerable rhetorical intensity, indicate the special quality of these poets' language: no image of time is adequate to them that does not include random, unfocused contingency; neither is a version of space that excludes the shifting inner space of the mind. The lines suggest that the transition from outer to inner space, far from being schematic or analytical, involves a simultaneous blurring of the world's contours and weakening, loss of control by the mind that has defined those contours.

The "Biedermeier" casualness is as usual deceptive: risks are being taken. And here Mörike and Droste-Hülshoff diverge. Mörike's self is deliberately passive, open to the microcosmic shifts of nature, and accordingly situated on the open hillside in the daylight hours; the inward movement of "I think of this and that" is the prelude to a release of memory that generates the decisive movement of "Bildung" into history, a letting go and a weaving at the same time. Droste-Hülshoff's persona, by contrast, is literally enclosed in a single situation, filtering all natural detail through an actively controlling consciousness: what the move inward does here is to subvert the enclosed perspective by turning the mossy bed into a grave, the privileged moment into a paralyzing temporal hallucination.

If the coherent vision of Romantic "Bildung" is still a viable framework for Droste-Hülshoff—and I think it is—then the relevant term is clearly Schlegel's "self-destruction," not the even textural change articulated by Mörike. Droste-Hülshoff's world is deeply threatened, and the vehicle through which she expresses this threat is a special kind of interpretive narrative. Heselhaus comments that there is always something "balladesque" about her texts,[64] and although "Im Moose" is obviously not a ballad, the term helps one to grasp its perspective. Schlegel emphasizes the ironic freedom, the controlling "caprice" ("Willkür") of the poetic self: and caprice seems an appropriate word to define Droste-Hülshoff's starting point. She sets the stage, exercises freedom in its pure form, and controls every element in the situation. But what begins as serene stage setting, in which elements of evening allegories are elegantly blended with intimate local details, gradually becomes a "ballad" in which the self is condemned to be a character. Once inside the story the poem's speaker is as terrifyingly unfree as the doomed heroine of any ghost ballad ("Schauerballade"). The perspective shifts from absolute freedom and control to absolute imprisonment, and the only way forward is destruction. "Im Moose" is a narrative that must destroy itself in order to exist.

All the elements of Romantic "Bildung"—the flexible, self-conscious language, the purposeful disruption of conventional time, the correlation of "chance" with "law"—are in place here. Missing is that sense, so strong in Eichendorff and Mörike, that a reflective, observing self is the instrument through which these elements can be made to coalesce into a continuum from contingency through interpretation to history. Instead, Droste-Hülshoff risks the viability of the self, and with it the possibility of "Bildung," by radicalizing the moment of rupture, entering an abyss of impossible time, and articulating a narrative as the sole alternative to madness. We see the self entering into its hubris of controlling time, then the horrific vision of what the realization of such hubris might mean; finally the ballad vision is banished, if only through physical escape, with the self's sole wisdom being sheer survival—and hence the reopening of time.

Beginning with the gentle rococo flourish of the first two lines, the opening stanza communicates a totally ordered situation. The word "alone" ("einsam") embodies the difference between Mörike's "I lie here on the springtime hill" and Droste-Hülshoff's "I lay alone still in the forest moss." Mörike's self is explicitly open to whatever spring may bring; Droste-Hülshoff's knows that it is alone, sealed off, intensely aware of time passing ("noch"), time that the self proposes to organize around a carefully chosen personal space ("*in* Waldes Moose"). The centralizing project is implicit in the last three lines, as nature's confiding intimacy is conveyed through each of the three main human senses in orderly sequence: "Nodded . . . whispered . . . exuded fragrance." Form, sense, and consciousness seem perfectly blended in the stately closure of the six-line stanza.

In the second stanza the speaker's perceptual empire is cautiously expanded. Distant realities are drawn into the same aura of intimacy as the nearby twigs and flowers. As a result, this stanza is almost analytic in its calibration of the exact nature of the perception: seeing, seeming, knowing—these are now the dominant verbs. But the opening to physical distance and mental image reinforces the sense that the self is in absolute control of its situation. Space and time are almost mathematically centralized, and there is nothing disturbing about the metamorphosis of the light into a "face in a dream." The speaker *knows* where she is, she knows every detail of the landscape, she knows the tricks played by the senses at twilight. She speaks of her "own chamber" and implicitly extends "ownership" to her whole complex of sensations. There is no tension here: the words "And yet I knew" emphasize that the premise of this "story" is the refusal of a story. To adapt Novalis's phrase, this is to be "a story out of nothing"—nothing, that is, but the human longing for control over time and space, a control that seems impregnable within the elaborate, rhyming gravity of the chosen stanza form. Postulated is an unbreakable continuity between organic time and the time of poetic consciousness: the one is laid upon the other in a perfect fit.

Both the completion and the impossibility of this control are articulated in stanza 3. If the second stanza insists on spatial relationships, the structure of the perceptual surface, now all surfaces are blurred. The virtual nonsound of the caterpillar's nibbling is carefully correlated with the speaker's awareness of her heartbeat; and the microscopic impact of the leaf particles is heightened by the incongruity of the emphatic verb "striking" ("trafen"). As speaker and world slip jointly into a realm of subtle intersections that elude the sensuous categories of day and night, inside and outside, the elaborate yet understated ritual language shapes the invisible motion of that realm into the all-absorbing temporal zone of the privileged experience. The second stanza established limits, the third abolishes them. The text is poised at the moment of ironic freedom, the moment of detachment through fullness of involvement, which might seem to fulfill a scenario of Romantic poetics.

But by situating the self so carefully inside a closed universe, by structuring the contingent to the point where it loses all autonomy within the interpretive narrative, Droste-Hülshoff has put freedom itself in question. The line "I lay and pondered, oh, such varied things" evokes the aimlessness at the center of the projecting, controlling self. The absolute quality of this ambition is what dooms it: no force in nature can resist the intensity of the human creative fantasy, and that is precisely the problem. The repetition of "own" ("eigen") is disquieting: "the beating of my own heart" has a very different impact from "my own chamber." As the speaker imposes "ownness" on the entire inner and outer universe, the word's premise of control begins to disintegrate, the singleness of the consciousness begins to fail, the privileged moment begins to lapse back into the randomness of time passing—and to open into a temporal abyss whence repressed contingency returns as nightmare. Although Margaret Mare stresses that "asleep" ("entschlafen") can be a euphemism for "dead,"[65] the more important point seems to be that sleep means loss of control as absolute as the control so far established. Certainly the imagery of death is present throughout the poem, but the self's exploration of the natural coffin in the moss implies that there is nothing passive about this dying. Controlling death is the ultimate fantasy, at the heart of the speaker's hubris.

Two striking atmospheric changes are announced by the first line of stanza 4. First, there is a subtle loss of directional force: the word "ich" controls neither the syntax nor the substance of these thoughts; and, further, the verb "arose" conveys a strongly vertical effect. The centralizing self has been explicitly horizontal, drawing the nominally elevated light of stanza 2 into the flattened perspective of a circle. But the turn inward has become an unpredictable journey downward and upward, a rupture of all horizontal continuities. In line 2 the memories are harmless; but in lines 3 and 4 the imagery becomes threatening, not in itself, but because it intervenes on a scene of rigid coherence. The remembered faces have "long ago become strange"; through them a clutter of long past moments invades the controlled present, imposing discontinuity and time quantities where all had been continuity and perfected spatial quality. The sounds of the past parody the whispering closeness of nature in stanza 1; the fusion of inner and outer worlds has been ominously "intensified," as the supposedly interior zones of the past manifest themselves as visual and aural perceptions. And finally, in an extraordinary image at the poem's very center, the present wells up again, having, within the space of a very few lines, undergone a metamorphosis from the horizontal, detailed, and controlled into the vertical, generalized, and threatening. The "ballad" has begun; the self is literally and helplessly swept along by the collapse of its centralizing project.

But the sweeping of the wave lasts only a moment. The collapse of interpretive control is to be articulated as paralysis, as the impossibility of narrative as such. The new vertical quality of the imagery is confirmed as the wave of the present is left standing, as if forever. In a fresh simile, the discontinuity of time is embodied in the aridity and meaningless eruption of the fountain jet in a wasteland of the future. The self's initial dream of projecting a seamless narration of the present is horribly parodied by the sterile control of the past exercised by the old lady with her mementoes. The vertical thrust of the fountain is echoed geometrically by the tense posture of the bent-over lady. The

62

images of time become detached from all intelligible time scales; the self is "suddenly" transported into the future, yet once there she sees a "family reliquary," as if some material continuity mockingly persisted, a disembodied pseudo-continuity refuting every ambition of the human consciousness.

A comparable terrifying meaninglessness is implicit in the words "I saw myself," which reflect back on the dissociation already present in "I heard the beating of my own heart." What is the self that is hearing and seeing? And what can it be that is heard and seen? The attempt at a totalized identity has yielded the horror of a self that must not be, a time that, with its ironic images of seamless continuity, cannot be. The impact of the orderly six-line stanza is heightened: how can such grotesque paradoxes be translated into such highly organized language? The project of control is fulfilled, with deadly irony, in the hallucination of a closed future: the moment of natural evening beauty is eternalized in the claustrophobic interior of the evening of life—an evening that is indistinguishable from death.

The sixth stanza intensifies these threatening visions. What can "out of fashion" mean in the second line? There is an obvious commonsense answer, but the evocation of a consciousness that could look back on the fashions of the present and deem them "veraltet" transgresses the possibilities of the temporal imagination. Fashion is so deeply embedded in daily time that, by definition, its future eludes control. Droste-Hülshoff's act of rupture has unleashed a narrative that, with its gravely elaborate rhyming, shatters the truce between language and life. In fact, the syntax draws attention to itself in this stanza: the separation of "Mich" (line 3) from "sah" (line 1) and the spreading out of "Sah . . . mir . . . die karge Träne" echo the wrenching discontinuities that this long sentence is translating into the illusion of linguistic coherence. This vision is made entirely of words, the words with which the self had sought to control and centralize time and space. And the words evoke their own porousness, the slippage of all imaginable experience out of these would-be containers. "Images" ("Die Bilder"), "extract" ("lösen"), "cases" ("Hüllen")—precisely because this language circumscribes an impossible future, which in itself is enacting the cancellation of life, the words seem to insist on their secondary meanings of phantasm, dissolution, emptiness. All life's props plunge into the vortex of loss, a loss embodied in its apparent opposite, the imagery of a deathly eternity: in another parody of the early stanzas' detailed intimacy, the self's gaze becomes trapped by the

63

slowly moving tear poised on the face's disintegrating surface. Once again the temporal abysses open: from which moment to which can this tear be flowing? How can there be any extension of time in this frozen "future" moment? To what emotion can the tear possibly relate?

The impossibilities culminate, in the seventh stanza, in the one outcome still possible: death. Although the hysteria breaks into the open and the terror is extreme, the language and imagery begin to release the self from the ultimate horror, death-in-life. The words are now focused on words as such, the names on the monument; and the vertical rigidity of stanzas 5 and 6 is exchanged for the renewed horizontal posture of prayer. Moreover, the event of death actually *is* an imaginable event, with a viable contributing scenario: "The quail cried! The cool breeze brushed me." The world is no longer paralyzed, the "ballad" finally begins to move at the moment of ending. And the crucial factor is that such a moment belongs in the contingent world; the return of living detail, however indifferent, restores to the self the possibility of reentering time, if only the time of death. Margaret Mare points out that the image of sinking into the earth is quite frequent in Droste-Hülshoff's poems;[66] perhaps even more important here than the ambivalent relationship between organic merging and the ritual of death is the fact of motion itself. We have noted the text's transition from the rigidly horizontal to the rigidly vertical; suddenly the two refusals of motion are fused in a satisfying acceptance, the vertical sinking of a horizontal body.

The verbs of the final stanza restore the vertical to some extent: "jerked awake . . . shook myself . . . staggered." But the speaker is visualized as staggering, bent over, not fully vertical. This suggests that the opening situation is restored, yet decisively modified. The fusion of vertical and horizontal in stanza 7 takes place within the closure of death. The lurching mixture of the two dimensions at the end connotes a retreat into contingency without direction; the poem's final formal gesture is the dismantling of form, the transformation of hallucinatory certainty into doubt without end. The momentum of the text toward total control has been such that it can only conclude in "self-destruction" (the word Schlegel aligns with "Bildung"). In destruction language persists, and the final principal verb, "doubting," holds all the tensions in balance. The phrase "And yet I knew" of stanza 2 is recalled; but now there is no knowledge. And the doubt is no mere figure of rhetoric: the self cannot be restored to its early self-confidence; the impossible vision, as the direct outcome of the centralizing dream, has invalidated the whole topography of the early stanzas. What the light is "in reality" has become genuinely undecidable. The self is stranded between a lost present and a future that became imaginable only as death. But because the death of stanza 7 finally admits genuine time, genuine events, into the vision, so the stranding of the self in no-man's-land frees it from its own sterility. The self will now always doubt, always oscillate, between two versions of the world. And as the speaker struggles out of the abyss she opened for herself, her utter inability to "interpret" the slightest contingent details opens her text up as a historical narrative, not gradually like Mörike's, but wrenchingly. To stage these extremes of domestication and exile conveys both the threatening enormity of this moment of rupture and the desperate power of the "Bildung" that precariously reconnects the collapsed time zones of past and future.

Schlegel seems to anticipate the limits probed by Droste-Hülshoff in this poem: "Space is the chain that binds nature, but for that very reason it ensures that nature does not disintegrate with infinite rapidity. Similarly, time is the chain binding spirit and creation, without which creation would occupy no space at all."[67] Space and time are in themselves the chains that bind experience, the limiting dimensions that keep the world intelligible. What Droste-Hülshoff does in this text is upset this balance. The perceptual links are calmly yet hubristically welded together in the first part of the poem: a closed space and a still moment are to be fused into a single entity identical with the perceiving consciousness. And the result is as Schlegel describes it: the world disintegrates into a pseudo-future, and the creative self, exiled from temporal continuity, is unable to reinsert itself into any viable space other than the grave. The world becomes unintelligible.

But the poem, despite its uncompromising move toward self-destruction, conveys a coherence belied by its destabilizing momentum, the coherence of "Bildung." Several voices appear to speak at once: the obsessive, centralizing self, the helpless character within the nightmare ballad—and a strongly moralistic, hortatory self, which speaks through the formal yet intimate language, providing the final intensification ("Potenzierung"), the mirroring act of the self that has survived its own story. These voices are held together only by the poem's own language; they are neither fused nor isolated into an intelligible hierarchy. Droste-Hülshoff provides no refuges.

One can argue that the poem, by the rigor of its logic, pushes the polarity between Schlegel and Novalis into the extreme of direct conflict: Novalis's reverence for the texture of discrete moments is undermined by the narrative of impossible time, which such isolating generates. There is no Schlegel-like reflexivity within this narrative, however, just a fixated, trapped quality that points only toward death.

The analysis has shown the multiple roles played by the elaborate stanza form; this multiplicity reduces ultimately to a single crucial function—reminding the reader of the shaping consciousness that both authorizes and contains the narrative project. Eichendorff and Mörike craft a temporality specific to their texts, achieving both closure and openness by a sudden release of energy, which renews the unity of mind and body, poem and world. Such multilayered expansiveness is absent from Droste-Hülshoff's poem; here the consciousness acknowledges no limits, and the very totality of its temporal claims is what nullifies them. Yet there is a robustness in the language, a barely perceptible detachment from the persona, which anchors the power of "Bildung" in the very possibility of reading and reenacting the self's disastrous project. "I lay alone still in the forest moss": a certain experimental time surrounds the poem, the time of the "still." The speaker has passed through the disaster of her vision in the moss, barely surviving it; the vision is now retold as a hallucination, from a distance, with self-analysis reduced to a minimum. The effect is to make these closed, dignified stanzas as porous as the mossy earth they evoke; the reader savors each contingent detail for its own sake, linking the images into the very interpretive narrative that the speaker withholds, a narrative that is also the history of this "universe." As they dismantle their projects of closure and control, Eichendorff, Mörike, and Droste-Hülshoff communicate the goal of "Bildung" as openness, as the unrealized but perpetually imaginable union of outer and inner worlds.

CHAPTER TWO

The Transmission of the Privileged Moment: Storm, Keller, Meyer

Historical categories are inherently in danger of congealing, limiting our response to a poem once its "discourse" is circumscribed. Conversely, of course, the historical relationship to a text, the sense of simultaneous closeness and distance, is indispensable to the life a reader gives it. In practice, the activity of interpretation tends to confirm, more or less, the usefulness of existing categories: the great debate between Lovejoy and Wellek over whether "Romanticism" is a singular or a plural concept has deprived us neither of the concept itself nor of the consensus that it designates a watershed in the story of Western culture. The value of hermeneutics lies in the fact that, while the process of change in our assessment of the past is continuous, such change is rarely abrupt or startling.

But the language in which we formulate our changing perceptions of the past has a constant tendency to wear thin, to become lifeless. Its reinvigoration can occasionally be achieved by the introduction of a new term, such as "mannerism"; but the most significant recent events in the self-description of modernity have been the disintegration of the idea of the avante-garde (the idea that to be modern is to be perpetually "conquering new territory"), and the renewed awareness of the complexity and open-endedness of Continental and English Romanticism. These events must be seen as interdependent. The abandonment of the claim for an autonomous, "modernist" poetry, one thriving exclusively on the inversion and distortion of bourgeois complacencies, actually restores to poetry the life of historical change: the disruption of modernism's canon does not detract from, say, Charles Baudelaire's greatness, but presses his language up against that of apparently remote contemporaries. (I shall be suggesting the value of juxtaposing his swan poem with that of Gottfried Keller.) And the installation of the Romantics as our "contemporaries" reminds us that the historical categories we deploy as descriptive of modern poems have been both actualized and called into question by the poems themselves. For not only is the production of literary texts inseparable, in Romantic eyes, from the will to produce history; the ironic anticipation of failure nourishes the production of an almost infinite encyclopedia of transformative possibilities. In the very act of crystallizing the moment of rupture Romantic language stages one of these possibilities. And no matter how far nineteenth-century poets withdrew behind the mask of privatism, they maintained a sense of language's magical-historical power. In the ebb of history, the coming flow is being continuously encoded. Just as, for Novalis, the disciplined focusing on any "chance" whatever can result in the production of historical truth, so the poets of mid-century became all the more committed to linguistic rigor as they felt compelled to speak of the isolation and rarity of authentic experience.

To focus on "experience," and the attenuation thereof, is of course to dwell in a subtly different time zone from that of Eichendorff, Mörike, and Droste-Hülshoff. In the previous chapter we explored an extraordinary variety of narrative shapes within just three poems written in the discourse of "Bildung." The authenticity of the contingent narrative, in these texts, is achieved through radically differing relationships with the narrative of interpretation. The slippage into "chaos" is more or less emphasized depending on the value implicit in interpretive weaving: Mörike ruptures the continuum of the present repeatedly yet almost unnoticeably, so flexible is his interpretive narrative, whereas Droste-Hülshoff's self-conscious control leads to the opening of an abyss. And this variety reflects both a categorical openness and a confidence in the possibility of history, of "Bildung" as a universal phenomenon, not a private attribute.

None of this is quite the same for the poets of this chapter. The validity of the contingent moment becomes both precarious and supremely precious, almost nursed into existence through stillness and memory. And while the interpretive narrative is suffused with tentativeness and doubt, it also acquires a clearly sequenced, describable structure. Moreover, the final stage of this narrative is a summarizing and redirection of the contingent details, as if to clothe the very uncertainty of the interpretive narrative in a language of metaphysical accord. Withdrawal, privatism, doubt—all are doubled by structural clarity, careful narrative sequencing and a paradoxically ambitious historical poetics.

All this reflects a profound shift in the master category of "Bildung." In the second part of the century the concept remains dominant, but the word's very authority is associated with new connotations. "Bildung" ceases to be a synthesizing value, Schlegel's "highest good," and begins to imply something strictly incomparable, a programmatic restatement of the moment of rupture as a moment of privilege. The privileged moment is then postulated as the highest public good, and the "Bildung of the earth," far from being abandoned to privatization, becomes directly imaginable as the aesthetic processing and dissemination of these moments.

In other words, there is a decisive shift away from the struggle to fuse Schlegel and Novalis and toward an aesthetic ontology dominated entirely by Novalis's mode of thought. Open-endedness, the insistence on freedom, which Schlegel called irony, becomes rare in this literature. Instead, a complex view of the self as isolated yet empirically constrained, of the world as alien yet imbued with inwardness, conditions both the sequencing of the contingent narrative and the self's interpretive response to it.

What Manfred Dick has argued in the case of Novalis himself[1] becomes implicit in all the major poetry of experience ("Erlebnislyrik") of this period: because the self is ceaselessly engaged in dialogue with the equally dynamic "self" of nature, to focus intently on the self implies involvement with the world, not withdrawal. The enemy is the empty time of the everyday, what Novalis calls "inertia," and the goal is the reproduction of the single intensified moment through a multilayered narration of the encounter between subjectivity and nature. "We are summoned to undertake the 'Bildung' of the earth," said Novalis; and the grandiosity of such a statement has become a simple assumption in this period, an aesthetic teleology that gives to the making of poems a definable function in the social order.

69

That there is nothing exclusive or escapist about "Erlebnislyrik" is made clear by Theodor Storm in his well-known preface to his anthology of 1870; in stressing the poem's audience, the bearers of its mission, he deploys all the key words of the time in a self-limiting coherence blended from religion and science, suggestion and precision:

> In its impact the lyrical poem is to grant the reader both a revelation and a release, or at least a satisfaction, which he could not have achieved for himself, whether because the poem expands and deepens our capacity for contemplation and feeling in an unimagined way, or because it makes psychic material, lying within us in a semiconscious half-light, appear with surprising clarity of outline.[2]

The reader is important to the poet, not as a passive receptacle of the poem, but as a symbolic element in the poem's conception, comparable to the creative figures, the poet's doubles, whom we will find at the center of each of the texts to be interpreted. For the dialectic of this new staking of "Bildung" on the self's specific experience generates a narrative of doubt concerning the receptacle of the crucial gift of experience, namely the persona who is speaking. But this doubt is productive, endowing the contingent with the life of the questioning language, and opening that language into the contingencies of the reader's own life. Uniqueness lives through subdivision and multiplication of the self. The goal is the putting into practice of Novalis's program for a dynamics of relationality: "We are not our Self, we can and should however become that Self. We are the seeds of Self-becoming. We should transform everything into a Thou, into a second Self; only thus do we intensify our own being toward the universal Self, which is both singular and all inclusive."[3]

Two other aspects of Storm's sentence clarify how the relational self can emerge through the poetic process. The term "contemplation" ("Anschauung") although not especially emphasized by Storm, is surely central to the ontological thinking of this period: the development of the so-called "thing poem" ("Dinggedicht") from Mörike to Rilke has been studied often enough. The paradox of "Anschauung" is that the self is systematically emptied of everything except its concentration on a given object. But the object is thereby transformed through the weight of the self's memories and associations—which redirect the reader's attention back to the observing self and generate precisely that "hovering" between outer and inner worlds imagined by Novalis.

Storm's notion of a sudden clarity arising out of a semiconscious, dreamlike state, although Goethean in origin, carries with it the non-Goethean implication that the central entity, the self, is dissolved without necessarily being reassembled. The dream state allows the whole life of the self, remote memories and instant impressions, to flood the poem's texture, while the resulting clarity can be an impersonal vision carrying no implications for the self's reintegration. The vision is the sole telos to be communicated. Karl Pestalozzi makes the contrast with Goethe in his discussion of Meyer's "Himmelsnähe": "But the opposites that concern Meyer are not complementary but contradictory. . . . . They cancel each other. Thus they cannot produce a third thing, but can only be intensified into paradox."[4] Goethe's truths are by definition "fruitful"; the value of these privileged moments, however, depends on their successful reproduction and transmission through narrative.

Pestalozzi also gives a valuable history of "poetry of the moment" ("Augenblickslyrik") and its origins in Catholic theology, but without special reference to Novalis. Yet it is Novalis who provides the framework that best illuminates these poets' concerns, their fascination with the visionary moment interwoven with their "realistic" contextualizing of all such moments. The moment is not just a theme, an experience to be evoked: it is the metaphysical goal of poetry itself, the special linguistic construct resulting from the bombardment of a given moment by all the reflective powers of the mind, by analysis, duplication, and skeptical reduction. Novalis evokes the proximity of privileged immediacy to the deadness of inert time—a proximity without mystical escape routes: "concerning the present moment, or the ceaseless congealing process of earthly time. It has a strange life flame. Time creates everything, as it also destroys, binds, and divides everything."[5]

Novalis's radical isolation of the moment is crucial for this poetics: in a single moment the forces of construction, destruction, and rigidification are not only simultaneously operative, they are instantaneously complete, exhausted. The continuum of presentness is thus not just threatening; it is a seductive falsehood, an illusion of comfort besieging the nineteenth-century mind at every level. The lyrical moment becomes then an absolute necessity, an act of rupture so openly and urgently staged that "chance" (Novalis's "Zufall") must be constituted within the narration: in the interpretive narrative subjectivity

can be interwoven with death, depersonalization, and the radical otherness of nature as dialogue partner. It is in this vein that Novalis continues the above fragment: "Like an electrical spark we spring across into
the other world. Intensified capacity. Death is transformation, overcoming of the principle of individuality, which now enters into a new,
more stable and productive relationality."

Critics exploring the intersections between Romantic philosophy
and poetry often tend to limit their examples to Romantic literary
practice.[6] But Novalis's dissolution of fixities such as individuality
and death into a dynamics of relational instants opens a path into the
poetic ontology of Storm, Keller, and Meyer. Novalis both histor-
icizes nature and imagines history itself as a sequence of self-purifying
moments. These three poets, all of them primarily storytellers probing
socio-empirical horizons, elevate the lyrical moment into the revelation of the half-hidden, "higher" narrative of nature's space. A juxtaposition of two sentences from Novalis gives us the beginning and the
end of this fundamental narrative: "Space as precipitate of time—as
necessary consequence of time."[7] "Time is intensification of space."[8]
Space is not just imbued with history: its status is provisional, to be intensified and transformed into a purified temporality accessible to the
privileged moment. Our image of a "real" world, a fixed space gov-
erned by independent laws, is historically produced, with the power
to control thought and language. The risk is always that the underly-
ing narrative of qualitative change will be submerged in the uniform
presentness that spatial "laws" impose. Nineteenth-century reality,
overdetermined by conventions of nature and private culture, cannot
be undermined until these conventions are installed, until the reader is
reading. The privileged moment, then, invades the consciousness of a
self embedded in conventions of presentness; simultaneously defend-
ing itself and probing new time zones, the self becomes gradually uprooted from past and future, in a time zone seemingly wholly other
than the "eternity" of surrounding nature. And it is this isolating
temporality, this acceleration of mortal processes, that certifies the
function of the privileged moment on the map of spiritual history projected by Novalis: "Everything is inherently eternal. Mortality and
mutability are precisely marks that distinguish higher natures. Eternity is a sign of spiritless beings."[9] This privileging of human temporality, of the transforming power of our fragility, culminates in the pathos of Rilke's *Ninth Elegy*:

72

Aber dieses
ein Mal gewesen zu sein, wenn auch nur *ein* Mal:
irdisch gewesen zu sein, scheint nicht widerrufbar.

But to have existed
this once, to have been of the earth but once
appears to be irrevocable.

The first stage of the narrative, the emergence of space from time, is fueled by the notion of "chance," the unpretentious, totally concrete happening so favored by Novalis: "It is not the essential, not the main elements, that are characteristic, but the inessential, the specific."[10] By situating a contingent event, a piece of autobiography, at the outset, the poets center their speaking on the principle of individuality.

But in the second stage, the speaker lets go of the experience; it becomes spatial and autonomous, and the self takes on the posture of observer. The given material of experience is heuristically "united" with the world's "laws"; through the interpretive gesture of "contemplation" the contingent mode in which the poem opened is transcended: "The world is the sphere of uncompleted unifications between spirit and nature."[11]

The third moment of the narrative involves the gradual reabsorption of the central scene into a new time zone, an intensification of the spatial, not by limiting it but by expanding it: the scene grows to absorb the entire life of the observer, emancipating him from his observer status even as it appears to deprive him of all autonomy. But in fact, the self's radical acceptance of his own reduction actually releases him back into the realm that is "his," even though all initial projections of identity are now suspended. Novalis evokes this dialectic thus: "The fate that oppresses us is the inertia of our spirit. Through expansion and heightening of our creative activity we will transform ourselves into our fate."[12]

If this reindividualization and retemporalization of space can be achieved, then a fourth and final stage in the narrative becomes possible: a turn from privileged to historical time in which the self endeavors to interpret its new authority, to become in effect the voice of its uniquely imagined space—time as "intensification of space." For the poetic movement is one of dialogue wherein the self alters the very texture of its chosen "partner" even as it abandons all the conventional props of subjectivity. The momentum of the text is thus toward widening the perilous dialogue, including the transmission of the privileged moment within its own processes. For there is indeed something to transmit: the rupture of such a well-established social space permits the emergence of strange, uncontrollable temporalities. What can happen in the course of the poetic narrative is that the hieroglyphs of the world are deciphered, past and future suddenly blended into potent meaning. The complexity of such a moment is compounded by the axiom that it lays no claim to "eternity," that the vision must be poised for immediate reentry into the flux. There is no Goethean order that it could serve to reveal. Paradoxically, there is a tinge of banality in the final stages of our texts, not because they fail, but because they succeed: at the very moment the poem's speaker achieves the authority of the "seer," he must shun the self-deception of such a role and redirect his language away from the achieved moment, toward morality and the everyday.

Theodor Storm's concern for a poem's impact is wholly consonant with his insistence on formal values, and with Novalis's view that the self is something to be "made," with privileged moments as scaffolding: "The Self is not a product of nature, not a naturally or historically determined being—but an artistic being, an art process, an artwork."[13]

Verloren
Theodor Storm

Was Holdes liegt mir in dem Sinn,
Das ich vor Zeit einmal besessen;
Ich weiss nicht, wo es kommen hin,
Auch, was es war, ist mir vergessen.
Vielleicht—am fernen Waldesrand,
Wo ich am lichten Junimorgen
—Die Kinder klein und klein die Sorgen—
Mit dir gesessen Hand in Hand,
Indes vom Fels die Quelle tropfte,
Die Amsel schallend schlug im Grund,
Mein Herz in gleichen Schlägen klopfte,
Und glücklich lächelnd schwieg dein Mund;
In grünen Schatten lag der Ort—
Wenn nur der weite Raum nicht trennte,
Wenn ich nur dort hinüber könnte,
Wer weiss!—vielleicht noch fänd ich's dort.[14]

(1873)

Lost

Something sweet is lying in my mind,
Which I at one time did possess;
I know not what has become of it,
I have even forgotten what it was.
Perhaps—at the far forest's edge,
Where I, one bright June morning
(Our children small, small too our cares)
Sat with you hand in hand,
While the spring dripped from the rock,
The blackbird's cry resounded beneath us,
My heart's beating synchronized with it,
And you were silent, smiling happily;
In green shadows lay this place—
Would that great distances did not cut me off,
If I could only reach across to that place,
Who knows!—perhaps still I'd find it there.

The tensions between formal and informal language, contingent and interpretive narration, which characterized the poems of the first chapter, are no longer in evidence. Yet the new ease of poetic discourse is curiously rootless, the omnipresence of memory dilutes instead of nourishes. The text is not a reflection on experience, but a narrative of longing for what experience might be. Of unusual interest is the tenacity with which the self clings to its own presence at every stage of the poem, a presence that generates all the distinctive features of the text, the thematic vagueness of both time and space and the elaborate, intricately tentative syntax, in which the reader gradually loses himself. The speaker is pushing his images as far away from his current self as possible, yet without being able to relinquish control of the images, and hence without opening himself to the transformation for which he explicitly yearns.

The conversational intimacy of the first four lines masks a radical disintegration of normal temporality; the sense of chance forcing things open is very much as Novalis envisioned it. We begin with virtually no distance between the rupturing moment and the everyday. The verb "lying" immediately domesticates "something sweet"; he seems to hold "it" in his mind as if it were a bird in his hand. The second line is equally informal, yet the word "possessed" ("besessen") begins to cause vibrations: how can something so imprecise have been "possessed"? A slight tension is evident between "liegt" and "besessen," as if the current tranquility were holding a more neurotic temperament at bay. The third line appears to resume the conversational tone. It is only in the fourth line that the reader becomes aware of what has happened. The accumulated negatives have gradually stripped away the speaker's protective covering. What had initially appeared as casual, comfortable, has now emerged as a challenge to the self's very existence. He cannot "remember" anything about the sweet something, yet this absent substance, through the simple alchemy of poetic movement, has laid absolute claim to him. The word "besessen," with its threatening double meaning of bourgeois control and neurotic obsession, has subtly invaded domestic time, opening an abyss under his thought process.

The word *abyss* seems appropriate to this stage of the poem, with the sudden emergence of immense yet detailed spatial dimensions from temporal musings ("space as a precipitate of time"). To counter the corrosion of the present through restless yet insubstantial memories, the speaker projects a faraway "remembered" scene from the past. From now until the end, the poem consists entirely of dependent clauses, which give the attempted depiction of peace and intimacy a nervous quality. The verbs are in the indicative, yet everything seems to stem from "perhaps"; and the stage setting, with birds and a dripping spring performing, stands in the way of the recapture of intimacy ostensibly being sought.

But it is through these tensions and apparently false notes that the poem's authenticity defines itself. For the self's existence is enlarged as it is forced out of its intimacy, put on stage, compelled to elaborate its spatial images in tortuous syntax. The phrases "at the far forest's edge" and "one bright June morning" enmesh the speaker in the willed harmonies of his own narration; he is forced to become the observer of his whole life, on the edge in the manner of Eichendorff, and to confront the "poetry" that sentimentalizes all images of the past, in order to wrest from it genuine images of at least a possible past. Through the gentle, seemingly random musings of the opening the speaker has stumbled into a poetic scene where his language, his memory, the very possibility of a coherent life narrative, are at stake.

At the poem's very center occurs the mention of the word "you" ("dir") and a concurrent rhythmic stabilization on the phrase "Hand in Hand" (the rhyme scheme, with the delaying rhyme of lines 6 and 7, provides a slight extra stress). There is no surprise at the entry of the poet's wife into the poem: the reader has been well prepared for it. But its effects are varied. The conversational tone of the opening is now explained, but also subtly estranged; the wife he finally mentions is the wife of another time and place, and the paradoxical result is that the nominal dialogue form makes the anxious isolation of the monologue all the more vivid. Or rather, the speaker's dialogue is not with his wife but with the entirety of his past. The problematic quality of the remembering has been so much in evidence by the time "dir" is spoken that the reader enters this past full of justified doubts, as if the intimate scene had become more an allegory of poetic resources than an experience. And this sense is reinforced by the role the wife plays. She is the creative second identity which we find at the heart of all these texts, the one who is at ease within the space that the poet's self-uprooting has produced, who simply lives her own being without possibility of loss. As the unmoved telos of the poet's quest, the wife of the past produces herself, effortlessly and forever.

The speaker's past self has become part of the scene, through the literal rhythm of the heartbeat, but this represents yet another stage of the self's devolution, in the special form of Storm's yearning. He longs to be part of the scene and so he is/was, and the stylized context of the bird song makes the reader conscious that such total fusion of external and internal belongs, not in the realm of experience, but only in the organizing action of poetry itself. The speaker intrudes on his own scene, and the poem subtly shifts from the second spatial stage of the narrative to the stage of temporal reabsorption. The wife's silence reinforces this. She is, as it were, the stage manager of the scene as it is evoked, creator of a moment that is for her in no need of narration. But she is also at the center of the elaborate, interpretive narrative being woven by her husband. Just as the remembered heartbeat is only an accompaniment, not the melody itself, so the wife's silence withholds the meaning of her own creation. The poet cannot be silent; he is made of words. And the words with which he must surround his vision lead him away from the center into the enveloping layers of time.

With the single line "In green shadows lay this place" two narrative shifts are instigated: the observing self moves away from the centrally focused scene, enclosing it from the outside; and the exaggerated clarity of the images enter the shadow, the realm of the indistinct and subconscious—the realm of temporal dissolution. The third stage of the ecstatic narrative is in process, the reabsorption of space into time. But the moment of this text generates sheer frustration, a failure of poetic language to achieve temporal intensification. For just as the speaker disrupted his own memory by the intrusion of his excessively harmonious heartbeat, so his manipulative closeness to the past stands in the way of temporal transcendence.

In the last three lines we are not in a new time zone; we are back at the beginning. One can look at the syntax as either in a state of collapse or in one of extreme complexity: either way the reader feels the speaker's mind and nothing but his mind. The moment is out of reach, it withholds itself from the ardent tentacles of linguistic organization. The phrase "great distances" maintains spatial linkage in the very act of withdrawal, although it is primarily temporal separation that is being evoked. But the fact that the speaker continues to perceive his loss as spatial is itself significant. The dynamics of the quest assume an opening into the deep past, a risk-taking plunge. Yet the past scene is like a hallucinatory extension of the present; time congeals into old space instead of producing new. In Novalis's terminology, the poem embodies a "congealing process," where what is sought is a consuming flame. "Chance" is the starting point, and in the model of this poetry it must be so. But the agony of this poem is that no transformation is achieved. The abyss rupturing presentness has opened, and there is only the insecure rope of the conditional clause to be thrown across it.

Refuge is also taken to some extent in a rhythmic lightening of the phrasing, especially the folksy "Who knows!" But when the reader reaches the final words, "perhaps still I'd find" ("fänd ich's dort"), he is literally returned to the uncertainty of the opening. The reader has not, after all, glimpsed "something sweet" in the past, but has merely accompanied the poet on his anxious, overcontrolled quest for it. The sentence that began with "Perhaps" in line 5 is "completed," but in such an emptiness of meaning that the poem seems open in a most dangerous way. If the poet cannot render secure the transition from the fixities of remembered images to the necessary immediacy of present identity, then time is his unrelenting enemy, engulfing him in sterile isolation.

The "it" of the final line is the goal embodied in the fourth stage of the narrative model; and for Storm it is that which is forever excluded from his poetry. The more he strives to direct his text toward the temporal regeneration of past beauty, the more his words speak only of the absence, the emptying out of the past. In poetic (as opposed to psychological) terms, the withdrawal of the past is intimately linked to the inability of the self to shed its own obsessive concerns at the outset. The process of "contemplation," the generation of a purified space, demands in this poetics that the speaker become functionally empty, a pure observer. This the poet could not do. Interpretation never loosens its grip on contingency, ultimately strangling it. Yet this anxious artifice vibrates as a historical narrative, anthologizing the possibilities and impossibilities of experience.

The probing insecurity of Storm's interpretive narration contrasts with the confident rhetoric of Gottfried Keller, as he actualizes an extreme moment of privilege through multiple narrative layering.

Stiller Augenblick
Gottfried Keller

Fliehendes Jahr, in duftigen Schleiern
Streifend an abendrötlichen Weihern,
Wallest du deine Bahn;
Siehst mich am kühlen Waldsee stehen,
Wo an herbstlichen Uferhöhen
Zieht entlang ein stummer Schwan.

Still und einsam schwingt er die Flügel,
Tauchet in den Wasserspiegel,
Hebt den Hals empor und lauscht;
Taucht zum andern Male nieder,
Richtet sich auf und lauschet wieder,
Wie's im flüsternden Schilfe rauscht.

Und in seinem Tun und Lassen
Wills mich wie ein Traum erfassen,
Als obs meine Seele wär,
Die verwundert über das Leben,
Über das Hin—und Wiederschweben,
Lugt und lauschte hin und her.

Atme nur in vollen Zügen
Dieses friedliche Genügen
Einsam auf der stillen Flur!
Und hast du dich klar empfunden,
Mögen enden deine Stunden,
Wie zerfliesst die Schwanenspur![15]

Still Moment

Fleeing year, in scented veils
Brushing against ponds tinged with evening red,
You wend your way;

79

See me standing by the cool forest lake,
Where, by the high autumnal banks,
A soundless swan proceeds.

Silent and alone it vibrates its wings,
Dives beneath the surface,
Raises its neck and listens;
Dives down a second time,
Reemerges and listens again
To what is rustling in the whispering reeds.

Absorbed in its action and inaction
I am seized as by a dream,
As if it were my soul,
Which, amazed at life,
At its oscillation back and forth,
Were looking and listening in all directions.

Only breathe in, in full measure,
This peaceful self-sufficiency
Alone on the quiet meadow!
And when you have clearly felt your being,
May the hours of your life conclude,
Just as the swan's trace dissolves behind it!

The foregrounding of narrative structure in the poems of this chapter is intimately linked to a decrease in vividness at the level of imagery. The language that produces the privileged moment is remarkable for its desire not to appear privileged, its conversational play with repertoire. But this apparent paradox reveals the double strength of this poetics. On the one hand, the speaker's easy familiarity with a conventionalized "nature" releases a rhythm of longing for specialness, a longing that in the course of the poem comes to *constitute* that specialness; and on the other hand, the persona's careful, self-limiting observation, the prowling around the central enigma, opens the text to readers as a kind of joint project, blending visual precision with moral reflection. Novalis suggests that the more the self becomes conscious of its isolation and separateness, the more its margins become permeated with the vibrant otherness of the surrounding world; for the poet this means that the presence of potential readers vibrates in his language: "Community and singularity. Everything can be Self, indeed is or should be Self."[16] In the privatized world delimited by the text of this chapter, the self is explicitly confined to empirical experience; and the dialectic of confinement drives poetic language to mythologize the empirical—by purifying the self into an observer without other motives, and by tightly focusing the act of observation. The interpretive narratives of these poets bind the self as closely as possible to a single contingency. And precisely because Storm, Keller, and Meyer lay claim to a privileged moment, their poetics is open and informal, securing that moment in as many ways as possible.

In his famous article on Eichendorff, cited in the previous chapter, Adorno argues that the very stylizations of vocabulary, the pastoral conventions, throw the repressed actuality of social conflict into relief. An analogous argument holds for the language of repertoire deployed by the poets of mid-century. Far from implying a stagnation or exhaustion of the idea of history, repertoire signifies its full establishment as a "formalized" discourse in Foucault's sense. Theodor Storm's 1870 preface, integrating private and public through the act of reading, reinforces the active understanding of repertoire poetics. For language as such, in this perspective, encodes the many possibilities of historical motion. The securing of the privileged moment thus enables the poet to tap into an already guaranteed, already "present" linguistic richness.

The structure of repertoire is anticipated by Novalis in his discussion of human creativity as a temporal fullness: "We call it instinct or genius, it is everywhere already actual. It is the fullness of future, temporal fullness as such—the equivalent in time to the philosopher's stone in space: Reason, fantasy, rationality, and meaning are only its individual functions."[17] If poetic language is to install the privileged moment in the historical process ("We are summoned to undertake the Bildung of the earth"), to narrate both the entry into fullness and the return from it, it is better that it *not* draw attention to itself, that the integration of the banality of the everyday with the unique moment be as unobtrusive as possible. A comparison with Charles Baudelaire's roughly contemporaneous "Le Cygne" illuminates the expressive range of repertoire poetics. Baudelaire's swan is in exile, ejected from its watery habitat into dry Parisian streets, reproaching God, refusing meaning, denatured in every sense. Whereas the harmonious typicality of Keller's swan is a given, this swan is also full of longing—but for the fullness in which it is already at home. The differences between Keller's swan poem and Baudelaire's "Le Cygne" could hardly be more radical. Yet it is only in the two texts taken together that Schlegel's "epoch" ("the universe as object") becomes fully intelligible. Baudelaire's foregrounding of repertoire as allegory, his leaps across the vast time zones of exile, live in polarity with Keller's cautious colonization of a single glimpse.

This polarity is illuminated by Walter Benjamin, for whom Baudelaire's swan, with its radical frailty ("Hinfälligkeit") in which antiquity and modernity are collapsed into a single dying, is the authentic emblem of the nineteenth century. For it is Gottfried Keller's remark, that "the truth will not run away from us," which Benjamin cites as irrevocably "historicist" in the fifth "Thesis on the Philosophy of History." In their own context, however, Keller's words do not sound complacent. Within nineteenth-century discourse his phrase invokes temporal continuities solely as the necessary source of the privileged moment ("truth") which must be enabled to float free and clear of these continuities. In this endangered world the countertruths of Baudelaire and Keller emerge through antithetical modes of temporal rupture. The teleology of the privileged moment—the poem by Meyer will make this point explicit—ultimately mirrors the Baudelairean diagnosis of social life as an infinity of unrecognized dying processes.

Keller immediately gives the quality of repertoire to his derivative opening images by modulating from one image of temporal movement to another. "Fleeing year": time is immediately spatialized and the reader given the sense of loss, of a continuous motion of time into the distance; but this effect is modified by the regular motion of "You wend your way." The year is vanishing into nothing, but it is also seasonal, touching the autumn leaves, regulating the human world even as it threatens it. More playful is the personification of the year: the first stanza depends entirely on it, yet a kind of collusion with the reader, an openness of manner, ensures that the centralizing year acts immediately to direct attention back toward the multiple, minute motions of the scene. "See me" links the year to the poem's speaker, effectively dissolving the year-as-Gestalt at the very moment when it is endowed with "eyes." Seeing, observing, is to be the governing movement of the text, leading from the seeing year through the intently observing persona to the listening swan itself. In this sense the "still moment" of the title is never actually still, but is only constituted through the movement between the observers of stillness, the flow from one nuance to the next of a wholly convention-bound natural scene. The word "standing" does *not* interrupt the flow; the poem's speaker is lacking in all presence except the function of pure perception. He has the poet's allegorical position on the edge, "by the cool forest lake," and represents nothing more than a point between sky and water, between time and space, between

82

fluidity and the longing for stillness. In the last line this longing produces the swan. The rhythm becomes stately, the trochaic gravity of the meter heightened by the gently contrasting dactyls in lines 1, 5, and 6. A swan's movements have always suggested allegory to human beings, and this one is clearly no exception. But Novalis's poetics, which condition the functioning of the privileged moment in these texts, requires that the swan's presence be in a crucial sense accidental, empirical: its allegorical strength can only emerge from the poem's elaboration of its singular movements, from a prolonged lingering on the bird's surface as it explores the surfaces around it, from a refusal of "higher" mysteries.

The movement of the first stanza culminates in a vertical sign (the swan), which is now reinforced by the (conventional) image of the lake as a mirror; everything that has been restlessly in motion above the surface is somehow concentrated in the tiny space of water in front of the swan. And then this extreme compression of reality into a single space itself generates a kind of violation, which is yet wholly contained in the spatial vision. For the swan plunges its neck "into" the sustaining surface, precisely not in order to dwell in the depths, but to reemerge as an explorer of surfaces; and then it "listens," listens to the universe, as if the brief plunge had transformed it into a seismograph through which the whispering reeds might speak of coherence, of the stillness at the heart of things, which the mutual stillness of swan and human observer yearn to approximate. The swan has become, in fact, the poet's "double," concentrating into its own silent being a gestural dream of the creative quest: it moves in its own time zone, and the suddenness of its movements suggests a purposefulness denied to all human motion. But at this divide between the human and the natural, the moment that would seem to make silence inescapable, the language of mutual longing (the longing even of the reeds) persists. Through the interpretive posture attributed to it the swan magically links its own contingency to the historical narrative implicit in its allegorical role. This last characteristic, this opening outward, enables the speaker finally to move inward toward his magnetic double, to begin establishing some kind of presence, to reabsorb absolute space into the structured "fate" of narrated time.

The "intensification" ("Potenzierung") of space into time is not a recentering, not a stabilization; rather, it is a narrative of dissolution, an absorption of the observer into its object of contemplation. Keller's poem is a very precise enactment of the narrative model. And again it is his use of the repertoire that enables him to move forward so concisely. In the first two stanzas the self lacks all presence; but in the third it is suddenly prominent, as Keller switches to a confessional style. Without the style change the language would be pale and flat ("dream," "soul," etc.). But the reader is alerted to read against the grain, to shun psychology, and to focus on the speaker's words as an event, the inner event that corresponds to the event of the swan's probing ritual. Then the phrasing can be taken literally: "in its action and inaction"—the self's absorption in the spectacle is total, the dreamlike state arises from his being *inside* the swan's movements.

As Novalis teaches, the fullness of space is ultimately identical with the fullness of time, because no action ever finally enters oblivion: "Nature is nothing but the accumulated past, the freedom of other times, hence it is most certainly the ground of history."[18] This insight translates the subtlest natural events into echoes of the past, in a narrated continuum perpetually transforming memory into the possibility of new history; and Keller's stylistic shifts intensify the audibility of such echoes. In particular, he suggests gaps in the text where words are momentarily transcended. One senses such a gap at the end of line 2; with the words "As if" the "dream" that is neither the externality of the swan nor the interior of the observing consciousness but an "oscillation" between the two, attains verbal reality. It is an "interpretation," an inward shift that yet remains wholly within the contemplated scene; the interpretive narrative is immediately reabsorbed into the contingent.

Once the state of identity with the swan is registered, the identity itself becomes a fiction, a new stage in the narrative. And Keller communicates this shift most subtly, by attributing inwardness to the swan's movements. In stanza 2 we learned only of the swan's intense attentiveness; now the word "amazed" is used, transforming the human emotion of externality, even alienation, into a dream of oneness-with-Being possible only through the swan, as the self's perfected double. And the abstraction "life" is now glossed as "oscillation [hovering] back and forth," a precise usage of the word "Schweben," so important to Novalis. The conceptualization involved is minimal, neither purposefulness nor emptiness is implied. But the swan's world is self-contained; in order for the human mind to gain access to this allegory of purity, the temporal fullness compressed in the image must be released through contingent sequencing within its world. This already occurs in stanza 2, with the simple enumeration of the two plunges of the neck into the lake. And now the entry of the "soul" into the swan becomes simultaneously the activation of a universal temporality, a contextualizing of the bird as being at one with the shifting rhythm of the world around it.

There is another gap, a wordless moment, between stanzas 3 and 4. And then Keller changes styles again, shifting to an imperative mode, the tone of Goethe the sage. There can be no doubt that "This peaceful self-sufficiency" is somewhat banal, a letting go of the concentrated moment. But as the speaker withdraws from the privileged moment itself, he moves, not into the long-dissolved presentness of the empirical, but into a hypothetical future in which the observing self, the observed swan, and the reader are equally partners in dialogue. In contrast to the nightmare future of Droste-Hülshoff's poem, this temporality is the gift of the privileged moment, both sealing in the poem's images and opening them outward into a public space where the reader can "end his days." On one level Keller is completing the circle of the poem, evoking the "fleeing year" of the opening and converting the perfection of the swan's presence into a comparably perfect absence, as satisfying as the disappearance of autumn leaves in winter. But on another level the speaker is linking the key word "clearly," a crystallization of the dream clarity of stanza 3, to the image of death as being readily accepted. Keller's "intensified time" is expressed in the swift, programmatic transition from concreteness to metaphysics: the refusal of melancholy in the face of death, indeed the viewing of death as an active, energized process. Novalis puts it thus: "If our physical life is a burning up of energy, then our spiritual life is doubtless also a combustion process. Death is thus perhaps a change in spiritual capacity."[19]

Seen in this light, the completion of the circle implied in these closing images is achieved at a level higher than mere acceptance. The term "dissolves" is more drastic, more clearly evocative of destruction, than the gently melancholic "fleeing year"; and the narrative of the poem, the absorption of the self into the mirror of the swan's totally pure creativity, has engendered a thrust toward absence and death that transcends familiar fears. The very perfection of the observed scene leads the speaker to relinquish it, as the speaker of Storm's poem was unable to do. For Novalis, individuation and self-destruction are synonymous processes: "All life is a proliferating process of renewal, which only from the side has the appearance of a process of destruction."[20] At poem's end, the speaker invokes death and loss with the stabilized knowledge that his words are spoken "from the side," from his spectator's post at the water's edge. The narrative itself has been freed to culminate in "dissolution," in an energetic fusion of the sensory and the hieratic.

From Keller's lake to the mountains of Conrad Ferdinand Meyer is a foreshortened textual journey. For whereas the swan's significance spreads outward in concentric linguistic ripples, the open, skyward perspectives Meyer introduces are gradually, obsessively blocked by a single, fragile human figure.

Die Bank des Alten
C. F. Meyer

Ich bin einmal in einem Tal gegangen,
Das fern der Welt, dem Himmel nahe war,
Durch das Gelände seiner Wiesen klangen
Die Sensen rings der zweiten Mahd im Jahr.

Ich schritt durch eines Dörfchens stille Gassen.
Kein Laut. Vor einer Hütte sass allein
Ein alter Mann, von seiner Kraft verlassen,
Und schaute feiernd auf den Firneschein.

Zuweilen, in die Hand gelegt die Stirne,
Seh ich den Himmel jenes Tales blaun,
Den Müden seh ich wieder auf die Firne,
Die nahen, selig klaren Firne schaun.

's ist nur ein Traum. Wohl ist der Greis geschieden
Aus dieser Sonne Licht, von Jahren schwer;
Er schlummert wohl in seines Grabes Frieden
Und seine Bank steht vor der Hütte leer.

Noch pulst mein Leben feurig. Wie den andern
Kommt mir ein Tag, da mich die Kraft verrät;
Dann will ich langsam in die Berge wandern
Und suchen, wo die Bank des Alten steht.[21]

The Old Man's Bench

Once I went walking in a valley,
Far from the world and close to the heavens,
Through its meadows' expanse there sounded
The scythes at work on the year's second harvest.

I walked through the quiet streets of a tiny village.
No sound. Before a hut there sat alone

An old man, deserted by his strength,
Gazing solemnly at the light of the glacier snow.

On occasion, with my forehead in my hand,
I see the bluing of that valley's sky,
I see the tired man gazing at the snow,
At the nearby, serenely clear glacier snow.

It's only a dream. The old man has surely departed,
Loaded down with years, from the light of our sun;
Surely he slumbers in the peace of his grave
And his bench stands empty before the hut.

The beat of my life is still fiery. But as to others,
So there will come to me a day when strength betrays me;
Then will I slowly wander into the mountains
And seek out the old man's bench, where it stands.

To transmit the privileged moment into the realm of potentially universal "Bildung" involves a journey through repertoire. Visionary images are not invented so much as reinvented, awakened to new narrative life. The poem doubles, contextualizes, communalizes the moment. The chance event, the subordination of self to autonomous space, the intensification of space into time, and the attempt to speak with clarity, in a time zone bridging poem and world: all these elements are necessary to a poetics of privileged vision, and Keller draws attention to the movement between them by deploying a variety of styles, setting the images in new verbal contexts, ensuring that the reader cannot limit the speaker's vision to the merely psychological level. Meyer's strategy is the opposite: he maintains the tightest possible continuity, both stylistic and psychological, between the speaker and his "double," the old man. Keller deploys a full range of conventional "nature" images, focusing on instants of juncture and dissolution; Meyer stages his quest in a landscape seemingly colonized as his "own" imagistic repertoire, yet its very closure is a threat to the life he longs for.

Much scholarship has been devoted to making an inventory of Meyer's images and their connotations. The harvest, for example, that dominates the opening stanza of our text is said by Jürgen Fährmann to connote "Ripeness, sacredness, fulfillment, excess, endangeredness, death."[22] Yet one wonders what is achieved by such a list. Like Storm and Keller, Meyer accepts the mission of the empirical, the imperative of a purified contingency; his constant compression and refinement of images represents the striving for the "musical" narrative invoked by Novalis, the encoding of psychological pain as pure verbal figuration. Particularly misleading is Heinrich Henel's application of Gottfried Benn's provocative title *Static Poems* (*Statische Gedichte*) to Meyer's style, thereby freezing him into an assigned role as a quasi-modernist bridge from the French Symbolists to Benn. For Meyer's poems are overtly allegorical: the structuring of repertoire images into narrative is a necessarily open-ended process, in which the eruption of pure contingency can only occur by chance and cannot by definition be reintegrated into the world's daily time. Meyer confronts the destructiveness of his pursuit of the privileged moment, which must rupture the present without hope of return. His poems allegorize the success that must also be failure, and they can only do so as melancholy, skeptical narratives, distancing the visionary claim as far as possible from subjective anxiety. "Die Bank des Alten" is not even mentioned by Henel in a book that deals with almost all of Meyer's poems; obviously he deemed it a failure, and it probably fits the following description of Meyer's "failures":

> Meyer was so much a symbolist that, without suitable subject matter, he could not express himself at all, or only tentatively and very imprecisely. Hence his constant quest for motifs that fitted into his project. He used them not only as examples to amplify or explain themes already appropriated, but to take possession of himself, to render his thoughts concrete, hence richer and clearer. Only in his bad poems does the material not fulfill this task. There it remains mere clothing for intellectual content, which could have been said as well or better in dry prose; such poems are allegories.[23]

The notion of allegory has of course since been critically rehabilitated, notably by Paul de Man in "The Rhetoric of Temporality."[24] But in general, despite the sensitivity of his individual readings, Henel's approach does not do justice to Meyer's oppressive sense of temporal sterility. Meyer's language is knowingly imprisoned within the banality of conscious feeling in the face of nature's remote silence. His strategy, particularly evident in the collection *In the Mountains* (*In den Bergen*), from which "Die Bank des Alten" is drawn, is simultaneously to colonize the silence and to accept the implications of the banality. The poet's own death is never far from his narrations, an imaginative zone where the crumbling of experience can be forced to stop. "Closeness to Heaven" ("Himmelsnähe") opens with imagery reminiscent of Mörike and Droste-Hülshoff:

> In meiner Firne feierlichem Kreis
> Lagr' ich an schmalem Felsengrate hier.

> In the solemn encircling of my glacier snow
> I rest here on a narrow rocky ridge.

But this is now a "repertoire" situation. The longing for nature has been formalized as the contemplation of "my" glacier snow, while the mountainous self-exposure holds no threat for the speaker. What Meyer fears is sterility, the infinite repetition of a present in which pure contingency has become inaccessible.

Novalis has provided something like a program for "Die Bank des Alten":

> That individual will be the most perfect, the most purely systematic, whose individuality is defined exclusively by a single, absolute accident ("Zufall"), for example, by his birth. In this accident all his other accidents must find their determination, be identifiable as *his* accidents, his states of being. The greater the poet, the less freedom he allows himself, the more philosophically stringent he is. He is satisfied with the arbitrary choice of the first moment. Every seed is a dissonance, a relational clash, which is later to be overcome and balanced.[25]

Even though Meyer's speaker stays as close to his central memory as does Storm's, he is able, in poetic terms, to complete his quest by following Novalis's dictum and allowing his entire being to be absorbed by a single "Zufall," the chance encounter with the old man. The temporal gap between the speaker's remembered experience and his recounting of it is remarkable for its emptiness; the past event reaches into the present thought, controls it, excludes all other imaginative outlets. A totally reciprocal relationship, "purely systematic," is achieved: the meaning of the old man's contemplation is generated by the self, and the self permits and disciplines itself to become, stage by stage, a product of that contemplation. Novalis's interesting combination of organic, musical, and abstract imagery seems precisely relevant: the originating event is cast as the seed from which the poem's language blossoms, but the growth is accomplished by an impotent resistance to that event, a longing to reclaim some freedom for the self, to resolve the dissonance, to close the obsessive gap that the old man has opened in the speaker's life. The gap is a "relational clash," a revelation of inadequacy; the privileged moment is brought into textual being by the speaker's inability to set any viable counterliving in the scales against it.

The unobtrusive opening stanza links two groupings of imagery from Meyer's repertoire that point in opposite directions. The first two lines, very spare and formulaic, suggest the fairy-tale isolation, the stylized purity familiar from the earliest Romantics. But the second two lines, richer in domestic associations, fill the mythically remote valley with people. It is important that the speaker only hears the people, indeed only their scythes are mentioned: the fullness of the year's second harvest is embodied in a fullness of sound, which is itself filtered into the isolation of the landscape as perceived by the speaker. The stanza is a stage setting, but a most cunning one, evoking with entirely conventional images both visual emptiness and aural fullness. Novalis's "Dissonanz" is subtly installed even before the "seed" is perceived; and the speaker is thereby endowed with important characteristics—he is ready both for the role of observer and for a slightly dreamlike atmosphere, which lends a monumental quality to what he sees. Novalis writes: "Our life is not a dream, but it should and perhaps will become one."[26] And Meyer's narrative does suggest the teleological wandering of *Heinrich von Ofterdingen*, a journey into dream.

An old man is by definition a temporal construct, potentially full of stories. All the more striking, then, that Meyer's old man functions as an exclusively spatial element in the narrative. He is defined by two qualities only: his gaze, which points away from him to the splendor of the glacier snow; and his feebleness, which evokes only his literal and metaphorical exclusion from life. Far from being a repository of fairy-tale wisdom, as the opening lines lead one to expect, the old man is the embodiment of every kind of absence and emptiness, except for the unadorned presence of his physical being. The negative attributes simply accumulate—"quiet streets . . . no sound . . . alone . . . deserted"—and thereby generate a powerful momentum toward the last line of the second stanza: "Gazing solemnly . . ."

It is as if we have entered the deserted village of Keats's "Grecian Urn," a deathly mirror world from which only the vision outward can redeem us. The stanza as a whole has a halting quality, emphasizing both the tentative quality of the old man's existence and the careful, cameralike focus of the speaker. We do not grasp the reason for this close attention; the lines strip all possibility of interest from the old man—until suddenly the rhythmic grandeur of the last line is upon us, alliterative and broadly paced. The line's verbal weaving ("feiernd . . . Firneschein") connotes precisely the kind of unified spatial event that lies at the center of all these poems. The religious overtone, the two-way flow between the man's gaze and the snow's reflective gleaming, fills the scene with the compressed time of ritual. And the appropriateness of the old man to his function as the self's double needs no elaboration. Whereas Keller needed a stanza in which to naturalize his already ritualistic swan, Meyer is intent on keeping his glimpsed scene within the pure immediacy of its carefully established limits. For the "revelatory" line fulfills, rather than contradicts, the stanza's negative rhythm. There is nothing within the old man; he is indeed an image of absence. But in the unrestrained outpouring of his feebleness to the snow, he simply has that unity of perception and being that is denied to everyone engaged in the continuum of daily time.

If the second stage of the model is very concise in Meyer's version, the third stage, the effort to reabsorb the scene into the speaker's personal time, is elaborate indeed. The scene itself has been anticipated by a dreamlike atmosphere, and the dream frame is immediately completed by the effort of the speaker to restage his memory. The goal of fusing the remembered event with the self's present quest for meaning is more explicit here than in the other two texts, as is the strong suggestion that the old man is the poet's double, "creator" of a scene already perfect. In Keller's poem, the speaker subtly humanizes the swan's vision after the shift from an external to an internal viewpoint; here too the speaker, in his effort to absorb the old man's simplicity into himself, alters the imagery just slightly. The old man is now "tired," assigned an "inwardness" not hinted at in the second stanza; and the snow is now "close" and "clear," the quasi-religious quality of "Firneschein" has dissipated. Categories of psychology and realism take over the scene in retrospect, and the repeated efforts of the conscious self to penetrate the meaning of its vision essentially fail: the vision simply obsesses the speaker as he adopts the old man's contemplative posture. Yet the will to unity stalls the narration, draining strength from the repertoire language.

And then the rupture occurs, precisely at the moment when the self reaches for safety, for the return to everyday time from the enigmatic past. The first linguistic signals indicate that the rescue is successful. The speaker deliberately "lets go" of the memory. The phrase "It's only a dream" brushes aside the hallucination leading up to and away from the central scene. And the language immediately loses its focus, its intimacy. Meyer draws on his repertoire of resonant, rather hollow conventional language to dismantle the old man's presence and stow him safely in his grave. After all, the scene in the first place had rested on a paradox of absence; the stanza endeavors to consummate that absence in a vocabulary of pious common sense. But Novalis's "chance" suddenly imposes itself on the speaker as he abandons his control of the contingent; in a moment of almost Proustian decisiveness, the removal of the old man uncovers the bench beneath. The culmination of the thrust toward absence is after all not the grave, but the persisting emptiness of the object, which the old man has marked forever. The bench "stands," mutely centralizing upon itself the speaker's disoriented temporality.

The scene is now present again for the speaker, but in an entirely new temporal zone, one that is neither limited to memory nor available to him so long as his own life maintains its private purposefulness. Of the three poems discussed, this one communicates most effectively the fourth stage of the model, a language that no longer belongs to the speaker in any psychological sense, but opens up the specific revelation of the text to a historical narrative emancipated from the speaker's interpretive struggle; a language that includes the speaker's whole life and subordinates it to a movement (the journey into the mountains), which is not his alone but the world's—just as the old man's original gaze belonged to the glacier snow. As the opening gesture of the last stanza the phrase "The beat of my life is still fiery" recalls "It's only a dream." Never can the literal meaning of "feurig" have been so utterly undermined.

In the poem's context, active life appears as an empty ritual that has to be played out. But the scope of Meyer's narration is inseparable from the open quality of this last stanza. He is opening himself to death, but in a "future" temporality that is already fully actualized, emancipated from the self-protective conventional time of the fourth stanza: his last gesture is that of the quest, "seeking out," not the banality of repeating the old man's contemplative act. For the speaker is forever exiled from that original contemplation, even though he is also forever bound by it. The goal he assigns himself is not the old man's own, but the bench that the old man took for granted; the absence the bench embodies is definitive and will be confirmed by the speaker's will-to-death. Yet this compression of time to a single spatial point can only be accomplished through the temporal movement of the poem; the "absolute accident" of Novalis's programmatic fragment is reached through a doubling and redoubling of the interpretive narrative around the initial contingency. Thus the poem's mysteriousness-without-mystery, its obsessive replaying of a moment of pure contemplation ("Anschauung"), frees the reader from the speaker's personal melancholy at the very moment when it is being intensified into symbiosis with the empty bench. The old man's steady contemplation has simultaneously robbed the speaker of his autonomy and answered his longing for a communicable privileged moment. Novalis anticipates this complexity: "Some things can appear only once, because the 'once' belongs to their essence. Our life is at once absolute and dependent. We die only to a certain extent. Our life must thus be in part an element of a greater, collective life."[27] The speaker has rescued the uniqueness of the old man, but at the cost of his own entire conventional time span; the narrative journey on which he is to embark promises him not the inaccessible duplication of the old man's vision but the pure duplication of the dissolution of his life. To reach the bench would be to die. The journey into the mountains has something of the aura of the journey of Abraham and Isaac; the speaker has willed the sacrifice of his own life in order to respond unflinchingly to the "commandment" of a single contingency.

In all three of our texts the central scene is one of absolute, self-contained peace—and for that very reason it disrupts the speaker-observer's life. He has had the vision of peace, but it eludes him by virtue of his very humanness; yet he knows that he must find a way, *not* to incorporate the experience into his life—that would dilute and degrade it—but to absorb his life into the texture of the unique experience. This poetics is directed at the time zone "after" the moment of rupture, the achievement of a temporality that will be no mere sterile return to the "before" of the empirical frame. Words are not exterior to this process, they constitute it, they are the "spirit" of which Novalis speaks when he writes: "Our spirit should become a physical, tangible machine, not within us, but in the world."[28]

The poetic self must be dissolved before this textual machine can reassemble it; and all three poets use a sequence of vertical and horizontal imagery to convey, first the dissolution and absorption into a quasi-mystical central point, and then the temporal distance that both separates and connects the speaker to his vision. Storm's vertical images are unobtrusive—the sitting posture of the speaker and his wife, the water dripping from the rock—but the anguished evocation of distance at the end lends a hieratic quality to the remembered scene. Keller, in contrast, emphasizes the vertical by reinforcing the given image of the swan's dipping and stretching neck through evocations of the standing self, the high banks, and the surrounding reeds. The horizontal images enter the text only gradually: "the oscillation back and forth," "on the quiet meadow." But with the strikingly dynamic "the swan's trace dissolves" the insistently vertical swan itself vanishes in a horizontal continuum. Meyer sets both the old man and the posture of the speaker obsessed by him in a vertical relationship to the world; and the process of contemplating an act of contemplation becomes concretized in the bench, which "stands" at the end of both stanzas 4 and 5: it is the vision's spatio-temporal legacy, an emptiness that is also the goal of the speaker's dissolving life, the imagined point at the end of the ritual journey. Keller and Meyer achieve the "hovering" ("Schweben") envisaged by Novalis, the time zone produced by a single pure "chance," but that does not lay claim to the vision's initial purity. In order for the vision to be communicable, it must be experienced as absence; and once absent its validity can be confirmed and reconfirmed by the narrative toward and away from it, the movement through closure to openness of the poem itself. The concept of "Bildung" is thus sustained, precariously, by the poem's power to transmit the privileged vision into the realm of potential history.

CHAPTER THREE

Cold Apocalypse: Rilke, Heym, Trakl

T he privileged moment is, to adopt Frank Kermode's phrase,[1] the principal concord fiction of the nineteenth century. This fiction aligns the rupture of the temporal continuum with a glimpse of full existence, whether distant or immediate; and a narrative of "Bildung" is maintained and codified through strategies of translating the contingent glimpse, nursed by a self-effacing interpretive narrative, into a dream of history shared by a lyrical community. But this consensual poetics made precarious assumptions about contingency, "Zufall": that it could be recovered as narration, and that its sheer vividness guaranteed communicable meaning.

In the early years of the twentieth century this concord fiction came rather suddenly to be seen as artificial, an arbitrary isolation of the contingent; and it was the suddenness of the shift, together with the absolute strangeness of a world whence the once all-powerful temporality of "Bildung" has completely drained away, which generated the "literary revolution" still being worked through in our century.[2] Shifts in rhetoric notwithstanding, to read Expressionist literary

95

essays is to be struck repeatedly by how culture remains dominated by that negative event, the loss of the narrative stability of "Bildung."

It might seem dubious to link Romantic theory to a poetics constituted by an overturning of the tradition that derived itself from Romantic principles. And indeed there are passages in Friedrich Schlegel's work that have become irrelevant to Expressionism: "Nature is the image of divinity coming into being"[3]; "Bildung is to a certain extent a process of limitation"[4]; "The only infallible mode of contemplation is self-contemplation; the essence of self, however, as it is being contemplated, is remembrance."[5] Synthesis of natural and teleological becoming; self-disciplined, Goethean "Bildung"; the validation of the self through memory—such hitherto powerful notions retain validity only for a poet like Rilke, who is in conscious resistance to the "chaos" of his own "epoch."

It is not necessary to fall back on negative dialectics, however, in order to argue that the Romantic epistemology of historical and productive consciousness, the fundamental revolution of modernity, continues to underlie and shape even as drastic an upheaval as Expressionism. Romanticism knows both revolution and ennui, both progressivism and nihilism; its texts glimpse all the possible worlds that the "Ich" makes and remakes. Romantic theory is so subtle and comprehensive in its speculative range that it includes all imaginable antitheses, all the subsequent combative moves of the Western mind. Schlegel saw quite clearly the shadows that darkened the generally exhilarating future he projected. It would be pointless to argue that he "anticipated" Expressionism. What can be said is that he and Novalis formulated the modern situation in categories that illuminate not only the culture of "Bildung" but also the energies released by its collapse.

First and most important: Friedrich Schlegel did think apocalyptically and did imagine a final epoch ("Endzeit"): "The whole of humanity is oriented toward the single moment of self-destruction."[6] And while Schlegel saw this final moment as one of fullness, a "tragedy of joy" ("Trauerspiel der Freude") opening onto a "future humanity," he also identified a counterpossibility, a negative apocalypse involving the gradual rigidification of the impulses to ecstatic disruption ("rigidity," "congealing into stone") and the homogenization of "presentness" ("Gegenwart"), the "world's fundamental sickness" ("Grundübel der Welt").[7] This image of presentness as a force in its own right, opposing the dynamic interplay of past and future as emergent "Bildung," is linked by Schlegel to the potential death of consciousness: "There are two kinds of eternity: through destruction of polar tensions (of future and past) and through destruction of presentness—as binding, circumscribing indifference. Total presentness would be death. Eternity is infinite temporal fullness, not absence of time."[8] Here can be seen the full dangerousness of "Gegenwart," namely its claim, buttressed by mystical urges toward timelessness, to what Schlegel saw as a counterfeit eternity, a paralysis of life. And this is precisely the metaphysical event that precipitates Expressionism: "Bildung" and history are suddenly experienced as directionless, ludicrous, empty words. The past is perceived as an opaque, shapeless mass of signs without illumination, instantly swallowing up the future, robbing the remembering process of its vitality, blurring all distinctions between itself and the undifferentiated present in which consciousness is imprisoned.

Because Schlegel was so aware of the deathliness of the present as a threat to the entire weave of narrative permutations enabling the invention and reinvention of history, he sought ways of absorbing that threat into an "ironic" totality. For him revolutionary thinking is ontological rather than political, an essential imaginative direction for the ironic consciousness. The threat of "Gegenwart," with its deathly passivity, can only be met by a reconceptualization of "nowness" as disruption, an ecstasy fusing fatalism, confrontation of chaos, and ironic impetuosity: "Basis for an eternal revolution (Christ is still waging war). The chaos, which in the modern world has been hitherto unconscious and passive, must return as conscious action: eternal revolution. . . . The 'natural' state of things is embrace of chaos, and poetry is the natural state of things."[9] If the ontology of nature can thus be claimed for the cause of a revolutionary version of the world, then death itself can be reclaimed as an immense event, liberated from the passivity of the empty present: "Probability of a great *revolution in consciousness* at the moment of death."[10]

The affirmation of chaos, of permanent revolution, produces the opposite of "chaos" in the conventional sense; humanity has concentrated its history in its languages, its semantic codes, and the emancipation from presentness frees that history, decongeals all systems: "Man is *spirit and language* at all levels of intensity. Man is a number. . . . Every moment thus brushes against an unknown eternity, like the moment of death. . . . It is not things but humans who are numbers and all things are humans."[11] It is false to speak of the material or the immaterial, as if the temporal dimension could ever be excluded from such perceptions; both things and consciousness are engaged in an incessant process of materialization and dematerialization, weaving ecstatic narrative relationships between systems and time zones that ultimately define the "universe": "We are aware of nothing but activity, we contemplate nothing but interactive effects— we can imagine things only in space, we conceptualize them only in time. . . . Truth is expressed through relationships, not through things in isolation."[12]

Powerful though Schlegel's arguments are for an open-ended universe of temporal "relationships," he is always in search of the formulation that will fuse such arguments with the necessity of a final epoch, of "infinite temporal fullness." Without a concept of fertile eternity as the historically imagined goal of human experience, the logic of collapse into a merely additive temporality will perpetually reassert itself: "The world's final revolution will be an infinite birth; the world itself would then be an eternal process of conception, in which all previous conceptions recur. Death—the final birth."[13] The significance of art is that it can intelligibly distill the chaos into narratives of death and rebirth, generating models of form and value in the very process of pulverizing repressive order and empty values. The integration of "eternal revolution" with "the final revolution" is rendered imaginable through the simultaneity of construction and reduction, the hierarchical elimination of the superfluous embodied in the action of art. Schlegel thus inaugurates a potently "activist" poetics: art's double role is to demolish the illusory continuum of order and to "construct" a counterworld entirely out of chaos where the truth of history swirls: "To construct the world out of chaos and allegory";[14] "To construct time accurately is a magical art"[15]; "In space we are perhaps surrounded by the ideal of time. Through the process of fantasy a formless form could perhaps be constructed."[16]

This ambitious use of the notion of construction is the key to the importance of Schlegel for understanding Expressionism. For such construction unites a necessary assault on the world as it is with an ideal of value inseparable from the premise of Romantic theory: historical narratives are mandated by the rupture of the present and the resultant need to project fullness, community between humanity and things. Schlegel uses the word "love" to define this value ideal and locates it at the beginning and at the end of time: "The emergence of chaos out of love."[17] Value "was" once and has been lost; and the need to regain it is what generates both the longing embodied in narrative and the Promethean detachment that is capable of destroying its own invention, of putting all imagery of achieved value in question. This simultaneity of construction and destruction is what constitutes "art"; and the more art claims, as it should, autonomy for itself, the more it points beyond itself toward the goal of "temporal fullness," which is implicit in every phase of its existence.

The key historical change separating Schlegel's apocalyptic vocabulary from that of the Expressionists is compressed in the word "history" itself. Schlegel's history is defined by its openness to the future; futurity is its essence. Whereas for the Expressionists history is foreclosed, an apocalypse that has already passed, leaving a temporality transformed not into fullness, but into the dead present anathematized by Schlegel. As an event the apocalypse is obsolete; as a fact of life it is everywhere, transforming all history and all individual dreams into a ghastly sickness. Schlegel's positive image of the "final epoch," in which a temporality ever more conscious of "value" accelerates its thrust toward an end that finally reappropriates the beginning, is a totality of all the accumulating self-assertions of human freedom. For the Expressionists such totalities have become "totalitarian," an imprisonment of all ideals, all language, all experience—a mockery of "Bildung." The negating process of irony is no longer adequate for them, because irony presupposes a viable, or at least modifiable, "universe." One can hardly call Dadaism ironic in this sense: it is an antisystem, a dislocation of the Expressionists' systematic assault. And in fact the Expressionist assault is already definable as the refusal of Romantic irony, which means in turn the impossibility of history—even Nietzsche's "critical history." The cold detachment of the Expressionist perspective is not the detachment of the judge (which would yield a Nietzschean dynamics); these texts speak from *within* the sick society, reproducing all the categories that have lost their power to nourish, categories of wholeness, of the organic, of visionary uniqueness.

We have seen that the key assumption of nineteenth-century poetics was the notion of the privileged moment. The Expressionists, realizing that this assumption pervaded every aspect of the historical outlook now become so burdensome and poisonous, were able to generate tremendous energy in the laconic pulverizing of the privileged moment. Ludwig Rubiner displays the force of this dialectic in his invocation, not of any new continuities, but of moments that are *not* privileged, random moments perpetually on the edge of devastation, moments that emerge from and merge back into the shapeless cell mass that is the totality of all moments:

We refuse to work, because the process is too slow. We are incorrigible about progress, for us it simply doesn't exist. We believe in the marvelous, in the shedding of everything that is fluid in us, in the sudden burning consumption of our bodies by the fiery spirit, in an eternal satiation in a single moment. We search our whole lives for marks of the fire in our memory, plunge after every fiery color, yearn to enter alien spaces, to thrust ourselves into alien bodies, we transform ourselves into organ voices, into the soaring of instruments, we slip through all the cell clusters of music, in all directions, like bolts of lightning.[18]

Such language is intoxicated but by no means vague. The persistence of notions important to Romanticism—magic, biology, music, and the encyclopedic consciousness—is apparent. Precisely because no individual structures of space or time are any longer plausible, the idea of a (chaotic) totality of *all* these unstructurable entities has returned with a new force.

Perched on the collapsing structure of privileged moments has been the privileged human self. Hugo Ball, in a remarkable 1916 lecture, portrays the new landscape, where outsize as well as microscopic forces of consciousness trample on human selves suddenly shrunken into insignificance:

> The world revealed itself as a blind clash and chaos of unleashed forces. Man lost his divine face, became material, chance, conglomeration, animal, insane product of inadequate, abruptly convulsive thoughts. Man lost the special position granted him by Reason. He became ordinary, no more interesting than a stone, constructed and controlled by the same laws; he disappeared within nature. . . . A revolution took place against God and his creatures. The result: an anarchy of unleashed demons and natural forces: the titans arose and pulverized the fortresses of heaven.[19]

Another central element in late nineteenth-century poetics is the status of the autonomous object, the perfect, self-contained reality to be both precisely contemplated and absorbed into memory. The privileged moment, the privileged self, and the privileged object are a mutually supporting tripod sustaining the tenuous persistence of "Bildung." Thus the collapse of one provokes the collapse of the others: there is no ref-

100

uge in "things." In the same lecture Hugo Ball evokes a world in which stable objects are no more conceivable than isolated selves, a dead present that is terrifyingly alive:

> But not only the walls were pulverized; even grains of sand were broken up, crushed, disintegrated. Not only were the stones not left standing one upon another; no grain, no atom remained attached to its neighbor. Everything fixed dissolved. Stone, wood, metal dissolved. The world became monstrous, uncanny; relationships of reason and convention, indeed all standards of valuation, disappeared. The doctrine of electrons imported a strange vibration into all surfaces, lines, forms. Objects changed their shape, their weight, their distinctions of class and hierarchy.[20]

Defamiliarization of the world was of course the original Romantic project, and it is reenacted by the Expressionists as a radical attack on the empty present, as the only form of defense against it. And again, it is the Romantic conception of a magical or encyclopedic set of analogies between macrocosm and any and all microcosms, which alone makes the attack sustainable. The imagination can transgress all limits, distort all shapes, precisely because rupture, "eternal revolution," is the only viable category; imaginative freedom becomes a most urgent task, the task of imposing allegorical structures on the chaos, constructing in the act of dissolving. Such is the energy the Expressionists absorb from a metaphysics of rupture that Rudolf Pannwitz can reclaim a version of history from the very process of its collapse; history is cyclical, explosive, sheer emptiness. History is virtually anything that makes linguistic sense *except* a structure of orderly development, the one version that is definitively obsolete:

> History is compressed psyche, with the explosive force of radium. Our modernity knows: no given world retains its validity, all fixities are dispersed, the great flood has broken upon us, there is no longer even the belief structure fashioned by our surest organ, the eye, but only the play of perspectives and mirrors, fabulous stimuli and crazy arbitrariness. We, however, stand between the old and the new truths, can renounce none and can be satisfied with none. This world, no longer one world and not yet another, this gap in the universe fills our art or yearns to fill it, a theatrical art in its grandeur, mediocrity or pettiness, but the person who can genuinely act out this theater is solely the artist vain

101

in the certainty of his impoverishment, the radical solitary, the uncompromising truth seeker, the Protean nihilist.[21]

"Protean nihilist": the phrase communicates essential self-images of the artist in our century. "Subjectivity," like "nature" or "the city," is a concept that has broken free of its moorings and become an unpredictable force, the force of what used to be called man, in the new chaos. Psychology, as Nietzsche noted, has become of central importance precisely because it bursts open the exhausted entity called the individual. Heidegger remarks of Nietzsche: "The conception of the subject as ego, self, which is the 'egoistic' interpretation of the subject, is for Nietzsche not yet subjectivist enough."[22] A near contemporary of Storm, Keller, and Meyer, Nietzsche had already radically undermined their understanding of subjectivity as defined by empirical norms. And Friedrich Schlegel foreshadows the violent psychology of the new literature with the vivid imagery of swallowing: "Absolute balance between idealism and realism remains impossible for human beings. Harmony must always emerge through the process of the one swallowing the other, the swallower always dominates the swallowed."[23]

Expressionism is indeed a new "idealism," but one that has, so to speak, forced itself on the artists concerned. The discourse of "Bildung" in the nineteenth century had achieved "formalization" (Foucault's term for an ideology at the moment of its universal acceptance) through the linkage of such incompatibles as history and privacy, memory and science, nationalism and tolerance—with the result that the synthesis of outside and inside through "Bildung" had become ever more precarious, passive, and potentially solipsistic. The metamorphosis of intelligible, renewable history into the festering sickness of the present leaves artists stranded, armed only with their liberated but also rootless and undefined subjectivity; their involuntary idealism does indeed "swallow" all realisms—but it must, given the dynamics of its liberation, open itself to being swallowed in its turn by any and all forces it encounters. Hugo Ball conveys very well the circularity, the spiral-like rhythm of expansion and collapse in which the artist must whirl perpetually; "inwardness" can only be defined in terms of its antitheses, the monsters it generates and the monsters that devour it:

> Artists in this age are directed inward. Their life is a struggle with madness. They are split, torn, broken apart, unless they succeed in finding, for one moment, equilibrium, balance, neces-

sity and harmony in their work. . . . Artists in this age are ascetics of spirituality in their confrontation with the world. They lead a subterranean existence. They are forerunners, prophets, of a new world. Their works resound in a language only now becoming known to themselves. . . . Artists in this age turn against themselves and against art. Even the ultimate, hitherto least vulnerable basis of thought becomes a problem for them. How can they still be useful, conciliatory, neutrally descriptive or socially supportive? . . . They are becoming creators of new beings, who have no model in the familiar world. They create images, which are no longer mimetic at all, but add to nature's species new, hitherto unknown secrets and forms of existence.[24]

The artist becomes a prophet, *not* because he has any new gospel to spread, but because the temporal calamity of being exiled within the deadness of the present forces him into radical innovation, into the allegorical construction of "new beings." Hugo Ball is speaking of Kandinsky, but what he says about art populating space with secret new forms renews Romantic imperatives at the moment of convergence between inert history and visions of new chaos. For this "space" exists only in the temporal crisis; these are monsters engendered by time. The original Romantic insight, expressed by Novalis in the phrase "Space as precipitate of time—as necessary consequence of time," has gained a new and terrible force with the collapse of the stable space of the bourgeois era.

The preeminence of the lyric poem as the voice of Expressionism derives from the rigor with which the major writers focused on the historical crisis as an absolute and systematic inversion of what had gone before. As the theoretical statements (those quoted are from 1916–17, slightly later than the greatest poetry) suggest, it is the precision of the negative vision that enables the language to speak. Friedrich Schlegel's striking phrase had been "structured chaos" ("gebildetes Chaos").[25] It is because the poem was structurally and emotionally so closely bound to the ethos of the privileged moment that a strict inversion of its established procedures constitutes a legitimate shaping of the chaos. In three specific respects the new lyric structures gain validity as negations of their poetic predecessors. The linear movement of a poem is deployed by writers like Storm, Keller, and Meyer as a narrative vehicle for the privileged moment: the poem will lead toward the moment and away from it into the dimension of its historical potential, frameworks of memory and contemplative detail bridge the abyss that initially opened onto the moment, rendering the contingent and interpretive narratives mutually reflective and coherent. The Expressionist poem, working antithetically, blocks the linear flow toward meaning; through devices such as repetition of motifs and rhythmic uniformity, no one moment is allowed to impose itself as more significant than the others. And no opening is made toward any realm of possibility outside the text; the reader is forced to confront without mediation the sarcasm, wildness, and estrangement of the poem's visions.

Another key convention of nineteenth-century poetics is that of the "lyric of experience" ("Erlebnislyrik"), the way texts situate, for example, the "objective" contemplative moment (stage 2 of my structural model) in a relationship of tension with the observing self, thereby enhancing the scope and subtlety of the speaking voice. The Expressionist poem, on the other hand, explicitly rejects the implication of subjective continuity. It blurs the location and functions of the speaker, either moving in and out of an enigmatic scene or articulating horrors with a laconic aloofness. The poems' visual force (often very great) will seem to emerge directly from the play of words against each other, without the presence of a mediating, organizing, experiencing voice; and if the self is named, either as such or through doubling, it is generally a disintegrating or paralyzed entity, helplessly stuck in the derangement of its own imagery.

And finally, the poetry of, say, Meyer takes up with a delighted intensity the baroque notion of the poem-as-object, establishing analogies and equivalences between its own structures and those of objects or scenes in the external world. The goal of the so-called "Dinggedicht" is to establish a rhythmic harmony between the poem's linguistic closure and an activation of the life latent within the privileged object; as Rilke formalized this project, the invisible should become visible and vice versa. The Expressionist reaction to this is made explicit in the sentences quoted from Hugo Ball: objects are in the grip of time, their surface conceals a swirling of chaotic particles and hallucinations absorbed from the newly unleashed forces of consciousness. Art cuts through the surface in quest of this chaos, knowing that all narration is provisional and unstable, that it must "construct the whole" in order to exist at all. The crumbling of "Bildung" has rendered the apocalyptic project inescapable. As the coherence of the Expressionist essays suggest, the new poetics of aggression is a cogent, even systematic response to the imperatives of Romantic temporality.

The difficulty of Expressionist texts derives chiefly from their rejection of development; they view the truth, with its double image of sickening stasis and eruptive chaos, as always and absolutely present in every line. It has to be indivisible because no categories of division, no parts of the whole, are defensible or even comprehensible. Heselhaus's term "line composition" ("Zeilenkomposition")[26] underlines the necessity of the line's autonomy. Thus it makes no sense to speak of a model for these poems, as was done in the previous chapter: such sequencing is by definition antithetical to their mode of speaking.

However, since Expressionist temporality inverts its predecessor, the assault on history is itself historical and generates describable procedures. The language of Expressionism is in fact fueled by a specific tension. On the one hand the words seek to become related only to each other; images merge into each other through a series of connotative chains, associative impulses that insist on remaining private, not as biographical markers, but as pure "constructions," in Schlegel's sense, of the perceived chaos. A part of this strategy is to limit the kinds of images used and to reuse them, ever more esoteric yet also familiar through their controlled textual history, in many different poems; the paradoxical effect of this procedure (as Killy and other Trakl interpreters have pointed out) is to force the readers still more tightly into the closure of the specific poem. For the related texts "explain" nothing: they deploy their own quite different connotative chains and silently direct the reader back toward the specificity from which he has been seeking relief. Another element in this strategy is the almost exclusive use of the present tense, the vivid focusing on a series of microevents. The very intensity of the visual cues encourages the reader to make connections, priorities, climactic structures in his mind. But always the text defeats this impulse, the climaxes dissipate instantly, images become laconic just when expansiveness is expected.

The connotative chain thus encodes the closure of the tradition, the paralysis of history. Yet it becomes a powerful, not an esoteric, poetics through a permanent tension with its virtual antithesis, namely the infusion of every line by what for want of a better word may be termed value. The weight it carries is of course Nietzsche's, and is reinforced by Heidegger's elucidation of Nietzschean nihilism as a *process*, the process of value degradation, which constitutes Western history as a whole.[27] For the Expressionists this process is tangibly complete, identifiable with the attenuation and collapse of bourgeois "Bildung." And the apocalypse of Western history, which for them is an irrefutable actuality, is revealed through the negative but universal saturation of all phenomena with value. In these texts there is no viable distinction between man and things, between description and feeling, between private and public. These distinctions have collapsed, not into a void, but into a kind of metaphysical fluid penetrating and decomposing all experience, a place that is all places, where meaning is always plural, never privileged.

Once such logic is accepted—the logic that the tradition totalized at its end point implies the presence of value in every microevent—the dynamics of this world vision force a further step, the step that makes Expressionism the decisive movement of our century. Both elements in its poetics, the connotative chain and the saturation of texts with value, endow language with a tremendous privileged status, thrusting it as far as possible from its conventional denotative function. Yet language, for all its flexibility and its historical-mythical porousness, imposes its own wholeness, its systematicity. And if this systematic instrument can, in its heightened state, aspire to the encoding of history in a single text, then that history is not closed after all. The more poetic language insists on its autonomy, its absolute emancipation from daily usage, the more it necessarily translates history's perceived finality into a vast repertoire of events either actual or potential, stories worthy of retelling. Expressionism drains this repertoire of life, reduces multiple narratives to single symbols, but in doing so it fills these symbols with a new, unmanageable potency. Nothing is more nourishing to the historical narrative than poetic death sentences and suicides. Even as Trakl's language seals in history's last illness with hermetic rigor, it also signals, as Heidegger has shown,[28] the possibilities of new rupture. Linguistic silence is impossible. When a text successfully puts an entire language system in question, it necessarily inaugurates the quest for alternatives. And so it is that the Expressionist paralysis, the refusal of a contingent narrative leads to a radical foregrounding of the narrative hitherto only implicit, the narrative of history as such.

This situation is prefigured in Romantic texts. Novalis writes, in a famous fragment: "Everything we experience is a process of communication. Thus the world itself is one continuous communicative process. A process of revealing the spirit. The time is no more, when God's spirit was directly comprehended. The meaning of the world has become lost. We have remained stuck at the letter of the text. . . . The significance of the hieroglyph is lacking. We are living still on the harvest of better times."[29] And Friedrich Schlegel remarks: "The true hieroglyph is an analogy for the universe, its approximation in a religious form."[30] The two uses of the word "Hieroglyphe" are complementary. For Novalis the word itself, without revealed truth, has become a hieroglyph, an enigma; while Schlegel imagines a man-made hieroglyph, the compression of an entire cultural and linguistic system into an actively willed enigma.

Expressionist texts are totalized hieroglyphs in Schlegel's sense; but the cultural pessimism present in Novalis's text has of course been radicalized. The world the Romantics sought to "analogize" is no longer merely enigmatic and withdrawn; it has become a monstrous chaos that disfigures everything old and instantly consumes anything new. Trakl writes, in what his editors nervously call an aphorism: "Feeling in moments of deathlike existence: All people are worthy of love."[31] This is a hieroglyph in Schlegel's sense: the "value" of human beings is an indispensable vision, but one that can only be formulated with maximum abstraction, from a perspective that denies the very possibility of this or any vision of value. The devouring monster of presentness, which the Expressionists confronted with such pure, paralyzed clarity, has become, in our time, ever more efficient in its consumption of value and experience. Consequently, the totalizing hieroglyphs of Expressionism gain both in urgency and in strangeness, as the dying of the Western tradition becomes a remote memory.

The purpose of opening a discussion of Expressionist temporality with a little-known, uncharacteristic poem by Rainer Maria Rilke is to evoke the flexibility, the tenacity, and the sickening of the discourse of privatized, privileged time that Expressionism confronted. Rilke's text stands for many others—by poets such as Hofmannsthal, Stefan George, or the young Ernst Stadler—in its dream-ridden structuring of this moment of malaise.

Aus einer Sturmnacht, 1
Rainer Maria Rilke

In solchen Nächten kannst du in den Gassen
Zukünftigen begegnen, schmalen blassen
Gesichtern, die dich nicht erkennen
und dich schweigend vorüberlassen.
Aber wenn sie zu reden begännen,
wärst du ein Langevergangener
wie du da stehst,
langeverwest.

107

Doch sie bleiben im Schweigen wie Tote,
obwohl sie die Kommenden sind.
Zukunft beginnt noch nicht.
Sie halten nur ihr Gesicht in die Zeit
und können, wie unter Wasser, nicht schauen;
und ertragen sie's doch eine Weile,
sehn sie wie unter den Wellen: die Eile
von Fischen und das Tauchen von Tauen.[32]

(1901)

From a Stormy Night

In such nights you can meet, in the back streets,
future people, narrow pale
faces, who do not know you
and silently let you pass.
But if they were to begin speaking,
you would be as one long dead
even as you stand there,
long consumed by decay.
Yet they remain silent as the dead,
even though they are yet to come.
Future is not yet beginning.
They merely press their face against the time
and, as if under water, can see nothing;
and if they endure a little longer,
become able to see beneath the waves:
the hastening of fish and the lowering of ropes.

I have referred frequently to Rilke's project as a strategic renewal of the language of "Bildung." And indeed his *New Poems* and later visionary works constitute a major attempt to rescue the temporality of the nineteenth century, the threefold privilege of moment, self, and object. But in an earlier poem like this one, where, so to speak, his guard is down, he lives more vividly in our century's time zone than he does in the grandiose, prophetic later work (which gains much of its power from the monumental struggle to preserve, against all odds, the viability of privilege and coherence).

If it were not for the phrase "in the back streets," this poem would barely qualify as a cityscape; yet just because it is such a fanciful, hallucinatory poem, freely acknowledging its literary past (most notably Baudelaire), it seems to me far superior to the controlled, pretentious *Book of Poverty and Death,* written more than two years later. Rilke gives us both a ghostly story in the manner of Poe and E.T.A. Hoffmann and a rather rigorous minimalist exercise, in which each verbal event is triggered by the language of the preceding series. The poem is clearly divided into four sections, and each section seems to be cued by a purely linguistic element in the previous one. Thus "silently" (line 4) provokes the speculation concerning "speaking" (line 5); this movement is one of antithesis, but the second one, from "long consumed by decay" (line 8) to "as the dead" (line 9), derives from close parallelism; finally the insistent rigidity of "remain" (line 9) is intensified in the unyielding "press" (line 12). The poem manages, with this linguistic introversion, to turn the nominal openness of the storm and the streets and the science-fictional premise ("future people") into an abstract, claustrophobic texture. The final underwater imagery is superbly appropriate, with its literally unbreathable atmosphere. Rilke seems to be almost sleepwalking here, telling us more than he means to tell; the other poems in the series "From a Stormy Night" are relatively bland, with the exception of number 3 (concerning fire at an opera house).

The contingent narrative, then, is almost entirely generated by the process of interpretation; the speaker's linguistic control is absolute. At the same time the interpretive narrative seems incapable of the kind of autonomy that would entitle the speaker to the status of "self" in the process of "Bildung." Gradually the interpretation "drowns" in a contingent sequence it has itself produced.

The scene is structurally linked to Droste-Hülshoff's meditation in the moss: in both texts an "impossible" future is actualized in concrete images. But whereas that future is articulated by Droste-Hülshoff as rupture, radical otherness, here there is no rupture at all, just a slippage into indistinctness, into the impossibility of living contingency. Rilke's future people seem to emanate from E.T.A. Hoffman's estranged gestural world, and inevitably evoke the "Doppelgänger." The opening scene immediately fractures the kind of coherence that might limit the scene to the confines of dream. Why do these figures not "know" the self? Are they moving or not? What does their silence connote? It is as if the poet has launched a decorative, "romantic" idea, which immediately begins to grow like a proliferating cell structure. The word "let pass" is already ironic: the self cannot walk past, but neither can he play, as Hoffmann used to play, with the problems of time and identity. Once released from under life's fragile surface, these images overwhelm everything, leaving no space for an authorial, observing self.

The second sentence maintains the framework of dual time zones as well as the presence of a self contemplating the conundrum it has evoked. But the very simplicity of the initial conceit is what makes it threatening. The "future people" lack Hoffmann's monsters' habit of stealing shadows or reflections; they are themselves shadowlike, anonymous. Productions of the cityscape, defined by their futurity yet seeming to refute the term's meaning, they fatally provoke the self's imagination. The speaker in "In the Moss" is driven by impossible future images toward horror and a struggle to rescue the self; but Rilke's persona, anticipating figures in Trakl's apocalyptic world, passively enacts the dying of time itself. As often in Rilke (though normally with constructive implications), the subjunctive shifts into the indicative, the self becomes what it is imagining. As the lines shorten, the adverb "lange" is reiterated and "langeverwest," standing alone at the poem's center, seems immovable in its claim to presence.

And the rest of the poem bears this out. As if to awaken from a bad dream, the speaker's "Yet" tries to reopen a gap between the self and the apparitions. But deathliness ("wie Tote") has filled in all gaps; contingency and interpretation have stifled each other. Through the "Telegrammstil" of "Future is not yet beginning," the ghosts are, as it were, officially banished. But the self does not reappear, does not resume his stroll. From this line the poem tumbles into the strangeness of the final section, with the self totally absorbed into the consuming presence of the doubles he has evoked. Their silence has become action, almost heroic action. Baudelaire's Parisian street people are evoked, particularly the blind men who defy "nature" with the sheer directionality of their sightless gaze:

> Their eyes are quenched, and yet they seem to stare
> at something, somewhere, questioning the sky
> and never bending their benighted heads
> in reverie toward the cobblestones.[33]

But Rilke's self cannot maintain distance, his perspective is drawn into an identification with the impossible gaze of the "future people." Thus the rigid abstraction of the last image, with the fish moving horizontally and the ropes descending vertically, again suggests Baudelaire, this time the mathematical horror of the seven old men:

> He wasn't bent, he was *broken,* and his spine
> formed so sharp an angle with his legs.

Yet whereas Baudelaire's strolling self rushes away in terror, speaking rationally of his loss of reason, the Rilkean voice is submerged by its own images. Interpretation has become helpless identification; the speaker's "seeing" is completely at one with the surreal visions attributed to the phantoms. The underwater scene implies the distortion and dissolution that the sea perpetrates on all solid objects. And indeed, like Baudelaire's characters, the "future people" are, at the end, evoked as fascinating objects—but without any saving distance. Their rigidity under water transforms the world into a nightmare fusion between watery chaos and the abstract shapes that defy it. And this culmination is precisely paralleled by what happens to the motif of time with which the poem began. The telescoping of present and future causes the self to disintegrate; but the apparitions sharpen their contours, they "press their face against the time." What kind of time can this be? It can only be time as pure element, analogous to the water, time as the horrible eternity of presentness, uninhabitable except that the self is forced to inhabit it. There is no escape, no vantage point outside the flux and certainly no viable perspective within it. The apparitions do not themselves drown, but they drown the self.

In a 1914 poem, "Ach aus eines Engels Fühlung" (from *Poems to the Night*), Rilke returns to the underwater imagery:

> Strömung zögert, Strömung drängt hinüber,
> Tiefe wirkt und Hindernis.
>
> Aus dem starren fühllos Alten drehn
> sich Geschöpfe, plötzlich auserlesen,
> und das ewig Stumme aller Wesen
> überstürzt ein dröhnendes Geschehn.[34]

> Current hesitates, current surges away,
> Obstructions in the depths intrude.
>
> From out of the ancient, rigid sludge emerge
> creatures, suddenly elected,

111

and a droning happening overwhelms
the eternal silence of all beings.

The scene is filled with the same tensions as in the earlier text: absolute sameness and silence is punctuated with sudden, irrational motion; and the incessant decay and dissolution is resisted by the rigidity of isolated, abstract shapes. It is no accident that a fable about time culminates in such scenery: for the temporality of Expressionism, the paralyzing apocalypse of history glimpsed through a mutual collapse of contingency and interpretation, suffuses these Rilkean images, as it does parts of *The Notebooks of Malte Laurids Brigge*. Such texts illuminate the terror against which Rilke struggled in his resolute development of a metaphysics of extreme privilege, of a language (in the *Elegies* and *Sonnets*) strong enough to impose its rescue of "Bildung" on a historical moment that has driven all imagery of coherence into the realm of paradox.

Rilke's project of rescue became fully conscious at about the time when, with the publication of his *New Poems* in December 1907, his poetic prestige began to become a factor in the vision of other writers. Reaching his maturity at precisely this moment, Georg Heym despised Rilke. Heym's radicalism gives full and harsh life to the deathly hallucinations Rilke struggles to repress.

Die Märkte
Georg Heym

Schleifender Füsse sind tausend auf ihnen getreten.
Hohe Karossen rollten wie Donner so hohl.
Immer lagen sie bleich nur und schüchtern. Und flehten
Um die übrigen Rüben und grünlichen Kohl.

Die in dem Schauen so vieler der Sommer ergreiset,
Im ritzenden Froste der bitteren Winter zernagt,
Vom winzigen Brosam des Frühwinds trübe gespeiset,
Wenn märzlich das Jahr mit blauem Sturme getagt.

Ewig nur hängende Särge krochen daruber.
Ihre Stirnen waren von Fackeln oft rot.
Tränen, die grossen, schlugen voll Hitze hernieder,
Und sie schwanden in sie, die so trocken wie Brot.

Viele Gesänge sie hörten und silberne Tänze,
Aus hellen Palästen oft schallte ein Saitenspiel,
Im Grunde der braunen Gemächer sahen sie glänzen
Fröhlicher Zeiten Ernte und Mähler viel.

112

Oben im Grauen oft sahn sie die Vögel kehren
Unruhig um—wie Spreu durch die Himmel vorbei.
Die, ach, trieben hinaus mit den Wolken, den schweren,
Über die schwellenden Herbste mit scharfem Geschrei.

Ihrer dachte doch niemand. Die kümmerlich assen
Nur der Dächer Unrat mit hungrigem Mund.
Wer sich nachts dort erbrach, die in Finsternis sassen,
Und sie lagen beschmutzt auf dem schneeigen Grund

Zur Mitternacht dann—die Mäuse schoben die Knochen
Über sie sanft. Die Raben schleuderten Mist.
Mit knickenden Beinen die Spinnen krochen
Zärtlich über ihr zitterndes Angesicht.

So sperrten sie immer empor ihre riesigen Lippen.
Und schrien nach einem Heiland der tollen Zeit,
Und hörten den Wind am Tage—im Abend ein Regentrippen—
Weisser Sterne Geräusche—durch Dunkel der Räume verschneit.[35]

(1912)

The Marketplaces

Thousands of dragging feet have pounded on them.
High carriage wheels resounded, hollow as thunder.
Always they lay there, pale and shy. And begged
For the left-over beets and greenish cabbage.

Made old by the gaze of so many in summer,
Gnawed into by the scraping frost of bitter winters,
Muddily fed by the minute crumbs of spring winds,
When the year announced its rebirth in March's blue storm.

Precariously carried coffins lurched across them.
Their foreheads often reddened by torches' glare.
Tears, large ones, struck hotly down,
Dissolving into their surface, dry as bread.

Many songs they heard and silvery dances,
From bright-lit palaces often the string's sound echoed,
Deep in the brown chambers they glimpsed the gleam
Of the harvest and feasting of joyful times.

In the gray sky above they often saw the birds turn round
Restlessly—driven like chaff through the heavens.
O lucky birds, moving out with the clouds, the heavy ones,
Crossing the swelling autumn landscape with sharp cries.

113

No one thought of the marketplaces. Hungrily gulping
Their wretched food, the garbage from the roof.
In the dark they were fed by those who vomited,
And their snowy surface lay covered with filth.

Midnight: the mice pushed bones
Gently across them. The ravens flung their dung.
The spiders, with their folding legs, crawled
Tenderly over their quivering face.

And so they always forced their giant lips upward.
Screamed for a redeemer in the time of madness,
And heard the daytime wind—the rain's drip in evening—
The sounds of white stars—snowflakes scattered through dark spaces.

In this text, written just days before his death, Heym creates a genuine hieroglyph of a world simultaneously rigid and chaotic, centralized and dispersed. Every facet of the marketplace, as concept and as physical reality, is exploited, and the contradictions that emerge become emblematic of the new paralysis, the impossibility of directional narrative. Thus the marketplace is the center of a town, its focal point; but it is a center that exists only as empty space, as the place where roads meet, where houses stop, where people cross to and fro, in perpetual transition. In short, its symbolic (interpretive) centrality is defined by contingencies accumulating and dispersing without any prospect of the binding singularity of "chance." A feature of the marketplace particularly stressed by Heym is its flatness: it is seen as a place of memory and history, where human events converge and are absorbed. Yet it is at the same time nothing but a surface; it cannot be entered; the tears at the funeral are absorbed only in the sense that they instantly disappear. And finally the market is a fluid, imprecise verbal entity, shifting between space and time. In the poem, the phrase "No one thought of the marketplaces" makes the reader start uneasily, with feelings analogous to those provoked by Kafka's "Metamorphosis" (written later in 1912), when the reader suddenly realizes he has been nodding in agreement with Gregor's perspective as if it were the only possible one. For what is the persona in a marketplace that people could or should "think about"? Like Kafka, Heym has created an imaginary creature that can launch a provisional narrative on the basis of its nonbeing, its exclusion from all possibility of being.

In this cityscape Heym makes a direct connection to one of the originating texts of modern seeing, Hoffmann's story "The Cousin's

114

Corner Window" ("Des Vetters Eckfenster," 1822), a perpendicular perspective on a market day, which crisscrosses between the evocation of shifting patterns and the imagining of the lives of participants. The actual word "market" is almost always used by Hoffmann in its temporal sense. And it is of course the word's temporal substratum that enables Heym, by rigid spatialization, to deploy the market image as an emblem of temporal crisis. "Space as precipitate of time": Novalis's phrase is taken as literally as possible by Heym. Hoffmann does frame his story with spatial imagery suggesting, by what it does not say, the territory Heym seeks to occupy. Here is the first impression of the marketplace gleaned by Hoffmann's observer: "The whole marketplace seemed to be a single, tightly compressed mass of people, so that one had to believe, an apple thrown into it could never reach the ground." The apple image is interestingly cosmic, an allegorical glimpse that the story quickly hurries away from; but at the end the allegorical note returns, with explicit solemnity:

> "This marketplace," said the cousin, "is even now a faithful image of eternally changing life. Energetic activity, the need of the moment, drove the mass of people together; in a few minutes everything has become desolate, the voices, incessantly drowning each other out in the racket, have died away, and every abandoned spot speaks all too vividly the fearful message: It is past."[36]

By refusing Hoffmann's anthropocentric perspective, Heym radicalizes these hints at the rigidity, the deathliness, beneath all the movement. From the point of view of the marketplace itself, it is pointless to talk of the beginning and ending, the rise and fall, of human activity. Such activity is always in meaningless process, with fragments of ritual and continuities of garbage mingling indiscriminately.

"Die Märkte" represents an advance from Heym's own earlier efforts at emancipating the cityscape from the customary deluded preoccupation with human "feeling":

Der Dächer Schattenrisse, und verloren
Ein Vogelruf im Raum, dem regenmüden.
Der flattert in die gelbe Nacht vorauf.
Still sind die Höfe und wie abgeschieden.

Ein Fenster tut sich zu.[37]

115

The roofs' shadowy outlines, a bird cry
Lost in the empty world, exhausted with rain.
The bird flutters up into the yellow night.
The courtyards are silent, as if deceased.

A window closes.

Windows are prominent in Heym's verse, and although they are used to dehumanizing effect, they retain an element of pathos, a temptation to empathy. There are no windows in "Die Märkte"; the marketplaces can "see" the human world in an unmediated, purely allegorical manner. In general "The Roofs' Shadowy Outlines," from October 1911, tends toward mood painting, its elements blending visually in a coherence not always appropriate to Heym's disruptive aims. "The City of Torment," written in September, uses an opposite strategy, turning the city itself into a character in the apocalyptic mode derived from Rimbaud's "Parisian Orgy":

Der Hunger warf Gerippe auf mich hin.
Der Brunnen Röhren waren alle leer;
Mit langen Zungen hingen sie dahin,
Blutig und rauh. Doch kam kein Tropfen mehr.

Und gelbe Seuchen blies ich über mich.
Die Leichenzüge gingen auf mir her,
Ameisen gleich mit einem kleinen Sarg,
Und winzige Pfeiferleute bliesen quer.[38]

Hunger hurled skeletons upon me.
The fountains' pipes were all empty.
Their long tongues hung outward,
Bloody and raw. Yet no more drops came.

And I blew yellow pestilence upon myself.
Funeral processions trudged across me,
Like ants with a tiny coffin,
And tiny pipers blew diagonally.

Many details in "Die Märkte" are already present here (a key Expressionist strategy is to develop and reuse a restricted series of motifs), particularly the perspective from underneath on both human sadness and human residues. But the perspective is not sustained, as it is in "Die

Märkte," so that the imagery is never free of the danger of becoming emptily rhetorical.

In "Die Märkte" Heym fuses the overtones of apocalypse with the imagistic precision of "The Roofs' Shadowy Outlines." Not that the poem is coherent in the conventional sense. Rather, the text generates its own structural categories on the basis of a single, rigidly sustained central image. Indeed, the word "central" is appropriate in several ways. The poem is not so much a connotative chain as a connotative whirlpool: images of intense vividness are hurled up, only to be sucked back down again. Heym maintains a counterpoint between the flatness of the marketplace and a violently perpendicular relationship between market and world that dominates all the stanzas except the first and seventh. His central market motif, with its cancellation of all singular directions, enables him to fill each stanza with a profusion of images and simultaneously to seal off the stanza from its successor: each embodies a single expansion and contraction of the mobile-immobile marketplace. The reader feels both trapped by the imagery and absorbed in the entrapment "felt" by the allegorical marketplace itself. The claustrophobic quality of the sickened present is fully realized in this text.

Expressionist poetics is founded on a systematic negation of the tradition it inherited. And Heym's rigid use of the traditional stanza form, in order to negate its forward-moving qualities, is well known. What the strict maintenance of the market's perspective enables him to do, in this very late poem, is to initiate and defeat several interpretive narratives simultaneously. Thus the reader is invited to discover at least three levels of linear forward movement in the text: each frustrates the anticipations it arouses, thereby intensifying the whirlpool effect, the collapse into an empty center. On one level there seems to be a seasonal structure: stanza 2 emphasizes the meager springtime; stanzas 4 and 5 have autumn scenes; and the final stanzas, with the advent of snow, are clearly wintry, with the nighttime reinforcing the bleak atmosphere. But this progression has no discernible significance: there is no nourishing element, no lightness, with which the end could contrast; only a compression of all individual images, with their potential for life, into the plural form of spasmodic, essentially lifeless repetition.

A second apparent structural movement builds toward and away from stanzas 4 and 5, the symmetrical center of an eight-stanza poem. Before and after these stanzas the atmosphere is one of oppression and victimization; time, whether generalized and monotonous (the early stanzas), or as the detailed midnight sequence of stanza 7, hems in the consciousness. The tears vanish in stanza 3; the spiders weave their web in stanza 7: whether the markets are oppressor or oppressed, the movement of time is fractured and void. By contrast, the central stanzas, in which the markets hear and see so much, are full of rhythmic breathing, seeming to expand the scope of time toward the mythic, the celebration of harvest and the enigma of bird flight. We suddenly hear of the "harvest of joyful times" and "the swelling autumnal landscape"; nature imagery is invoked with full force and without apparent reservation.

But the suddenness is the point. Despite the symmetry, there is literally no connection between these stanzas and the others; stanza 4, in particular, with its Anacreontic echoes, obtrudes in the total text like a collage element. Heym is giving us, not a developing sequence, but necessary elements in an antiencyclopedia of narratives now become impossible. What is left of the many human stories is language uprooted from contingency. Images of harvest perpetuated in language belong to the total consciousness absorbed and refracted by the marketplace. But they are also absolutely other; the harvest celebration has no more impact on the repetitions of human existence than does the bird flight with which it is bracketed. By using his marketplace perspective as a device for including "everything," Heym radicalizes his version of the microcosm: no war, no apocalypse, can cure this sickness, because the time relations imagined in the text are reducible to systematic dislocation between isolated objects and occurrences. The world's fragments are unified only in the semantic, temporal, and spatial exile of the marketplace.

There seems to be a third progression, from the shyness of the marketplace at the beginning to its cry for salvation at the end. But the process of sabotaging this particular expectation of change, of development, leads us to the heart of Heym's achievement in his poem. For the cry with open lips is not really different in kind from the "hungry gulping" of garbage in stanza 6, which in turn is qualitatively comparable to the instant absorption of tears by the parched surface. And this series, which is open to the world, giving out and taking in, stands in counterpoint to the market's opposite characteristics, which are sealed off, confined to observing the world and receiving its blows. The marketplace is shy and full of longing, and also aggressive, predatory; it is ascetic, beaten down by the seasons' harsh treatment, as well as inseparable (like Gregor Samsa) from the processing of organic, decaying matter; it contemplates the otherness of the world, and it consumes whatever comes into contact with it; it is a closed, blank surface and an infinitely vulnerable quasi-organism. The final stanza juxtaposes the two visions of the marketplace without possibility of synthesis: the organic, open entity is caught in a single perpetual gesture of protest, while the impersonal perspective registers the multiplicity and repetition of the world in a final encyclopedic sweep.

The marketplace has an identity both insistent and elusive: it is a monster that can both speak the poet's protest and bring the world's sickness into the open. The very immensity of its repertoire relentlessly obliterates the metaphysics of "Dinggedichte," the dream of integrated "contemplation" developed by nineteenth-century poetics. The poem is built entirely of moments, and their visual intensity often suggests the "special" moments of the tradition. Yet at the same time there are no moments here, only seasons—seasons generated within the frame of a single stanza, then collapsed and sealed off by the stanza's conclusion. The whirlpool rhythm throws up events without discriminating between general and particular, then sucks them back in; no time can escape the marketplace, which produces temporality unceasingly, in order to leave it stranded in the sterility of the perpetual present. There is no life here, because there is no death, all events are "often" or "always." The marketplace makes indefatigable inventories of the world while severing all the links that might give meaning to phenomena; it longs to consume the world in passionate hunger, yet leaves the frozen garbage untouched on its surface. The accumulation of sealed events culminates in the paralysis of the cry; the one category of phenomena that the marketplace, image of directionless totality, has successfully consumed is the category of binary oppositions on which all narratives of rupture and ecstasy depend: past and future, movement and stasis, life and death.

Although the market's version of the world maintains the necessary links to familiar objects and events, the intensity with which it seizes on them generates a radical semantic and metaphysical estrangement. Oppositions are no longer binary, but clashing lunges of a chaos that has rendered all outlines of objects, indeed the objects themselves, momentary and unpredictable. Every stanza of the text is saturated with value concepts, with the compression of qualities the Western tradition has held sacred: the almost sacramental imagery of food in the first two stanzas (again, the analogy with Gregor Samsa's food longings suggests itself), the tears in stanza 3, the fulfilled joy of stanza 4,

119

the radical contrast between the remote bird flight of stanza 5 and the filthy immediacy of stanza 6, and the imprisonment and emancipatory longing of the final stanzas. But this inventory of values, like the inventory of objects, "dissolves" (to recall Novalis's valorization of music) in the proliferating discords of the marketplace, in its incessant alternation between an all-consuming openness and a collapse into surface blankness. Value is everywhere and nowhere in this world, drenching the imagery of a specific stanza, dying before the next one can begin.

If Heym's violent accelerations drive everything nominally alive toward extinction, the proliferating stasis of Georg Trakl's images prevents the nominally dying from ever reaching the release of death itself.

Vorhölle
Georg Trakl

An herbstlichen Mauern, es suchen Schatten dort
Am Hügel das tönende Gold
Weidende Abendwolken
In der Ruh verdorrter Platanen.
Dunklere Tränen odmet diese Zeit,
Verdammnis, da des Träumers Herz
Überfliesst von purpurner Abendröte,
Der Schwermut der rauchenden Stadt;
Dem Schreitenden nachweht goldene Kühle,
Dem Fremdling, vom Friedhof,
Als folgte im Schatten ein zarter Leichnam.

Leise läutet der steinerne Bau;
Der Garten der Waisen, das dunkle Spital,
Ein rotes Schiff am Kanal.
Träumend steigen und sinken im Dunkel
Verwesende Menschen
Und aus schwärzlichen Toren
Treten Engel mit kalten Stirnen hervor;
Bläue, die Todesklagen der Mütter.
Es rollt durch ihr langes Haar,
Ein feuriges Rad, der runde Tag
Der Erde Qual ohne Ende.

In kühlen Zimmern ohne Sinn
Modert Gerät, mit knöchernen Händen
Tastet im Blau nach Märchen
Unheilige Kindheit,
Benagt die fette Ratte Tür und Truh,

Ein Herz
Erstarrt in schneeiger Stille.
Nachhallen die purpurnen Flüche
Des Hungers in faulendem Dunkel,
Die schwarzen Schwerter der Lüge,
Als schlüge zusammen ein ehernes Tor.[39]

(1914)

Prelude to Hell

By autumnal walls, shadows seek there
By the hill the sounding gold
Grazing evening clouds
In the peace of withered sycamores.
This age breathes darker tears,
Damnation, as the dreamer's heart
Overflows with purple sunset,
With the melancholy of the smoking city;
Golden coolness breathes after the striding man,
The stranger, from the cemetery,
As if a tender corpse were following in the shade.

Quietly the stone structure resounds;
The orphans' garden, the dark hospital,
A red ship on the canal.
Dreaming in the darkness rise and fall
Rotting humans
And through black doorways
Emerge angels with cold foreheads;
Blueness, the mothers' death laments.
Through their long hair rolls
A fiery wheel, the rounded earth day
The world's unending torment.

In cool rooms without meaning
Tools decay, with bony hands
In the blue a groping for stories
By unholy childhood,
The fat rat gnaws at door and woodwork,
A heart
Congeals in snowy silence.
The purple curses of hunger
Echo on in the putrid darkness,
The black swords of the lie,
As if an iron gate were slamming shut.

121

The immediate contrasts between Heym and Trakl are extreme and not, I think, exaggerated by the present choice of texts. Heym centers his poem on a single obsessive motif; associated images accumulate around it, while individual stanzas function like barriers, both blocking the temptations to harmony inherent in certain words and building toward a final eruptive intensity. Trakl prevents any image, no matter how explicitly charged, from becoming central to his meaning, by a process of ceaseless diversion and shifting along a connotative chain. His images do not accumulate; they subdivide like cells, blurring all structural and thematic lines of demarcation. And whereas Heym's world is always present, with a visual insistence that becomes hallucinatory, Trakl's world is always slipping into absence, blending its rural and urban landmarks into a metaphorical texture that initially appears neutral but gradually darkens into a blankness of corruption and loss.

But Trakl and Heym are united by the temporal crisis of the Western tradition; their texts convey the nightmare induced by the disintegration of privileged experience. All moments are now equally privileged, which means that the category cripples instead of nourishes experience. All objects and human beings are now prone to rupture, so that the struggle to describe and narrate results in a ceaseless tearing and dissolving of physical identities. And the elaborate repertoire of images, which had underpinned the privilege of the lyric persona, has become a language swallowing up the nominal user.

Poetic language seems endowed with a monstrous vitality—and Trakl is the poet who most fully accepts its terms, abandoning all claims to an independent, controlling persona. This results, however, in severe problems of critical procedure, diagnosed by Killy and others. Since Trakl systematically dissolves all the categories of a conventional descriptive syntax, how can criticism justify the kind of coherent statement that must presuppose the continuing viability of that syntax? But the opposite difficulty is just as striking. Given Trakl's insistent deployment of an allegorizing, totalizing vocabulary and the care with which he constructs his texts, how can one justify a cautious response, one that limits itself to annotating his linguistic usage and registering the ways in which his images elude conventional categories? Here is a poem with three carefully organized eleven-line sections, with an apocalyptic title and strategically placed phraseology ("Damnation," "torment," "without meaning," "lie") implying ultimate questions of value. Unless the reader can devise a comparably ambitious hermeneutic response, a reimagining of the poem's sequences that somehow does not violate its closure, the interpretive challenges have not been genuinely confronted. The text is more than a harmonious or dissonant interweaving of thematic fragments. It is an attempt to actualize the narrative of history itself in the very corrosion of contingency and interpretation that appears to immobilize experience as such. Criticism simply has to find an adequate way of speaking about such a text.

One way forward is through Trakl's well-known propensity for generating new permutations of the motifs of an existing piece of literature. If Heym centers his poem on a specific image, it is sometimes the case that Trakl's "center" is the absent text that has brought his own into being as counterrhythm and commentary; such procedures have been noticed particularly in relation to Hölderlin and Rimbaud.

A way into the center of "Vorhölle" is provided by the fable of Wackenroder and Tieck, published in 1799, entitled "A Strange Eastern Fairy Tale about a Naked Saint."[40] The fairy tale concerns a hermit who is obsessed by a vision of the wheel of time, slaughters people who presume to do normal things without regard for the wheel of time, but is finally released from his enslavement to the vision through the power of music. Trakl gives a direct cue for the possibility of linking his poem to the "Märchen" in the last two lines of the second section; following through on such a link is, of course, only worthwhile if the total structure of Trakl's text is illuminated in the process. I believe this to be the case. Wackenroder's "Märchen" is a powerful concentration of Romantic temporality: modern existence as potentially sealed in empty reiteration of patterns that once cohered, with the consequently urgent need to view that repetition as "chaotic" (the wheel of time) and to generate, through rupture, a myth of progressivity and/or purification.

There are roughly three phases in the "Märchen": the hermit's horrible vision of the wheel and resultant suffering; a substantial middle section of "expectation," in which the final change is anticipated by moments when the hermit longs for release; and the transformation of time, through the hermit's death and elevation, into a kind of cosmic music. The "Märchen" portrays both a genuine hell on earth and, with its clothing of Christian sacrificial motifs in Eastern garb, a release into a ritually purified, paradisal history. Trakl's title, however, is "Prelude to Hell," a precise situating of the totality of human time as he now saw it. All visions of hell are blurred and compromised by the ever-present suggestions of purity and wholeness. However, there is no release from the endless process of blurring; neither glimpse of darkness nor glimpse of light can ever become decisive. As our memories of purity become ever more completely overlaid with the paralyzing clutter of lifeless contingencies, so the totality of inverse purgatory, the prelude to hell, becomes a time zone without exit, with no death and no resurrection.

What a counterpointing rhythm with the "Märchen" enables Trakl to do is to illuminate, through structural analogy and verbal echo, the paralysis of experience in which historical memory persists in the form of hieroglyphs. In broad terms he inverts the sequence of the "Märchen" by beginning at the middle stage, the stage of expectation, and moving backward: the central section of the poem concerns the ordinary hell analogous to that perceived by the hermit; and the last section imagines a temporal world even more nightmarish, a world of interiors (Wackenroder's hermit, although he has a cave, is always seen in the open) in which time is actually accelerated, speeding humanity from innocence to corruption without even the familiar anguish offered by the wheel of time.

At the "Märchen's" nocturnal moment of transformation the world is evoked thus: "The trees were suspended in the magical glow like wandering clouds on their trunks, and the dwellings of humanity were transformed into dark, rocky shapes and twilit ghost palaces. Human beings, no longer blinded by the sun, dwelt with their gazes in the firmament, and their souls were already mirrored in the heavenly clarity of the moonlit night." And at the hermit's apotheosis as the spirit of love of music: "Then all the stars rang out and sounded a radiantly bright, divine note through the air, until the genius dissolved into the infinite firmament." Such language, with its ecstatic fusion of inner and outer worlds, its dissolving of distinctions in order to give new vividness to a word like "souls," brings us very close to the opening section of Trakl's poem.

Trakl's images are full of connection, motion, anticipation: the shadows make a continuous entity out of the human "walls" and the natural "hill"; the fusion between trees and clouds is as close and as anthropomorphic as it is in Wackenroder's landscape. But the inclusion of the "smoking city" disrupts the pastoral in the very process of invoking it. Trakl's verbs are dynamic in the extreme: "seek," "sounding," "breathes," "overflows," "smoking," "striding." The prominence of present participles certifies a world in process; even the discordant "darker tears" flow organically within the imagistic framework of "withered sycamores" and "breathes." The trees are justifiably "at peace," being at the end of the organic cycle, but the "age" continues to "breathe." The same enclosing effect is achieved with the word "damnation," strategically situated in the central sixth line yet almost consumed by the ecstatic "overflows."

But gradually Trakl's lines lose momentum, the synthesis of nature and humanity cannot be sustained. Specifically, Wackenroder's transformation of human dwellings into "dark rocky shapes and twilit ghost palaces" is now out of reach, the "melancholy of the smoking city" blocks and attenuates the movement of the opening lines. It is not the city itself with which Trakl is concerned (his cities are always as close to those in the Bible as they are to a modern metropolis), but its linkage of decay with self-perpetuating pseudo-life, its resistance to the completion of death, which has thereby rendered the transforming power of organic death inaccessible. The last three lines are abstract, an allegory without a referent. The verbs ("breathes after," "following") are now without strength, and the governing image is one of doubling: as the "stranger" walks, his steps are doubled, mocked, by a corpse that is not dead. This strictly human movement, a movement that is "away from" the cemetery, haunted by death yet in flight from it, nullifies the earlier dynamism and forces all process into a paralysis of circularity. The "Märchen" amplifies what has happened. During his obsession we are told of the hermit: "he could take no step with his feet like other people." And at the end, during his apotheosis: "he launched himself ever higher, with dancing feet, into the heavens." Trakl echoes the imagery of the feet, but for him there is no release from paralysis to cosmic dance. On the contrary, the dreamer of line six is nominally static, but still imbued with fullness, whereas the subsequent emblematic stranger (strangeness is now universal) "walks" perpetually into an inner paralysis without imaginable end. The biblical "damnation" can now be interpreted: it is a condemnation, not to hell, but precisely to "Vorhölle," to hell's antechamber.

The temporal zone of the first section is that of process, expectation, the human quest, the possibility of change even when, at the end, that possibility becomes radically attenuated. And the landscape is entirely external—human preoccupations feed directly into nature—while the dominant colors, gold and purple, are both transitional as colors and suggestive of the possibility of grace, the openness of time.

In the second section we move backwards into the obsessive time of the hermit's wheel itself, time as repetition and closure. The colors—red, black, and blue—are now primary, fixed in their nature; and the fluid landscape of the first part is replaced by a double vision, with an immobile cityscape shifting at the center of the section toward a dark interior, the imprisonment of human reproduction ("The mothers' death laments") within the unyielding geometry of city tenements. It is not necessary to import one's knowledge of other Trakl contexts in order to sense the deathliness of "the stone structure"; the opening of the first section is here subtly inverted, as the "Mauern" are intensified, rendered concrete and threateningly autonomous, while "the sounding gold" echoes passively in "Quietly resounds."

The next lines evoke a single set of images, a cityscape, but also, with the juxtaposition of the orphans and the commercial vessel, the breaking of the threads that could bind these motifs of urban "living" into an imaginable contingent narrative. Human activity as such is "orphaned," without the parentage of a temporal mythos. This hieroglyph of presentness submits blankly to the hermit's obsession; he is so furious at people who carry on "these trivial earthly preoccupations" that he kills them if he can. And lines 4 and 5 embody his perspective precisely, as human beings "rise and fall" on the rhythmic wheel of time, ignoring their own incessant decay. However, paraphrasing Trakl's images in this manner imputes to them a dynamism of which they are in fact completely drained. Trakl's cityscape is deliberately static, the wheel of time is so inexorably at work that it has become invisible.

At the sixth line we seem to move into an allegorized interior of the city. The movement is a double one. The angels "emerge" from the large black doorways; the image suggests abandonment, the irrevocable separation of whatever is within from the possibility of salvation. Certainly the eighth line, with its compression of death and birth into a single image, takes us inside the buildings, where these ultimate human processes take place. The external cityscape is realized concretely; this interior, however, is set on a metaphorical level. Although it is pointless with Trakl to speak of a time of day as if it were a given, he does maintain in this poem an evening atmosphere: the human beings move "in the darkness." Thus the line "A fiery wheel, the rounded earth day" intervenes garishly, converting the deepening darkness of the world behind the "black doorways" into an interior of the mind rather than of the buildings. The mothers see what no one else sees. They see the wheel of time; at the moment of giving birth they share the hermit's vision of a death that *is* calculable, inexorable. In the first section Trakl has evoked the oneness of the dreamer's heart with the process of evening; here he uses a much more drastic image—"through their long hair rolls"—to suggest the total invasion of the mothers' being by their vision of time. Here there is no organic flow from inside to outside and back, no giving and receiving; this is a crushing, a dissolving of all individuality into "the world's torment."

With the double structure of this section Trakl "dissolves," in the vocabulary of Novalis, the music of the hermit-saint, which functioned as both crisis (the wheel's horrible sound) and resolution. Now the wheel of time is both silent and omnivorous, absent from the city's impersonal walls, yet obsessively present to the residual humans struggling to perpetuate the dream (now the illusion) of organic continuity behind those walls. This endless "prelude" enacts a "chaos" whence neither birth nor death can emerge into narrative life.

In the final section the landscape is entirely interior and the experience of time is shifted to a level of horror not imagined even by Wackenroder's hermit. In all his poems Trakl follows the principle of the connotative chain, the use of the associative power of words themselves to generate new images. Here he takes literally the terrible truth of the mothers, the interlocking of birth and death, and fills the private rooms of humanity with an accelerated time process, in which the decay of everything from children to household equipment can be experienced directly, as with X-ray vision.

The lines gain intensity from being a virtual anthology of images already encountered: the poem, as it were, accelerates the consumption of its own possibilities, embodies the temporal crisis in its own process. In noting the linked images, one has no need to claim correlations of meaning: this would imply the existence of some stable outside world, some normative criteria, whereas in Trakl the words generate their own worlds, their own tonal contrasts. Thus "In cool rooms" recalls "golden coolness"; the connection almost prevents the reader from thinking of temperature (in Trakl a commonsense meaning, such as suddenly becomes available in this phrase, seems enigmatic, precarious), and directs attention to the neutralizing, antiorganic quality of the phrase in the first section. The connection is reinforced in the next lines: the child that is already old and bony is analogous to the corpse that is not dead. But here, and for the remainder of the poem, the human element is unable to become incarnated as a full, singular being. The concept of a person has become fragmented by the acceleration of

127

time, and the hazy singularity implicit in the early reiteration of "the striding man . . . the stranger" seems remote and ironically full of richness in this ultimate circle of "Vorhölle." The "Märchen" for which this "childhood" is groping would appear to be the fairy tale of existence itself, a human existence now obsolete, in vivid contrast to the energetic decaying of the implements and the eager gnawing of the rat. We find this sort of scene in actual fairy tales, for example, the loom covered with cobwebs in "The Sleeping Beauty." But there, of course, the scene is invariably a prelude to transformation, whereas here it is "without meaning"; the residues of humanity are trapped within this sleep from which there will no longer be an awakening, and they grope for the lost key, the squandered fairy tales.

"A heart" fills the central sixth line, and here the symmetry with the first section, where "the dreamer's heart" is similarly placed, is clear. The shift from "overflows" to "congeals" is dramatic, the openness of cosmic expectation has been succeeded by a paralysis that enters consciousness exclusively through the antisystem of poetic language. And the systemic rigidity implies drastic changes in every other element in the world: the context accentuates the semantic isolation of "a heart" both as existential solitude and as an internal breakdown of the human organism, a disintegration of the connective tissue.

The last four lines seem to draw the poem's gestures together in a kind of inventory, without actually repeating major motifs ("purple" and "darkness" appear in new combinations). They are dominated by sound, as if in this accelerated world "silence" and (the very next word in the German text) "Echo" were no longer mutually exclusive. (They are of course not to be understood as successive, Trakl always transmits a given group of events as simultaneous, essentially a single event.) The bee's hum, in Mörike's "Im Frühling," connoted a drop below the semantic threshold into a zone of renewal. Now, regeneration is unimaginable; instead, noise and echoes dissolve all residual connective structures. The hermit in the "Märchen" already conveys the aural invasion launched by the wheel of time, in its rigid, unyielding rhythm: "the uniform sounds piled on top of each other in ever more monstrous wildness." The echoing "purple curses" recall "the sounding gold" of the poem's opening; although Trakl does not use a precise color coding, we sense the darkening into claustrophobia, the "wild" passivity of humanity as it is forced in upon itself, into the interiors of its rooms and its bodies.

The motif of hunger provides a semantic X-ray of the cityscape at the beginning of section two, as Trakl concentrates social, biological, and metaphysical resonances into a single image. As human intentionality disintegrates, language begins to encode the ruined tradition with a new density; the very paralysis of human projects releases unused energies into words themselves. The immediate shift from hunger to the "swords of the lie" illuminates the level to which the poem has moved, the level of the Bible. Friedrich Schlegel remarks, "the constructed works of poetry constitute in fact a bible,"[41] and Trakl hints at a biblical encyclopedia of culture-bound sensations, an emergence into the open of all the value-constructs of the Western tradition. Such emergence can be invoked because the stories that secured Western values are no longer tellable. Trakl's claustrophobic interior resembles Heym's marketplaces as they "scream for a redeemer in the time of madness." Grotesquely parodying the "privileged objects" of the culture of "Bildung," these human environments resound with the language that can no longer be spoken.

The swords sever one human component from another; in their blackness they reverse the memory of the romance of the quest, a memory still present in the "seek" of the poem's opening line. And they also resound metallically; the word "Nachhallen" achieves its full effect in this "echo"; lying has become the small change of this cosmos, echoing long-forgotten "truths" that once could shape contingencies into an interpretive narrative. But of course the binary structure of interpretation is obsolete. Values exist, indeed they "resound" ritualistically, but only as components of the universal decay.

The concluding image similarly operates on several levels. The door's clanging raises the infernal racket to a new intensity, impressing on the reader that there is nothing monochromatic about this prelude to hell: as the human paralysis turns into disintegration, every other element (like the "fat rat") acts as if released from the bondage of man's control and fills the atmosphere with threatening energy and unpredictable movement. There is also something definitive about the door's closing, as if the whole of time were suddenly concentrated into a single moment. Biblical images of the Last Judgment are present, but Trakl does not rely on them. The whole sequence of his poem has led us from a dreamy if troubled expansiveness to this radical point of extreme contraction. Rather like Kafka's door in "Before the Law," this door excludes rather than includes: there is no movement from "Vorhölle" into some other state, just an irrevocable dwindling of the human world. Trakl's poem renders the imagery of any other kind of hell superfluous.

This sealing of signifiers into an irrefutable "construction," a totality without wholeness, a density without harmony, suggests a kinship between Expressionist techniques and Schlegel's combinatory art ("Kombinatorik"); the dynamics of combining renders viable, for Schlegel, a language speaking simultaneously of encyclopedia and chaos: "Are intensifying and combining perhaps identical processes? When intensifying one combines the quantity with itself."[42] Expressionist poetry is essentially a combining, a hypnotic inventory of the fragments of the Western tradition, which yield a direct reading of the collapsing ideologies of "Bildung" and privileged time. Schlegel's encyclopedic project is of course fueled by the confidence of "Progressivität"; its linguistic combining is free to be playful, arbitrary.

But to the Expressionists history speaks of the impossibility of freedom; it is grimly singular. Yet its very singularity rules out all narratives of contingency. It has become a chaos that does not know it is one, the presentness of an "order" that has forgotten all reasons for acting and being. In order to "live" this history, the imagination must surrender to it unreservedly, speaking its language of nonliving without mediation, coldly. What emerges is a narrative in which the poem's speaker, the self as user of words, is drastically redefined. Friedrich Schlegel, radical differences of perspective notwithstanding, is able to evoke the energy infusing this language: "Should a human being will to change the world? Can, may, that be his purpose? Logically speaking, the central concern of a human being can only be humanity itself. It must become individuated. The human being should strive to actualize totality in himself and individuality in humanity."[43] The structure of values that underpinned the code of "Bildung" has collapsed, but the values themselves have not vanished; they have been reabsorbed by the language, a language that speaks through the poet with a hermetic, intransitive potency. The process of taking inventory becomes a "Kombinatorik" as intense as that envisaged by Schlegel; for the very act of singling out both present and absent phenomena, of finding words for them and organizing them as a sequence, becomes an act charged with significance.

To the Expressionists history is not so much a project as an immanent experience: it is inherent in their sense of themselves, stranded in the impotence of tradition yet equipped with a language saturated with its accumulated values and dreams. Their experience is "express-ible" because it has ceased to be personal, because individuality, whether as premise or goal, no longer limits them; the self's language is not "parole" but "langue," the entirety of the language system. And the other pole of Schlegel's dual assignment is activated with a compa-rable logic: as Heym and Trakl transform the first person speaking of the privileged moment into a multiplicity of dying narratives, so hu-manity, collapsed into the impersonal energy of its language, becomes reimaginable as "Individualität," a singularity guaranteed by the unique power of these texts.

CHAPTER FOUR

Double Time, Double Language: Benn, Celan, Enzensberger

It is becoming possible to view the period roughly from 1920 to 1970 (the lifetime of Paul Celan) as essentially closed, historically describable. Celan's extraordinary poetic enterprise, so wholly and desperately logical while in process, is unimaginable now; its cultural premises have ceased to exist. The question remains whether or not one can say anything reasonably coherent about a period so recent and filled with so many clashing voices. One risks banality, a statement so cautious and generalized that it fails to advance understanding; one also risks making a formulation that is so esoteric it does not seem applicable to specific major voices of the epoch.

My starting point will certainly seem close to the banal when I outline three key paradoxes that are central to the intellectual atmosphere of these years. First, the individual is predictable, repetitive, sociologically determined—yet also a marvelous instrument for surviving, observing, transforming the world. Second, the Western tradition is moribund, weighing down humanity with obsolete ideas and reflexes—yet the function of traditions in the plural sense, anthropologically delimited, then culturally combined, is more stimulative than

133

ever. And third, language, in the age of fascist and media politics, has become debased, rendered impotent—yet this is also the age of linguistics, of the exploration of language both as a flexible, systematic structure and as the archaeological vessel of cultural experience.

The major poets of this period both articulate these paradoxes vividly and insist on maintaining them as paradoxes, refusing all premature synthesis. This does not mean, however, that they write like mandarins, perpetually transforming the predictable into the unique and jeweled, the world into language. For the situation is temporal in its essence. The negative side of the paradox—the sickness of the individual and of tradition, the decay of language—constitutes precisely the world of paralyzed horror in which the Expressionist writers felt themselves trapped. And the positive side—the sense that a new version of humanity is imaginable through a kind of sociolinguistic encyclopedia—has emerged directly from the Expressionist transformation of intentional into linguistic energy and established itself as the powerful concord fiction of the new period.

The poets of 1920 to 1970 are "outside" the Expressionist experience of narrative immobility; the paralysis of history is not an obsession but rather a premise, a problem to be confronted incessantly but also a rich poetic storehouse available for play as well as melancholy. For the Expressionists, the abyss is visible through the transparence of impotent, intransitive language; from 1920 to 1970 the abyss has become the basic fact of consciousness, and like all facts it has become routine.

But a world of postapocalyptic routine was strangely fruitful for poetry. As the grip of bourgeois custom loosened its hold everywhere, the Expressionist paralysis gave way to a sense of new functions for an interpretive narrative, new extremes of unacknowledged social dislocation requiring the complexities of poetic language. This complexity is "political" from the outset, in that the lyrical self speaks necessarily from anonymity and flux, from cracks that have suddenly opened between blocks of social realities now become unstable. The collapse of privatized "Bildung" forces poets to redefine human individuality in the context of social norms that are simultaneously arbitrary, oppressive, and provisional. An explicitly political poetry emerges from the new possibilities for interpretive narrative. Brecht's quest for a political style is nourished by the multiple linguistic gestures available to him, from collages of "personal" moments through laconic reportage to the stylizations of ballad and proverb. Harsh cynicism and images

134

of innocence become all the more inseparable in Brecht's work as the doubleness of his political language, the fusion of immediate and remote time zones, achieves full focus. This poetry is political precisely because it is both in exile from nonexistent or grotesque public language—and has as its historical mission the projection of images of value. The quest for values is necessarily archaeological, even when, as in the Romantic "Märchen," the truth is right nearby.

"Wherefore poets in wretched times?" ("Wozu Dichter in dürftiger Zeit?") Hölderlin's question is answered by the phenomenon of poetry in this half century: what Walter Benjamin says of the opportunities afforded by close-up photography is applicable to poetry—the poets do indeed "calmly and adventurously go traveling" among the "far-flung ruins and debris" of the Western tradition.[1] And the result is that the monstrous events of the 1940s, far from making poetry look irrelevant or esoteric, may be genuinely accessible only through the narration of poets like Celan and Nelly Sachs. Complexity and political consciousness are equally inherent in this language, which is more than seismographic. It becomes a civilizational life-support system. The Expressionists have desperately inverted the language of "Bildung" and privileged time; these poets take up the challenge of Expressionist rupture, accept the central event, which is the absorption of historical contingency into the system of language. Yet they postulate the reenergizing of that language, the coalescence of disintegrated historical fragments into new narratives of sociohistorical potency.

The Romantics speculated frequently on the metaphysics of totalized endings and open beginnings, projecting the fiction of a conflict between space and time, and assigning ontological priority to time. Friedrich Schlegel argues that an open future is not just preceded but actually constituted by an assault on the imprisoning illusions of finitude: "The consciousness of the infinite must be constituted—by annihilating its opposite. One must constitute oneself through a decisive act, and that act is none other than the destruction of the illusion of finitude."[2] More explicitly, Schlegel suggests that the act of "annihilation" can be seen metaphysically as the annihilation of space by time: "In theorizing the world the essential move is to destroy mass and space and to reduce everything to time and activity."[3]

For the post-Expressionist poets the immediate need is to radicalize the dying of the Western tradition, to "annihilate" it, to reimagine its hospitals as cemeteries. For in its infinitely long drawn out ending, the tradition has become a pervasive memory, filling the minds of men,

135

the scenery of nature, the structure of daily language. Although produced by the accumulation of history it has ceased to move forward; it spreads through the world like a dying river becoming ever shallower. In short, the tradition is now best understood as a "space," a space that is so omnipresent as to have become invisible. To quote Novalis once again: "space as precipitate of time." This endlessly dying mental landscape, Eliot's wasteland, is the residue of the Expressionist apocalypse. Here political upheavals give an illusion of history, but all such temporal convulsions succumb to the paralysis of spatialized experience, confirming Schlegel's dictum: "Space is congealed, distorted, decayed, dead time."[4]

For the poets of this infinite decay, the necessary rupture is actualized by a structured conflict between space and time. Much misunderstanding has been generated by the conceptual function of purity and absence in this conflict, terms that are indeed essential to this poetry. The poets often appear to be laying claim to an autonomous aesthetic realm, but in fact this is only the first stage of an authentically temporal dialectic. These poems aim to *become,* to bring into immediate textual existence ("constituiren" is Schlegel's term) the possibility of history that the dying tradition has already systematized, spatialized, diluted into inauthentic life. A double version of time is the key to understanding this process. To be suspended, forced into absence, is the time of the tradition in its endless dilution, the repetitions that must be understood as spatial, as "decayed time"; to be generated by the poem is a time livable yet not actually lived, a time zone that, simply because it constitutes itself as an aggressive compression and abstraction of everyday details, has a quality of "purity." But pure does not mean empty. The poem's time claims a narrative singularity not otherwise available. This claim (which since 1970 has come to seem strange, hubristic) is not reducible to the idea of an experiential privileged moment, which the poem would simply transmit; that poetics died in the furnace of Expressionism. But the conception of poetic language as in itself privileged certainly reaches a climax in the self-understanding of these poets. The new temporality of the poem can only emerge from a double mode of struggle with the spatial paralysis afflicting all contemporary experience: a strategic engagement in both destruction and colonization.

It is this fundamental aggressiveness, wherein the Expressionist gesture of revolt has become normative, that differentiates the twentieth-century privileging of poetry from that of the Romantics. Marshall

Brown has shown that the Romantic purification of language was re-generative in its essence, a project to restore the unity of a world fallen silent.

> The center of time has opened; that is, the organization of nature is imperceptible. In language man still has a trace of the divine spirit. Logic provides the principle of organization, and speech provides the principle that human organization will be temporal and successive. In language man still has a center, but only an external one, only the principle of organization without its realization, only the form of his destiny without its content. Man's aim must be to bring meaning to nature, to naturalize, and in so doing to humanize the Word.
>
> To thus purify language is the role of poetry. It is, I believe, because poetry was to restore integrity to our experience that the romantics so often called it central.[5]

The parallels between Romantic ambitions for poetry and modernist poetics serve to identify the differences. In the twentieth century there is too little silence, too much organization; the sick omnipresence of tradition, together with the decisive assault on individual experience by the technologies of war and mass society, have invalidated the ancient goals of integrity and centrality. What remains is a fascination with history shorn of all teleological dreams, a sense that poetry must speak wholly autonomously, without the Romantic aspiration toward synthesis with other modes of discourse. Such speaking occurs not in a void, but in the oppressive context of ceaseless everyday speaking, a context that allows no escape from trivialization; "history," like "tragedy," is an ever-present cliché. Moreover, the poem cannot generate a private language, cannot seal itself off, however much it may deploy such movements strategically. As Paul Celan, a master of such strategies, insisted: "The absolute poem—no, that certainly does not exist, that cannot exist!"[6]

To assault the world and to colonize it with new narrative potency must be a simultaneous process. The image of conventional time and conventional experience as spatial is the premise for a systematic pulverization of that space (Gottfried Benn's famous term is "reducing reality to rubble," "Wirklichkeitszertrümmerung"). But the alternative time, the militant self-isolation of the poem can only come into existence if the process of destruction is matched by a colonization of particular fragments of experience, a linguistic intensification without illusions, fueled only by destruction. Novalis's "worship of chance" regains its importance: but whereas in the late nineteenth century it was a starting point, an occasion for revelation, now the contingent is characteristically a telos, a single image emerging from and guaranteed by an elaborate interpretive narrative.

Although the temporal claim of these texts is inseparable from the reader's function (as their historical executant), there can be no narrative of revelation here such as underpins the poetry of Storm, Keller, and Meyer. The poem's aggressive momentum leaves no space for an autonomous "self"; its act of colonization is necessarily and knowingly linguistic. The poem's language is double in that, more than earlier poetry, it is a "dialogue" (Celan's term); even as it draws its reader out of the inhibiting space of tradition, it must constantly test and strengthen the mountaineer's rope of language that binds the reader to it. The risk of severing the rope is never absent. And the poem's time is also double; even as its imagery maps a world devoid of temporal direction, a vast landscape of repetition, these images are anthologized, isolated and ultimately recombined in a linguistic moment dense with the potentiality of value.

The paradoxes of our century, with which this discussion began, are never absent: the poem annihilates the conventional first-person expression of feeling, but it also struggles toward a viable new way of saying "I" and "you." The tenacious memory of tradition is dismantled in order to open the way for a new kind of memory, nourished by forgetting and by the "shocks" (Benjamin's term) of urban space. And the formlessness of everyday language is abstracted into a skeleton of ascetic imagery so that a new fascination with the pure structure, the almost magical flexibility of the language system, can begin to extract the diachronic and contingent from the synchronic and spatial. But although the poem thrusts toward these transformational goals, it also knows that the historical moment in which it must speak is not the moment of their achievement; indeed, that the lure of easy and total mythic transformation (fascism) must be passionately resisted. The spatialized repetition of the everyday is by no means the worst that can be imagined.

During this period there existed a "world language of modern poetry," in Enzensberger's memorable phrase,[7] and it might be helpful to approach the narrative ambitions of German poetry from the perspective of another language. The work of Wallace Stevens is more didactic, more confident, more seamless in its texture than anything compa-

rable in German. Yet in its unhurried, rather formal way, his poetry operates on the same double level of time and language, embarks on the
same quest for an alternative temporality. Here is section 12 of the
1949 poem "An Ordinary Evening in New Haven":

The poem is the cry of its occasion,
Part of the res itself and not about it.
The poet speaks the poem as it is,

Not as it was: part of the reverberation
Of a windy night as it is, when the marble statues
Are like newspapers blown by the wind. He speaks

By sight and insight as they are. There is no
Tomorrow for him. The wind will have passed by,
The statues will have gone back to be things about.

The mobile and the immobile flickering
In the area between is and was are leaves,
Leaves burnished in autumnal burnished trees

And leaves in whirlings in the gutters, whirlings
Around and away, resembling the presence of thought,
Resembling the presences of thoughts, as if,

In the end, in the whole psychology, the self,
The town, the weather, in a casual litter,
Together, said words of the world are the life of the world.[8]

It is almost impossible to quote specific phrases or stanzas in isolation.
The poem exists as a continuous reflection on what it is to be a poem
and, simultaneously, as a complex play with the formal possibilities of
the three-line stanza, particularly enjambment. The images seem informal, accessible—yet they are articulated cautiously, self-consciously:

part of the *reverberation*
Of a windy night *as it is* [my italics].

Indeed, this multiple mediation of the images is the key to their
vividness; the central *topos* of the leaves would be a mere echo of Shel-
ley's "Ode to the West Wind" were it not for the reverse simile (the
leaves resemble "the presence of thought," not vice versa).

What the poem does is narrate the movement from a cerebral
self-description, which seems limited to the notion of the privileged mo-

ment, to an ambitious claim to an identity as "the life of the world." The distance is temporal, the transformation is that of the private "occasion" into the occasion of history. Stevens is not extracting his specific moment from the flow of time; rather, he is imposing his own time on the world through imperious and persistent disruption, driving the reader toward the insight that the time of ordinary life, marked by disparate objects of the cityscape, is decentered presentness, an alienated space ("things about") obliterating the coexistent but temporally vitalized space, "the area between is and was." The poem turns what might easily seem mystical into sheer common sense. Initially, the comparing of the statues to "newspapers blown by the wind" resembles a conceit. But the speaker *knows* it is a conceit. His language grasps it, imposing structure on what is most fragile, transforming a conceit into a truth-bearing fiction. The flickering, vanishing image becomes, through repetition and transformation, something seen clearly and steadily. And in a subtle countermovement the self's elaborate equipment of analytic categories gradually becomes a jumble, a "casual litter." Thus the poem simultaneously hardens and dissolves: the glimpse and the argument about the glimpse merge into a serious claim that the poem's language, by absorbing into itself the scattered remnants of time persisting in an otherwise blank daily space, has indeed become "the life of the world."

The tension between poetological meditation and an intact convention of private experience in Stevens's text is not available to his German-language contemporaries. The legacy of Expressionism is such that the imagining of an alternative world time is inseparable from a poetics of aggression. Just before Gottfried Benn, in his address "Problems of the Lyric," settles on the misleading phrase "the absolute poem" (a phrase with which he was subsequently identified), he has this to say about the poetic process: "It is impossible for the lyricist to know enough or to work enough, he must be close in to everything, he must be focused on the exact point where the world is today, the exact hour standing at this noon above the earth. One must fight close in to the bull, say the great matadors, then perhaps victory will come. There must be nothing accidental in a poem."[9] The spatializing of time is here radicalized, so that the time of the poem can be released; the analogue to Stevens's "occasion" is a static midday or the plunging bull, a locus of struggle and nothing but struggle. The poet is locked into history; no experience can be imagined apart from it. Yet history is only intelligible as the impossibility of experience, the dissolution of all au-

thentic contingency. These poets move forward by radicalizing their
sense of entrapment, by literalizing the stagnation of history as narrated space.

In his speech accepting the Büchner Prize, Paul Celan articulates
a kind of antihistory, praising Lucile's cry "Long live the King!" in
"Dantons Death" as "the counterword . . . an act of desperation."[10]
And Dietlind Meinecke comments legitimately: "Celan designates the
moment of poetic origination as a rising up in a strategic act of rebel-
lion against historical time."[11] But while Celan's argument insists on a
kind of armed solitude for the poem, it does not stop there; it does not
press the poem into a static "beyond." Rather, it curves backward toward this struggle with history, invoking Benjamin's word "attentiveness" as Benn had invoked Nietzsche's "nostrils"—as the poet's essential equipment. In this poetics the world's details are abstracted into
the poem's space, where the alchemy of the interpretive narrative, the
moment of writing itself, subtly introduces the otherness of the contingent into the prison of self-interpretation:

> The poem becomes . . . conversation. . . . Only within the
> space of this conversation does the object addressed constitute it-
> self; it coalesces around the self that is talking to it and naming it.
> But the object addressed, which in the act of being named has as
> it were become a "thou," brings with it into this presentness its
> otherness. Even in the here and now of the poem—the poem it-
> self always has only the one, singular, punctual present time—
> even in this directness and immediacy the poem permits its part-
> ner, its other, to speak what is most peculiarly its own: namely
> its time.[12]

The first use of the word presentness ("Gegenwart") is primarily spatial: the deathliness of the present, the impossibility of "Bildung,"
must first be crystallized as linguistic space. But "punktuelle Gegenwart" is clearly temporal; the time of the poem is released. Like Wallace Stevens, Celan stresses the singularity, the contingency, of the object being formed in the interpretive "conversation." But the passage
ends with the dialogical openness of "speaking its own time"
("mitsprechen"): the time of history has been compressed, yet at the
same time released, in the time of the text.

With the early Enzensberger the poetics of double time culminates in a new anxiety. Whereas for Benn and Celan the interpretive

narrative yields a new semantic fluidity between the contingent and the historical, Enzensberger maintains the interpretive process in the foreground of his texts. For modernism has become an identifiable whole, forcing him to speak from outside as well as inside its dynamics; and to interpret from the outside is to be historically vulnerable in a new sense. Although the autonomy of poetic language remains for him a sine qua non of its vitality, the political freedom of such language, its claim to pulverize and colonize the contingent, has become both precarious and questionable. Paradoxically, the tradition of the new, the cumulative achievement of poetry since 1920, has become almost dangerously powerful. The richness, the compelling logic, the self-reflective history of this poetry—all have given it, for Enzensberger, the polyphonic authenticity of a kind of counterworld. Such autonomy, as we have seen, is precisely what this poetry does not seek, as if anticipating that "autonomy" would render it vulnerable to the ultimate defeat, cooptation into the dead presentness of the consumer society. Enzensberger's strategy of resistance is polemical stylization, an intensification of the tradition's aggressiveness, as he anthologizes it into the ambivalently titled *Museum der modernen Poesie:*

> Whoever does not tire of interrogating modern poetry (while shaking the head) concerning "the positive"—such a person overlooks the obvious: "negative" action is poetically impossible; the reverse side of every poetic destruction is the construction of a new poetics. . . . Like history in general, the history of poetry is irreversible. It does not repeat itself. This fact can only be ignored by ahistorical thinking, which confines itself to the dilettantish contemplation of phenomenological models; and it does this not without the intention of drawing the teeth of the still disquieting modern style, of domesticating it.[13]

For Enzensberger the post-Expressionist era has attained, by 1960, a state of calm insanity. The more the modern tradition speaks the truth of history, compressing its disguised horrors into irrefutably vivid images, the more skilled does the world become at orchestrating an appropriate reception for these images, to the point of subverting Enzensberger's final article of faith: "The poem is anticommodity pure and simple."[14] For Benn and Celan a counterhistory involves a linguistic quest, an assault on surfaces in order to shake out remnants of an imprisoned past. For Enzensberger the world's hidden dimensions have dissolved. The truth of history has become transparent, the poem as "Antiware" is oppositional without metaphysical hope. The confrontation of time zones can, indeed must, become direct.

At the heart of his "inner emigration," entangled in the many bonds, visible and invisible, of his role as army doctor in the Third Reich, Gottfried Benn struggled to open a purely linguistic time zone, to structure a narrative exclusively from the imagery of modernism, understood by Benn as the encyclopedia of an alternative world.

Abschied
Gottfried Benn

Du füllst mich an wie Blut die frische Wunde
und rinnst hernieder seine dunkle Spur,
du dehnst dich aus wie Nacht in jener Stunde,
da sich die Matte färbt zur Schattenflur,
du blühst wie Rosen schwer in Gärten allen,
du Einsamkeit aus Alter und Verlust,
du Überleben, wenn die Träume fallen,
zuviel gelitten und zuviel gewusst.

Entfremdet früh dem Wahn der Wirklichkeiten,
versagend sich der schnell gegebenen Welt,
ermüdet von dem Trug der Einzelheiten,
da keine sich dem tiefen Ich gesellt;
nun aus der Tiefe selbst, durch nichts zu rühren,
und die kein Wort und Zeichen je verrät,
musst du dein Schweigen nehmen, Abwärtsführen
zu Nacht und Trauer und den Rosen spät.

Manchmal noch denkst du dich—: die eigene Sage—:
das warst du doch—? ach, wie du dich vergasst!
war das dein Bild? war das nicht deine Frage,
dein Wort, dein Himmelslicht, das du besasst?
Mein Wort, mein Himmelslicht, dereinst besessen,
mein Wort, mein Himmelslicht, zerstört, vertan—
wem das geschah, der muss sich wohl vergessen
und rührt nicht mehr die alten Stunden an.

Ein letzter Tag—: spätglühend, weite Räume,
ein Wasser führt dich zu entrücktem Ziel,
ein hohes Licht umströmt die alten Bäume
und schafft im Schatten sich ein Widerspiel,
von Früchten nichts, aus Ähren keine Krone
und auch nach Ernten hat er nicht gefragt—

er spielt sein Spiel, und fühlt sein Licht und ohne
Erinnern nieder—alles ist gesagt.[15]
(1941)

Farewell

You fill me as blood wells up in the fresh wound
and pour downward along its dark trace,
you expand as night does at that hour,
when the meadow dissolves into evening shadow,
you bloom like heavy roses in every garden,
you solitude of age and loss,
you living on when dreams fall away,
having suffered and known too much.

Estranged early on from the madness of realities,
renouncing the quickly used up world.
exhausted by the mirage of momentary hopes,
after none has nourished the deeper self;
now from the immobile depth itself,
never betrayed by word or sign,
you must draw your silence, your downward journey
to night, mourning, and late roses.

Sometimes you still think of yourself, your own story—
That was you? Oh, how profoundly you forgot yourself!
was that your image? was that not your question,
your word, your divine light, which you possessed?
My word, my divine light, one time possessed,
my word, my divine light, destroyed, wasted—
he to whom that happened must forget himself
and interferes no more with times past.

A final day: glowing late in vast expanses,
a stream leads you to the withdrawn goal,
a high light pours down round the old trees
playing a counterpoint of rays within the shadow,
the day speaks neither of fruit nor ears of corn,
poses no questions about harvest time—
it stages its play, feels its light, moves downward
without memory—everything is said.

The paradox of Gottfried Benn's work is easily stated: although
he developed early on a profound pessimism about all human activity,
he possessed an intellectual exuberance, a curiosity, a Baudelairean fas-

cination with life's surfaces, which ensured a continuously productive literary life. He was constantly repositioning himself in historical terms. A self-conscious survivor of the Expressionist generation, he strove to develop a formula that would blend the directionlessness of history's chaotic surface with a sophisticated renewal of narrative directionality. His nihilism was only a starting point; and in his quest for a version of history that would, in Romantic terms, "construct" the apparent chaos, he combined the retrospective insight that a historical period is defined by its art with a biologistic image of life as both genetically purposeful and modifiable (this view led to Benn's brief—but alarmingly eloquent—advocacy of the Nazi state). A juxtaposition of two such formulations illuminates the present poem. In some undated "marginalia" Benn notes: "Not wars but art controls the shape of history. . . . Even art is a renunciation, but one that receives everything within itself."[16] And a final version of "deep history," in a 1955 radio talk, reads as follows:

> Poetry does not improve the world, but it does something far more decisive: it changes it. Poetry has no powers of historical intervention, it works otherwise: it suspends time and history, its impact is felt in the gene, the hereditary material, the substantive depths—a long inward journey. . . . Poetry brings into fluid freedom what was hardened, blunted, weary—a fluidity that confuses, eludes rational categories, but that spreads seeds on banks that have become desolate, seeds of joy and seeds of mourning.[17]

The aggressive confrontation of sickened life by autonomous language, which dominates Benn's early collection *Morgue* (1912), is taken for granted in his later quest for a poetics. What interests him is the way poetry simultaneously absorbs the world into itself, renounces the world, replaces the world's time with its own—and generates the "seed" that alone will nourish the world of the future. The title "Abschied" turns out, on rereading, to contain the poem's multiplicity within itself; it is, precisely, not a farewell from another person (although this realization is delayed until the sixth line, in order, it would seem, to include that conventional possibility); it is a farewell from the self, a farewell from the world's emptiness, a farewell from the past—and the imagery of the last stanza suggests a farewell from life itself, an entry into death. For another poet all these kinds of farewell might

145

mean roughly the same thing, but for Benn they are almost infinitely differentiated. The very formal stanza structure, as well as the use of the second person, propels the intimacy of the self-questioning onto a public level: the closer the self comes to his own empty center, the more the desolation begins to look like a definitive opportunity. Saying farewell to the self becomes ritualized, an intensifying self-interpretation opening dialectically into a new zone of contingency. The farewell is neither gradual nor climactic but a series of convulsive shifts in the tone and focus, whereby a purified version of the self, wholly absorbed into the contingent moment, speaks the kind of historical narrative that, in Benn's view, only art can speak.

In the first stanza Benn gives a spatialized version of the process of aging. Indeed, the imagery is unhealthily organic (one thinks of Trakl); the decline of life is taunting the speaker with its obscene blossoming, its invasion of all his senses. And the point is radicalized by the term "living on" ("Überleben"). Essentially the speaker is already dead, living a mere afterlife. The movement toward a farewell is already disrupted, because the process of being released from living is suffused with sickness. This first stanza seems to refute the title altogether: no farewell is imaginable, because the self is already distended, barely recognizable as singular. And the poem's leisurely, formal manner appears to acknowledge the obsolescence of the contingent, moving immediately from self-interpretation to the historical stage through images that bind the experience of the self to that of the Western tradition as a whole. The blood, the evening modulating into night, the roses' heavy scent—these phrases establish a familiar landscape, the ancient landscape of religious and erotic longing. By delaying the moment when the "you" is identified, and then by counterpointing images of deathliness and loss to the earlier luxuriance, Benn imprisons the illusions of modern experience within an ornately rhythmic dance of death. The expansiveness is maintained to the very end of the stanza: "when dreams fall away" evokes a meaningless harvest, a psychic autumn deriding all imagery of renewal, and the last line maintains a vision of overripeness and surfeit.

With its shift from a mode of similes to an enumerative style ("too much") this concluding line leads into a second stanza, which is systematically opposed to the first: it counters the expansive with the negative, dismantling all experience into a heap of wreckage without connections (the first stanza embodies a proliferation of connections). Benn is probably trying to do too much in this stanza; phrases like "the madness of realities" and "the deeper self" are awkwardly schematic. The purpose is to counterpoint a second "story" to the first, this time the story of a lifetime's vain quest for meaning—and to reach exactly the same point, with the reprise of the first stanza's imagery in the last line. Both stories are presented spatially, as traversals of landscapes: fullness and emptiness are versions of the same static journey. And as Benn has intensified "solitude" into "living on," so in this stanza, too, he makes a radical move, situating the notion of pure negation at its very center. The deep self is that which does not experience, it is a postulate, a state of being that the negativity of experience compels one to imagine. This dialectic is central to Benn's version of double time. The deep self, as in Novalis's historical poetics, is blocked off by the intentionality of the everyday. But the project of "Farewell" is to overcome intentionality, to encode a whole life as "eternally recurrent." Far from being internal, the deep self is "public" in its essence, located in the depths of a hidden but inexorable biological-aesthetic history. Part of the stanza's awkwardness derives from these poetological hints. The reader needs to respond to the cue of Benn's depth concept in order to sense the paradoxical power of the negatives "no word . . . your silence." For the wordlessness is of course being narrated, the poem itself is bringing an ecstasy of silence into being.

As the stanza curves back toward the imagery of its predecessor, it is also staging a doubling of language. The slightly stale poetic similes of the first stanza are not so much echoed as shifted from sickened horizontal space into a vertical penumbra where temporal change seems once again imaginable. The destructive sequence of the second stanza, culminating in "silence," is simultaneously a rupture of bloated nonliving. No new possibility of living emerges, the negativity is total. But the movement of the stanza gives a dynamic accent to the nominally deterministic "you must" of line 7. The speaker has shifted from passive to active, from "when dreams fall away" to "downward journey," as he inscribes his will to lifelessness in the silence, a silence that is also the sound of poetry.

The biological time of the speaker in the first stanza is already stylized as the sick space of tradition; the vision of experience in the second stanza becomes a vertical space, its language strangely energetic yet bound to the paradox of silence, to an inaccessible depth. The third stanza attempts to instigate a language drawing on this vertical energy, the renouncing, generalizing narrative of individual history, individual memory. But the first two words seem to doom the attempt:

"Sometimes still." Since the perspective from which the self's life is to be narrated cannot be fixed, but shifts aimlessly in the spatialized present, the life itself cannot hope to attain the desired unity of the interpretive and the contingent.

But while the "story" cannot take root, it does further the poem's complex development of double time through double language. The function of linguistic repetition becomes clearer with the evolution of key words such as "word," "light," and "forget." The first use of forgetting connotes a collapse of identity: from the perspective of empty survival, "living on," the speaker can see a total discontinuity *within* the framework of the life that is supposed to have been lived. The disruption of everyday time is more drastic than in stanza 2 because the activity of forgetting becomes potent; the consciousness can, through cancelling the past rather than postulating recurrence, cut through the sick space of experience: "how profoundly you forgot yourself." Discontinuity generates its own momentum, as the temporal code ("question," "word") rejoins the spatial ("image," "light") in a newly alive assault on the futile anxieties of the singular self. With extreme irony the second person shifts to the first at the center of the stanza, at just the point where the poem's incantatory assault on the notion of possession renders the word "my" ("mein") meaningless.

The threefold repetition of potent words has a double function. First, it completes the fracturing of a coherent individuality based on the "possession" of such words: the poetic voice taunts the self with the accelerating rush of experience into abstraction. Second, the repetition, especially the third time, advances a purely linguistic consciousness. "Destroyed, wasted"—the verbs are somehow excessively strong, they seem no longer to refer to the dissipation of coherence. Rather they appear spoken from a new point of view, that of the poem's own time as it completes the destruction of the self's claim to narrate its own past. The poem's move into the past tense has generated only the static fragmentation of "was," "forgot," "possessed." The moment of destruction, however, is an authentic event ("happened"), and it immediately produces the word "forget" in a new sense. This is a projective forgetting, which frees the consciousness from its self-protective urge to occupy the time zone of the traditional self; the collapse of the self into spatially evoked fragments leads not to annihilation but to release. Again, as in the seventh line of the preceding stanza, the verb "must" implies active acceptance, the possibility of a new kind of reclamation of history. And the simple language of the last line opens

the door further: "die alten Stunden," the conventional past, is accepted as passively spatial, its otherness at last accepted, while "no
more" heightens our sense of a real event. "Happened," "must," "interferes no more": the past tense is drawn voluntarily into a present
moment which finally renounces the versions of identity through
which the poem has passed. Mörike's "old unnameable days" reverberate infinitely at the end of his poem, weaving the contingent and the interpretive into a rich narrative of "Bildung." Benn's unmysterious
"times past," in contrast, are literally untouched, relinquished. But
this closure, this renunciation of longing, has a structurally liberating
effect similar to that of Mörike's ecstatic self-embrace.

"A final day": with a drastic shift the poem enters its own time
zone, which is a kind of refutation of all that has preceded. The language is now full of singulars rather than plurals; everything is happening once only. The spaces are open, the journey by water, with its
mythical aura, seems to transform the landscape into an active, focused, temporal process. In the first stanza the shadow play was the
gradual emergence of evening, a horizontal spreading, almost like an
infection. Now the shadow play, freshly colonized by the double language, is generated vertically by a singular light from above; and it ne-
gates the earlier play by being free of all the imagery of growth and fru-
ition that had proliferated in the first stanza. The rhythm of negation
in the poem's last lines reminds the reader of the heaping negatives in
stanza 2; but now the negation is pure, in easy harmony with the singularity of these images. What happens here happens once only, contingency born of interpretation and released by it into a purely semantic
historical narration (which for Benn is the only possible history). The
potency of this linguistic event depends on the preceding otherness of
the poem, on the failed experiential quests that it transcends. Thus, at
the end memory is emptied out and the poem's language explicitly completes itself. The earlier notions of silence and forgetting are recalled in
this conclusion, their role in opening up the earlier stanzas from within
reaffirmed. But the language of the conclusion embeds the silence and
the forgetting within the activity of play: there is not so much silence
as a perpetually completed language, not so much forgetting as a single
direction of time without imaginable need of memory.

The ideal of play, always seductive, needs to be earned. With the
tightness of his language, the network of relationships between the first
three stanzas and the last, Benn does earn his final gleaming images. He
achieves the balance, and thus the release, articulated by Friedrich

Schlegel: "In mysticism the world appears as *nothingness*. In mythology it appears as *play*, as *poetry*. That is both the positive and highest perspective. Only the latter view is usable, but without a firm grounding in the former, mystical view, it cannot be sustained."[18] There is no doubt that the release is essentially linguistic. But language is at the center of this poetics: the interpretive narrative is acted out as paralysis, repetition, ironic dismantling; yet the very vocabulary of that narrative is stripped down, purified in the process of utterance, and reenergized as contingency. Poetic language has the alchemical power to translate the multiple inertness of a dead past into the singular farewell of verbal life.

The extreme changes in the world between the writing of Benn's "Abschied" and the publication of Paul Celan's *Die Niemandsrose* in 1963 throw the closeness of their poetic projects into sharp relief. The "productivity" of the modernist encyclopedia is as great as ever, indeed it increases toward the end of Celan's life; but it becomes a productivity of pain and paralysis, a refusal to budge from the moment of pain, which alone can authenticate an alternative time zone.

Die Silbe Schmerz
Paul Celan

Es gab sich Dir in die Hand:
ein Du, todlos,
an dem alles Ich zu sich kam. Es fuhren
wortfreie Stimmen rings, Leerformen, alles
ging in sie ein, gemischt
und entmischt
und wieder
gemischt.

Und Zahlen waren
mitverwoben in das
Unzählbare. Eins und Tausend und was
davor und dahinter
grösser war als es selbst, kleiner, aus-
gereift und
rück- und fort-
verwandelt in
keimendes Niemals.

Vergessenes griff
nach Zu-Vergessendem, Erdteile, Herzteile

schwammen,
sanken und schwammen. Kolumbus,
die Zeit-
lose im Aug, die Mutter-
Blume,
mordete Masten und Segel. Alles fuhr aus,

frei,
entdeckerisch,
blühte die Windrose ab, blätterte
ab, ein Weltmeer
blühte zuhauf und zutag, im Schwarzlicht
der Wildsteuerstriche. In Särgen,
Urnen, Kanopen
erwachten die Kindlein
Jaspis, Achat, Amethyst—Völker,
Stämme und Sippen, ein blindes

Es sei

knüpfte sich in
die schlangenköpfigen Frei-
Taue—: ein
Knoten
(und Wider- und Gegen- und Aber- und Zwillings- und Tau-
sendknoten), an dem
die fastnachtsäugige Brut
der Mardersterne im Abgrund
buch-, buch-, buch-,
stabierte, stabierte.[19]
(1963)

The Syllable Pain

It gave itself into your hand:
a Thou, deathless,
by which all Self came to itself. There circled
around wordless voices, empty forms, everything
entered them, mixed
and distilled
and again
mixed.

And numbers were
woven into

151

the uncountable. The one, the thousand, and whatever
before and behind
was greater than itself, smaller, overripened and
transformed
backward and forward into
the burgeoning Never.

The forgotten grasped
for what was yet to be forgotten, earth parts, heart parts
swam,
sank and swam. Columbus,
the time-
less one in his mind's eye, the mother-
flower,
murdered masts and sail. All was unleashed,

free,
full of discovery,
the rose compass faded, lost
its leaves, one world ocean
bloomed massively into the day, in the black light
of the tiller's wild strokes. In coffins,
urns, canopies
the little children awoke
jasper, agate, amethyst—peoples,
tribes and kinsmen, a blind

Let there be

wove itself into
the serpent-headed rigging
hanging free: one
knot
(and counter and inverse and multiple and twin and thousand knots), by which
the carnival-eyed brood
of marten stars in the depths
de-, de-, de-
ciphered, ciphered.

Key elements of Celan's project are vividly evoked by certain Romantic fragments, but whereas Romantic imagery is experimental, inviting other formulations, Celan's words are to be taken so literally that, in T. S. Eliot's phrase, they

152

strain,
Crack and sometimes break, under the burden.

Thus Schlegel articulates what any reader feels as the simultaneous breadth and abstraction of a Celan text: "Spiritually, the artist consumes other beings. He swallows in an instant whole masses of spiritual seeds and blossoms. In his feeling he always feels something higher along with it."[20] And a Novalis fragment suggests the fusion of rigidity and instability in Celan's images of history: "Where eternal unchangeable laws prevail, there you have antiquity, deep past. The process of history is a burning up. Mathematical nature consumes unmeasured nature."[21]

But it is the juxtaposition of the fragments that yields the truly significant word: "consume" ("verzehren"). Celan consumes history and is consumed by it. Although the temporality of both Benn and Celan is best conveyed by vertical imagery, with Benn a simple binary model is sufficiently descriptive: the fragmented, multiple surface is contrasted with a singular, inexorable historical depth ("Tiefe"), which is not mystical but perpetually emergent as the narrative of aesthetic and biological change. The poet's task is to emancipate language into this depth through a pulverization of the surface.

For Celan the antithetical framework of multiplicity versus singularity, spatialized surface versus temporal depth, has become inadequate. If Benn, the doctor, tends from the start toward the posture of the ironic seer for whom only renunciation, distance from experience, can activate historical meaning, Celan, his poetic existence forged by the event named Auschwitz, is incapable of distance, is pressed up close against an experience that must become language, yet is utterly hostile to it. Unlike Benn's melancholy sickening of the self, Celan's experiential space evokes a transparent wall, a compression of tradition and the self that is in perpetual danger of collapse. Celan's attempts to inscribe these wall fragments into the movement of a poem often appear desperate, precisely because such fragments *do* have integrity, potential meaning, hence are always losable.

To continue the wall metaphor for a moment: Celan finds embedded in it the intensities of remembered individual experience, and toward these he expresses none of Benn's detachment. Glimpses of passionate living are projected by his poems without any reservation as to their validity or durability—but also always with a profound sense of unfreedom, of inhibiting depths into which passion itself compels one

153

to stare. In these depths, at the foot of this compressing wall of consciousness, is the absolutely singular event Auschwitz, the event that is decisive for all subsequent experience but that does not seem to belong in the category "experience" at all. For Benn the singular depth of history can only be glimpsed through a radical disruption of the surface. For Celan singularity is a given. But—and this is central to his version of the ecstatic narrative—the event of Auschwitz has not yet entered history and may never do so. It is not a question of forgetting it, but of the possibility that adequate language, without which there is no authentically imagined reality, will never be found. It is a commonplace that the actuality of the death camps compels silence. What terrifies Celan is that language cannot do justice to *any* dimension of this event; and without the necessary language we are incapable of responding to the silent imperative of Auschwitz, namely that the temporality of our "universe," of our literally deadly tradition, be entirely reconceived. Instead, time simply washes over Auschwitz, as if it were some natural plague, horrible but ultimately best forgotten. As the postwar years simply accumulate, Novalis's sentence acquires a new and frightening meaning: "Mathematical nature consumes unmeasured nature." For Celan the spectacle of history is not inherently invalid, as Benn holds; it has been *made* invalid by Auschwitz and the subsequent failure of the collective imagination.

Celan's strategy is to freeze history, to stop time; the opening of time that his poems project is always also an effort to reenter the frozen moment. With the passing years this retrospective journey becomes ever more formidable, the poetic narration that of a sealed and inaccessible history. Indeed, in one sense his words can never reach their goal, must always shatter before the unique darkness of Auschwitz. As Meinecke puts it: "The more the word endeavors to approach the origin, the more opaque it becomes."[22] In this perspective Celan's texts condemn themselves to falling short, to speaking when only silence is adequate; theirs is the eloquence of knowing their own failure.

But Celan himself, in his Büchner Prize speech, does not talk of failure. For him the potentiality of a historical poetic narrative is always immanent; the journey into the unique historical moment and out again, the attainment of that point where the poem can not only speak the unimaginable to the world, but can reconstitute a "self," can speak the simplicities of "I" and "thou": "But there are also at the same time paths, among so many other paths, on which language achieves its voice, there are encounters, paths from a voice to a recipient Thou, creatural paths, perhaps sketches for existence, sending the self ahead of itself to its own being, on a quest for itself . . . a kind of journey home."[23] The very image of a journey is paradoxical if neither beginning nor end can be more than "sketches." Nevertheless Celan retains the Romantic imagery of homecoming, of the identity of inner and outer journeys. Overcoming the denial of Auschwitz, finding the language for its silence, is the ultimate challenge to the narrative imagination. It remains feasible because, although the uniqueness of Auschwitz is absolute ("the wholly other," in Celan's own phrase), it is not outside the world. The Western tradition has culminated in this horror and so there are myriad points of contact, both through imagistic analogy (the famous perversion of mystical longing in Celan's "Death Fugue") and through total antithesis, between the event itself and the complexities and contradictions of the tradition. The death camps are silent, but not mute.

Brutal animality, colorless bureaucracy, staggering nihilistic dreams—the complexity of Western experience is concentrated in Auschwitz, but as antiexperience, as silence. Thus, Celan's sense of this event as definitive, his own historical unfreedom, is what liberates his poetic urgency. He is always speaking this finality, he lacks all distance from it, he cannot select and juxtapose his material as Benn does: the more the world's time and language accumulate on top of the unique event, apparently weakening its impact, the harder it becomes to hear the authentic silence. Yet the goal of Celan's temporal poetics, his quest for "sketches for existence," remains binding: the narration of the end of time as the only possible beginning.

That is not to say that all his poems are "about" Auschwitz: "The Syllable Pain" clearly does not thematize the camps directly. But the event has converted the entire tradition into a binding repertoire; and whatever motif Celan draws from that repertoire, the poetics of speaking an ending is always at the text's center. All themes are transformed by the silence, their vehicle a language from which it can never be absent. Celan's insistence on this limit gives his texts an analytic fascination with sound and etymology that is never pedantic, an associative freedom that is never arbitrary. His poems also have a unique ability to release contingent narrative out of sheer verbal elan ("Die Silbe Schmerz" is very much a case in point); but the spontaneity of such movements always provokes a counterrhythm, the renewed stirring of the one story that puts all others in question, the story that subverts all potential history.

155

Textual hints in "Die Silbe Schmerz" suggest that the poem is conceived in part as a "refutation" ("Widerruf") of a well-known modern "story," the journey into the death realm in Rilke's Tenth Duino Elegy. The clear connection is made early in the poem with the word "deathless" which Rilke uses as the brand name of a beer that people drink to distract themselves from the fact of death. Celan then subtly reinforces the reference in line 12 through the word "behind" ("dahinter") a term stressed by Rilke immediately after mentioning the beer: "right in back of the billboard, right behind it, is reality." Verbal links are of course not in themselves significant. What Rilke offers in his poem is a kind of negative theology, a solemn celebration of images of passivity, melancholy, and nonlife. Although the word "suffering" ("Leid") is used frequently, there is no sense at all that dying involves pain; rather, it is viewed as the only avenue to "reality." It is not difficult to read such a poem as a kind of consolation in advance for the death camps, a picture of death as a place complete with a hierarchy of characters, landmarks, and ritual gestures. To say that is to say nothing whatever about Rilke's intention, but only about the historical function of his language.

Celan's title, then, acquires a polemical resonance. With its reduction of language to the syllable, experience to pain, its insistence on the primal and irreducible, the title demystifies any tendency to view death as a realm. It also denotes an impossibility: pain is precisely what cannot become language. But it is an impossibility that must be explored; if it is to become authentic, language must be doubled, confronted at every stage with the fact that it is language, always at one remove from the originating pain.

Celan has written the opposite of a death journey, namely a creation poem, as his Genesis-like landscape and language emphasize, an allegory of whatever possibilities for a new beginning are imaginable. And since all such imagining is inherently linguistic, the poem circles around its own language, putting in question its own emancipatory gestures. If a rhetorical space opened between the nonlanguage of pain and the imperative confidence of "Let there be" ("Es sei"), the poem would collapse. Initially all gaps are filled with echoes from the silent "chaos," the rupture of history that both demands a new creation poem and renders it paradoxical. Certainly Celan has rendered such suggestive phrases as "wordless voices," "numbers," and "the uncountable," so abstract that no thematic connections to the camps need be made. But my point is that such connections are, by definition, never absent, and that if the reader allows them to echo in his consciousness, certain "obscurities" in the text will become less obscure. Thus the disembodied, uncannily well-ordered quality of Celan's primal chaos connotes a landscape after Auschwitz: speaking is continuous, the metamorphosis from the material into the immaterial and back again is an incessant process. Yet the emergence into individuality, or even into identifiable species (as in Genesis), never takes place. The multiplication of "thou" and the quantification of "self" in the opening lines ensure that this landscape cancels all alternative perspectives. "I" and "thou" still exist—human speaking is impossible without them—but they no longer signify subject and object, creator and created.

Dietlind Meinecke comments on the interplay of the personal pronouns in this poem and the way in which the concept of identity is not so much abandoned as redefined: "Where anonymity can no longer be broken open, the poem must come to rest by the pure being of identity as such."[24] This identity is "pure" in the sense of being generated by the poem itself; but both its premise and its articulation are historical. The ease with which this unique configuration is "given" to the speaker, as well as its Protean variety and continuity, suggests the special problem posed by this history: the poetic self cannot embark on a journey, for the end of all journeys immediately surrounds him. The orientation of inherited language toward hierarchies, quests, and varieties of singular experience is obsolete. In this sense the reference to Rilke constitutes a necessary antithesis, a starting point. In the context of Auschwitz "deathless" means not a Rilkean critique of human superficiality, but a systematic denial of both death and life. The victims neither live nor die, their "death" is nothing but a dissolution. They become "empty forms."

Yet it is these "Leerformen" that inaugurate the narrative. Again unlike Rilke, Celan moves not toward lament ("Klage,") but toward a kind of allegorical remoteness, a linguistic completion of the tradition's systematic self-destruction. These first two sections of the poem have tremendous energy, as the multiplying verbs close all the gaps, complete all the circles. The landscape is essentially horizontal ("around," "before and behind"), the space of nonexperience endowed with purely verbal life. Its movement includes "everything"; all the temporal strands of the tradition have become pure spatial repetition ("repeatable matter," "Wiederholbares" is Meinecke's term).

In the second section however the circle begins to become a vortex. As prefigured in the title, the fundamental division in human consciousness between the exclusively abstract and the exclusively organic enters the poem. Numbers are projected by the system of "Leerformen," which strives to impose its circular rhythm on them ("greater . . . smaller"). But numbers are incorrigibly linear, they keep suggesting a story, even history. The abstractions become more intense more explicit ("the uncountable," "the Never"). But the verbs move in the opposite direction toward the organic, the generative: "woven into . . . overripened . . . transformed backward and forward . . . burgeoning." This section unites the beginning and ending of time in an allegory of symmetry and completion. But such intensification instigates life at the center of abstraction, in the numbers themselves; they are rounded off, then begin to run riot.

We may detect here an explicit reference to Novalis's fascination with mathematical symbols and his sense that the system life of mathematics, in its purity, offers the closest possible analogy to the primary structure of the absolute: "Everything real that is created from nothing, like for example numbers and abstract expressions, has a wondrous relationship with things of another world—with infinite series of strange combinations and linkages, with, as it were, a self-contained mathematical and abstract world, with a poetic, mathematical, and abstract world."[25] Celan is offering precisely that perspective on history that for Novalis remained within the realm of theory: history completed, rounded off, all time zones coalescing into a single oscillation. Moreover, Novalis's cosmology cements the links between the language of numbers and the poem's opening scenery of "Ich" and "Du," the language of self-realization: "Self-consciousness in the larger sense is a task, an ideal—it would be that condition in which linear time would cease to pass, a timeless, forever constant condition."[26]

Out of the heart of his allegory of completion, of time become empty but systematic space, Celan has extracted the possibility of a new event. It is of course also impossible: "burgeoning never." But poetic language, however negative, is both linear and visionary: differentiated time has been reshaped into the potentiality of narrative. The circle has become a vortex, the perspective of infinite flatness is yielding to the vertical. And the monochrome texture implicit in the term "deathless" is being replaced by the sharp antitheses that endow life's contingent sequences with the possibility of meaning: a "lot" ("Los") including death, but not paralyzed by it.

With a masterly transition from the "Never" to "The forgotten," and maintaining the rhythm of oscillating completion ("sank and swam"), Celan directs the energy of the first two sections upward (and downward) into a reopened time zone. The generative force of forgetting, already evident at a crucial point in Benn's poem, operates here on the largest possible scale. What is wholly forgotten can be wholly remembered. Things "to be forgotten" have escaped the obliterating closure of "deathless." And thus the "empty forms" are now "earth parts, heart parts"; they sink, they resurface.

In the presence of fragments, in the struggle with a newly imagined water there is the possibility of an originating human event: the disintegrative rhythm points now not toward the regularity of the void but toward the most ancient narratives of adventure, toward Sinbad and Odysseus. From the repertoire of the Western tradition, now opening in its singularities rather than its collective collapse, Columbus emerges: he *is* "the time." He also embodies the antithesis that is to dominate the poem, blending devout Catholic concentration on the Virgin with a resolute individualistic assault on the elements. At this point the verb "murdered" seems merely a strong image. The Virgin's "timelessness" is immediately qualified by her association with deeply temporal, even fragile, qualities as "mother flower": the purgatory of "deathless" is wrenched open in both directions. And in "All was unleashed," at the poem's approximate center, the reversal of the centripetal motion in section 1 is fueled by the cumulative energy of all the earlier verbs: the entire Western tradition is bursting out onto this one voyage.

In the fourth section the singular moment of creation is evoked as in essence a colonization, a transformation into narrative uniqueness of the spatial repetitions of the opening. Thus, the sequence "faded, lost its leaves . . . bloomed massively" simultaneously expands the organic imagery of section 2 and accelerates it into a single cosmic moment: "*one* world ocean." This "blooming" of the nominally sterile ocean is presented as a toweringly vertical event and also as intensely visual, with extreme light contrasts: "into the day, in the black light." The defining quality of the opening sections has been abstraction, refusal of the visual, as well as plurality and horizontal recurrence. The many smoothly linked verbs are transformed in effect into the single emphatic "bloomed," which is then echoed by "awoke." This blooming is indeed a resurrection (the "death," the "losing leaves" of the medieval world's compass is its prerequisite), and the images then cluster to confirm it. The meaning of Columbus's voyage is not so much that the medieval world ended, as that it was reborn in a new and vital form.

Celan conveys this vitality by filling his singular event with a series of "trinities," ritual groupings of medieval images, which the context renders specific, functional, full of future. Again the contrast is with the "empty forms": this historical moment is not empty but teeming. Yet it teems with delicacy: the "Weltmeer" has produced a most fragile resurrection. The children are perhaps a "refutation" of Rilke's "young dead, in the initial state of timeless indifference." However alchemically imagined, the children of this text are the opposite of timeless, they are awakening to the world, not withdrawing from it. Two aspects of the trinity of precious stones seem relevant. Albertus Magnus assigns a curative quality to each of them: jasper drives away fever, agate reveals the presence of poison, amethyst protects against drunkenness. A sealed-off, protected humanness is evoked. Moreover, jasper and amethyst have significant functions as, respectively, the first and last (twelfth) precious stones garnishing the foundation of the city of God (Revelation 21: 19–20). Columbus's tempestuous voyage has resurrected this ultimate and wholly static ancient vision, a vision based explicitly on purification and exclusion: "there was no more sea" (verse 1); "there shall be no night there" (verse 25).

Even as the structure of trinity sequences conveys synthesis, the poem's fundamental antithesis (between horizontal closure and vertical dynamism, deathly space and resurrected time) breaks into the open, as the counter-trinity of "peoples, tribes, and kinsmen" expresses the rush of energy, the indiscriminate colonization generated by Columbus's voyage. This section is dominated by the wave rhythm of the "Weltmeer," the stillness in the trough and the crashing breaker. The paradox of creation, of the narration of a new time zone, is the paradox of the poem's title: language alone releases the extremes of life (animals lack "syllables"), but it also functions as a system in which extremes can meet and the purely physical ("pain") can become a link in a newly conceptualized chain of being.

But this poem imagines the paradox through to its conclusion, imagines the death of the unique event generated by its own act of creative rupture. The climactic "Let there be" is isolated textually, but only textually. It is "blind" in the sense that Columbus himself was blind, bringing realities into being of which his late-medieval mind could have absolutely no conception. And immediately it is firmly attached ("wove itself") to the ambiguous intricacies of subsequent Western history. The moment of the poem is not the original voyage of Columbus, but the reemergence of that voyage in language at a time when the tradition, at the source of which the voyage stands, seemed finally extinguished. Such a moment is both singular in history and language—and multiple, in that it opens Columbus's violent purity to everything that followed. It is "one knot" and "thou-sand knots." It crystallizes Columbus's unique role in our mythology, establishing the liberating image of the New World at the center of Western consciousness. And it constitutes Columbus's story in a quite new way, both compressing its outline toward abstraction and bringing some thoroughly defamiliarized details of ship and sea into extreme close-up. This Columbus is a mythological skeleton, his original historical flesh eaten away by the unholy alliance of complacent forgetting and barbaric perversion of the adventurous spirit.

The language of poetry can convey such doubleness directly, but only by doubling itself without reservation, by narrating its own structure as language. The final section of the poem attempts the task, culminating in a kind of stammering, an openness both tentative and slightly sinister, decisive only in its refutation of the closure with which the poem began. The formidable difficulties of this ending fall into two specific areas: what is the resonance of this intensely vertical imagery, ranging from the stars down through the rigging on Columbus's ship into the depths? And what are "marten stars"? Some things can be said through an immanent reading: the imagery concentrates a multiplicity of concrete detail (details that expressly multiply themselves into the thousands) into its linguistic-temporal oneness. Thus, the open, potentially dissolving movement of the "deciphering" of "Let there be" remains bound by innumerable knots into an interpretive narration that can never end. The poem's language thematizes itself to the point of "becoming" the ship's ropes. But it also tells us that its aspiration toward such identity, toward becoming the historical moment, means that it must dissolve itself into the "world-ocean" of subsequent events, resisting the temptation of unitary creative gestures, prefigured in the opening lines. The poem's difficulty derives from the refusal of its own solutions, the refusal to say, with Benn, "Everything is said."

And so the reader is following the poem's own rhythm if he looks outside it for the illumination of its central enigmas. In two poems of

Celan's subsequent collection, *Atemwende* (1967), we encounter sea-scapes that can be seen as meditations on the concluding section of "Die Silbe Schmerz":

> Es scheren die Buchstaben aus,
> die letzten
> traumdichten Kähne—
> jeder mit einem
> Teil des noch
> zu versenkenden Zeichens
> im
> geierkralligen Schlepptau.
>
> The letters cut themselves loose,
> the last
> boats thick with dreams—
> each with a
> part of the still to be
> submerged sign
> in the
> vulture-clawed towline.
> —from "Flooding" ("Flutender," II, 37)

>   ein Wahndock,
> Schwimmend, davor
> abweltweiss die
> Buchstaben der
> Grosskräne einen
> Unnamen schreiben, an dem
> klettert sie hoch, zum Todessprung, die
> Laufkatze Leben,
> den baggern die sinn—
> gierigen Sätze nach Mitternacht aus,
> nach ihm
> wirft die neptunische Sünde ihr korn—
> schnapsfarbenes Schleppseil. . . .
>
> mirage of a dock,
> swimming, before it
> the unearthly white
> letters of the
> great cranes
> write a cipher, on which

it clambers up, ready for the death leap,
life's crane crab,
the cipher is dredged out after midnight
by the sentences hungry for meaning,
after it
Neptune's sin throws its
rye-colored towrope.
—from "Harbor" ("Hafen," II, 52–53)

What this imagery has in common is a powerfully vertical dimension, with movement both upward and downward, and a concretely imagined coincidence of impossibles, words, climbing creatures, and the sea. The rope is the unifying factor, and its power to link land, sea, and air in the functionality of the human voyage endows it with an animistic, slightly savage quality ("serpent-headed," "vulture-clawed"). In each passage Celan evokes the binding of words, of human creativity, into the rope—which, embodying the prehistoric discovery of how to generate strength from the binding of slender reeds, is perhaps to be seen as a human miracle analogous to that of language, its toughness resisting the sea as imaginative language resists silence. The difference, in "Die Silbe Schmerz," lies in the function of the words: here they are specific, identified as the creative formula "Let there be," whereas in the later poems they are obscure, slipping into the subverbal realm of "signs" or "ciphers," and provoking the longing of everything alive to grasp and consume them. In "Die Silbe Schmerz" the problem is in the very transparency and energy of the "Es sei." The world is galvanized, but which of its many dreams, dark or light, should it set about realizing? Certainly the ambivalence of the final lines seems total: the persistent struggle to "spell" the formula means that it is not lost, but also that it cannot be realized, that human understanding is never adequate to transform the vision of creation into a functioning, humane language.

For interpreting the enigmatic image of "marten stars," the poem's link to Rilke's Tenth Elegy offers a hint. Evoking the stars above the "grief land" ("Leidland"), Rilke mentions "the Staff" and "the Burning Book" (suggestive in the context of Celan's dismantling of his key—untranslatable—term, "buchstabieren"), and then:

pure as in the palm
of a blessed hand the clearly gleaming "M"
that signifies Mothers.

163

Such imagery may seem remote from the actuality of the "marten," an unpleasant variety of weasel, of whom *Grimms Wörterbuch* says: "The marten's name may have been derived by the Germans from murdering, since it strangles and murders everything." But earlier in Celan's text precisely this juxtaposition occurs:

> The mother-
> flower,
> murdered . . .

From the poem's title onward Celan has been projecting ways of making fruitful the paradox of purity and violence, the impossible truth of a history that cannot be rendered accessible through interpretive narration. The urgency of this contingent narrative does not seal language in, but drives it into ever more extreme contradiction. And in fact the etymology of "Marder," according to Kluge, suggests that the word itself embodies the central paradox. It is connected with the Lithuanian word "marti," meaning bride, and with other words denoting a young woman, and is in fact a taboo word used for community protection: "Name of the weasel that people fear and want to avoid attracting by the use of its true name."[27] This primitive use of a word is by no means foreign to Celan's intention: by linking the feared yet linguistically masked creature to the image of remote stars actualized in the abyss, the poet has given new potency to his rope/language in the very act of sealing in this enigmatic fusion of purity and violence ("Marder" occurs nowhere else in Celan).

The procedure may seem esoteric, but so was Columbus's original project; his driving of history toward a new "Let there be" pressed an entire tradition of illusions and rituals into a not-yet-imaginable generative moment. The poem suggests that the very creatures struggling to decipher history's text contain that text in their etymological being. Moreover it is language itself that can resist history's collapse into reductive uniformity. In the density of myth and etymology opposites coexist, maintaining the perpetual possibility of new narratives.

The key words at the beginning and end of this text, "deathless" and "marten stars," compel the reader to look toward other texts. This is entirely consonant with Celan's view of the poem as always "under way," to be actively embedded in history. In a sense we should speak of a tripling rather than a doubling of time and language by Celan. His disruptive force is directed against a destruction of history itself, which has already taken place and can never be masked; his colonization of that desolate completion opens the way not toward any new version of personal identity (we have seen how fragments, "heart parts," are all man has and all he now needs), but toward a vision of the ambiguity and incompleteness of all such colonizations. The poem's language reflects upon itself, but its self-sealing is also a self-opening. Its esoteric images confront the silence of the past with the noise of the escapist present. The poem makes no sense at all as a self-contained aesthetic object. It exists exclusively as a stimulus to dialogue between a past and a future that seem to have collapsed definitively into the machine of the present: the exhilaration of its emergent contingency is inseparable from its implicit historical narrative, which simultaneously closes and opens an endlessly festering event.

From the outset of his career, with the collection *Verteidigung der Wölfe* (*In Defense of Wolves*) in 1957, Hans Magnus Enzensberger has sought to reuse the modernist encyclopedia as the source of a historical narration that can no longer be merely implicit in an autonomous text. Enzensberger constructs surreal landscapes without escape routes, runs every kind of rhetorical risk in order to prevent the tradition of individual fantasy, the energies of irony, from becoming sterile.

Spur der Zukunft
Hans Magnus Enzensberger

was zieht mich über die brücken, beharrlich,
wie eine schnecke, wie einen hund
mit verbundenen augen, ausser mir
auf der spur der zukunft, nach verhängnis
scharrend, nach unsrer eigenen asche, nach dem,
was noch nicht auferstanden aus zeitgruben
und noch nicht erbärmlich vollstreckt ist?

aber die lampen rufen es schon, in der luft violett
bäht sichs, dämmerung, dieser duft.
und ich will es nicht leiden,
was wir langsam, langsam, langsam begehen,
was sich türmt wie wolken, und immer zunimmt.
nein. nein,
aus den häusern räuchern, aus dem himmel jagen,

was noch nicht verwirklicht ist, einholen, wenden;
ich, eine schnecke, den donner scheuchen,
ich, mit verbundenen augen, ein hagerer hund.[28]

(1960)

Trace of the Future

What draws me across the bridges, insistently,
like a snail, like a dog
with blindfolded eyes, beside myself
on the trail of the future, scratching the earth
for signs of destiny, for our own ashes, for
what has not yet been resurrected from pits of
time and has not yet been miserably lived through?

But the lamps tell of it already, in the air the
violet shade bleats it, the twilight, this scent.
And I will not accept
what we slowly, slowly, slowly are acting out,
what towers upward like clouds, ceaselessly growing.
No. No,
fumigate the houses, expel it from the sky,
stop, turn around whatever is not yet realized;
I, a snail, would scare away the thunder.
I, with blindfolded eyes, a haggard dog.

In his preface to the *Museum der modernen Poesie* Hans Magnus
Enzensberger wrote: "Poetry today presumes not only knowledge but
also a critical perspective on modern poetry." When revising the essay
for inclusion in his collection *Einzelheiten,* he added: "indeed production and criticism can no longer be separated."[29] The intensification is
symptomatic of Enzensberger's perception of the world. The critical,
ironic posture is so crucial to his poetics that it tends to colonize all
other modes of speaking, to be subtly present in the other poetic voices
for which Enzensberger has become famous: the voice of empirical directness and the voice of a committed politics. Hans Egon Holthusen
notes:

> This poetic consciousness is as far from being naive as was
> the consciousness of the Schlegels, Tieck, and Brentano: To the in-
> ward dialectic of his freedom there belongs that illusion-breaking
> irony, attacking his own formulations in the back, which, in the

context of literature around 1800, we name "romantic irony"; except of course that the climate prevailing in Enzensberger's poetry is anything but "romantic."[30]

The vague word "climate" lets this perceptive judgment fall back too readily into a limiting version of Romanticism. Enzensberger's insistence on a critical stance brings him very close indeed to the Romantics he knows so well (he wrote his dissertation on Brentano);[31] his irony embeds itself as faithfully in history as theirs, and as some Schlegel passages suggest, the restless Romantic conceptualizing illuminates Enzensberger's quest for nonesoteric images of the historical paralysis: "The unity of the fragment derives from individuality, to characterize is to produce a historical fragment. The characterizing act of the individual is tied in to the evolving characterization of the universe; every human being is a microcosm."[32] "When we have finally learned to understand better the history of the revolution, then the origins of the earth and of human beings must also become historically comprehensible."[33]

Enzensberger finds it indispensable to reanimate the rational quality of poetry (which makes him a key figure for the subsequent poetics of the 1970s). The notions of individual singleness and analyzable history may have collapsed metaphysically for Benn and Celan, but they persist in common sense and can perhaps be reimagined through a conscious deployment of the Romantic critical perspective, of (historical) "characterization." The urgency of such a project is traceable to a double premise of Enzensberger's poetics: the sick tradition, far from dying, has infiltrated all remaining space, establishing itself literally as a consuming machine. And poetry is no longer privileged; it cannot, indeed should not, project its own time zone. The saturation of language by the "consciousness industry" means that, in order to claim its function as "anticommodity" ("Antiware"), the poem must locate itself unflinchingly within the debased spatiality of "commodities"; although obviously not unusable, language requires devious strategies, termed "distortion" ("Entstellung") by Enzensberger, before it will yield a viable narrative. Moreover, Enzensberger's texts are formal, highly structured works; but the aura of the autonomous poem has completely dissolved. At the end of his "author's interpretation" of the poem "To all long-distance subscribers" ("an alle fernsprechteilnehmer"), the author comments casually: "It remains open to question, what a poem really is, whether, in the case of the present text, we are even talking of a poem at all. That is a title that it is not the place of the author to dispense."[34]

It is especially remarkable, given Enzensberger's stance as a political writer, that the idea of the future has completely lost its productive power. Discussing Enzensberger's parody of Brecht's "To Posterity" in his brief text entitled "continuation" ("weiterung"), Holthusen notes, in a striking phrase, "the liquidation of the principle of futurity."[35] For Enzensberger, in short, the spatial infiltration of human time is already complete: historical imagining can (indeed must) function strictly as a guerrilla operation.

The slippage in the idea of an autonomous, textually generated contingent narrative releases in the Enzensberger of the late 1950s and early 1960s an extraordinary negative energy. Every spectrum of contemporary opinion, from reactionary to radical, is assaulted in the essays collected in *Details* (*Einzelheiten*, 1962). But the question that troubled readers, then and since, is: from what perspective does the author himself speak? The answer is contained in the question; what makes Enzensberger so skilled a strategist of double language is, precisely, the impossibility of all single perspectives. In his essays this impossibility is masked by a deceptively rational, even bland, tone of discourse. Thus, in his discussion of "political poetry" he comments:

> Poetry and politics are not "areas of expertise" but historical processes, the one in the medium of language, the other in the medium of power. Both have direct access to history. The practice of literary criticism as "sociology" fails to recognize that it is language that defines the social character of poetry, not its involvement with political struggle. Bourgeois literary aesthetics ignores or conceals the fact that poetry is social in its essence.[36]

The difficulty with such symmetry, as Enzensberger's poems reveal so clearly, is that the critical middle way evoked in these sentences does not exist. History, in the poems, is not the orderly machine implied here, with the "processes" of language and politics humming quietly along on their separate assembly-line belts. History is more like a devouring monster that consumes the private and the public, instinct and language system, with equal voraciousness. In certain poems, notably "an alle fernsprechteilnehmer," Enzensberger suggests that there is a specific source for this universal encroachment, namely the invisible spread of radioactivity. In vivid contrast to Celan's Auschwitz, the temporal point of which is becoming invisible through forgetting, Enzensberger's initial "event" lacks all contours and definition; it is always underway, spreading into the world like a perverted religion, symbolic of history's self-transformation into indifferent space. Radioactivity is the destructiveness that cannot itself be destroyed.

Enzensberger confronts his diagnosis of hopelessness with only two weapons: a thoroughly demystified language, and the fact of consciousness itself. By renouncing critical distance and embedding consciousness in the very mechanisms of alienated, spatialized history, Enzensberger finds the possibility of narration in an almost entirely despairing interpretive process. There is no rupture, no opening in the time zone of these poems; but there is an intense longing for rupture, a negative urgency that enables Enzensberger's exclusively interpretive narratives to generate the energy of an anticipated, utopian contingency, a moment that has not occurred yet demands to be repeatedly imagined.

Consciousness may be free only to contemplate its unfreedom—Enzensberger is careful to avoid a dialectics of hope—but its access to language means that it can *describe,* can map the landscape of hopelessness with the certainty that its variety is infinite. And it can tell its own story. Enzensberger is especially interested in birth, the origin of consciousness. On the one hand, birth is connected to death in a rhythm of seamless determinism (the poem "birth notice" "geburtsanzeige"); but on the other hand, birth is a moment of freedom, a concentration of literally blind emotion:

> ich bin geblendet geboren, schaum in den augen,
> brüllend vor wehmut, ohne den himmel zu sehen.[37]

> I was born blinded, foam in my eyes,
> bellowing with sadness, unable to see the heavens.

The poetic consciousness remains embedded in that birth foam, like the genie moving from bottle to world in a cloud of smoke, its power of narration latent even though always bound by the rules of the world in which it finds itself. The doubleness of Enzensberger's language is defined by this fusion of determinism and negative energy.

Consciousness resembles Benn's matador in the way it holds tight to the chaotic specifics of the present; but it differs in that, for

Enzensberger, there is neither a "deep" rhythm of history to be revealed, nor a privileged linguistic zone in which the revealing can be situated. Instead, the time and perspective of an Enzensberger poem shift constantly, as the consciousness dons new masks, roaming the landscape of the present with the apparently total freedom granted it by the fully functioning machine of the consumer age. Unlike the detached voice of Benn's self-ironizing persona, Enzensberger's consciousness gains its energy from staying intently within its historical prison. The perspective is, of course, impossible. And this impossibility is Enzensberger's time zone; an analogy is perhaps available in the "angel of history" described by Walter Benjamin. The model of past-present-future has simply broken down for this kind of consciousness. It sees only wreckage but struggles distractedly to realize the remembered dreams of wholeness. It moves tempestuously yet stays in the same place. And it experiences the center of history, not through a privileged glimpse, but with an ironic, maddening directness—as a machine that has definitively malfunctioned:

> The face [of the angel of history] is turned toward the past. Where we perceive a chain of events, he sees one single catastrophe that keeps piling wreckage upon wreckage and hurls it in front of his feet. The angel would like to stay, awaken and dead, and make whole what has been smashed. But a storm is blowing from Paradise; it has got caught in his wings with such violence that the angel can no longer close them. This storm irresistibly propels him into the future to which his back is turned, while the pile of debris before him grows skyward. This storm is what we call progress.[38]

The speaker of "Spur der Zukunft" is ultimately as paralyzed as Benjamin's angel, but the road to paralysis is the reverse one: instead of a storm, there is silent encroachment; instead of history-as-wreckage there is history-as-cancerous-growth. And so the poem is constituted as a narration of frenetic and finally helpless activity. The language shifts from elaborate rhetorical questions to laconic withdrawal, from cogently developed images to jabbing, cinematic shifts. The second half of the poem is full of verbs, full of efforts to narrate the spread of the horror; but what is narrated instead is the spread of impotence, as the carefully calibrated imagery of the first part disintegrates into an impossibility of language. The last three verbs—"stop," "turn

170

around," "scare away the thunder"—tell only of emptiness: lifeless abstractions, a helpless proverbial gesture, sheer presentness has absorbed their narrative spasms, leaving the speaker with only a voice, confined once again to self-description.

The poem is thus in a sense circular; it ends exactly where it begins, with no progress whatever (Enzensberger uses this structure elsewhere, for example in the well-known "the end of the owls"), but the tight circle contains extremes of movement, extremes that know their impossibility from the outset. The title, indeed, has the antithetical power of Celan's "Die Silbe Schmerz." The future is precisely not what is normally "traced"; if an archaeology of the future makes sense, as the poem suggests, then the word *future* itself is denatured. The future is not the future, merely a spatial extension of the deathly present. The speaker's quest is not to create the future, but to prevent it. No alternative is imaginable; all imagery is compromised. All the speaker can do is utter an anticipatory "refutation" of Celan: "a blind 'Let there *not* be.' "

Several contradictions are compressed into the speaker's persona. His blindness, his persistence, his crossing of symbolic bridges—all this suggests a posture of insight, a summoning up of ancient virtues into a figuration of possible change. But the triviality, the marginality, of the snail and the dog imply a view from below, an impossibility of insight; the scavenging of dogs is always after the fact, a quest for bones discarded by the world's active processes. And then again, the dog's eyes are not just blind, they are "blindfolded." The nonseeing is a positive decision: dog and snail can be seen as residing within a "house" of private integrity, sealed off by their very limitations from involvement in history. However, Enzensberger undermines that image with the phrase "beside myself" ("ausser mir"): the speaker is not inside, but very much outside himself, not really able to see clearly, at least not at the outset, but not able *not* to see either. The energy of the first section derives from the way an embryonic narrative of resistance and its impossibility are articulated simultaneously. A free vision can only be reached through a radical acceptance of unfreedom, an unfreedom amounting to "doglike" dependence. It is only in this knowledge of his dependence ("*what* draws me . . . ?") that the dog can claim significance for his anguished scratching at the surface. His act is sufficiently ridiculous for the tattered mantle of the warning seer, which he dons, to become legitimate.

Unlike Celan, Enzensberger's poetics does not depend on the

resonance of specific words, not even on a sense that the words are particularly well chosen. He is expressly a storytelling poet, locating his narratives inside an allegorized history, with a clearly defined perspective and a continuity of argument. The fact that both perspective and argument are rooted in impossibility is what the poem is rhythmically organized to reveal, doubling the apparently plain language. Thus, Enzensberger cannot assign to Auschwitz the privilege accorded it by Celan; although his dog persona burrows under the surface of history's calm landscape, his narrations must remain conditioned by the infinite absorptive power of the new machine world. To offer any privileged perspective would be to flinch from the specificity of his vision: that history has already processed all singularities. Thus, the word "ashes" both evokes Auschwitz and absorbs it in the paradox of a future that is already written as deathliness. Our death is simply lying around in fragments, not yet magnetized by the engine we still call time but is now almost entirely spatial, with hollows and flat stretches.

Almost, but not quite. The meaning of the dog's otherwise ridiculous scratching is an encoding of the quest for rupture, for the narrative latent beneath time's cumulative inertia. Even if successful, his scratching, far from preventing the future, would *accelerate* it, bring to the surface what is not yet ready. And this acceleration could generate a figuration of rupture. The language here forces together acceleration and deceleration in a single rhythm. The commas, the shifting images, evoke the frenzy of the dog's "scratching," while the self-perpetuation of the sentence and the repetition of "not yet" hold things back, refuse completion. Both in content and rhythm the sentence is a perfection of impossibility: the dog is digging up what he dreads to dig up. But in doing so, by performing a parody of Benn's quest for deep history, he disrupts the smoothly functioning machine of spatialized time. A narrative of failure is the only ecstatic mode available to this poetics.

Without in any way betraying his premise of ontological imprisonment, Enzensberger converts this disruptive act into something extraordinarily, momentarily real at the center of his poem. Several elements fuse at the beginning of the second section: what was hidden is suddenly in the open, everywhere, and the simple vividness of the opening world provokes exhilaration. The vertical dimension of the poem is activated; from scrabbling below the surface, the speaker suddenly thrusts his gaze upward (this movement continues to the poem's end). The persona of the dog is set aside, as the sensory and judgmental

172

power of the self is broadened. And most important, the dead poetic tradition is allowed a brief afterlife, as the speaker savors the possibilities of synaesthesia and of such resonant words as "twilight . . . scent." The temporal opening, the magic of evening, is both real and impossible, for of course the "it" at its center is the horror itself. Celan encrusts his "Let there be" with negative elements, yet releases a narrative fusing the contingent and the historical in a virtually impenetrable singularity. Enzensberger immediately embeds the moment, which exists only as a skyward gaze, a last relishing of hallowed words, in the landscape of hopelessness. The fused elements come apart: the openness of the fearful future leaves no margin, no hiding place; it is a spreading sickness. The upward momentum of the images ("clouds . . . sky . . . thunder") leads to no gods, merely to cosmic enclosure; the released self, bearing full witness, can only say "no," its gestures becoming more empty as they broaden in scope—until finally it collapses back into the persona of the dog, now "haggard" rather than "insistent." And the language becomes, until the final collapse, helplessly abstract and strident. All the speaker can do is offer, in a negative tonality, a mimesis of the process in which he and the world are trapped: the threefold "slowly" retards the poem to the pace of the process it had briefly accelerated.

Just as the "future" of the first section is essentially no future, so the transitive "acting out" ("begehen") is really not transitive at all, and the "we" suggests no solidarity, no link of self to world. An appropriate image is found in "fumigate the houses," but it is immediately followed by the impossibility of "expel it from the sky." And the final imagined action—"stop, turn around whatever is not yet realized"—is pathetic in the woodenness, the feebleness of its abstractions. The imagery is pointing back to the original scrabbling in the dirt, but now it is rootless, without energy. The speaker falls silent, offering a final self-description without any of the movement that filled the poem's opening lines. What remains is still consciousness, but consciousness reduced to a single point, the minimal voice of a character in Beckett. The repetition of "with blindfolded eyes" illuminates the power of double language to accentuate closure, to exclude alternatives—and still, somehow, to refuse silence. At the beginning, we noted, the bound eyes encouraged many mystical-dialectical overtones; now they are strictly what they say they are, a mode of sealing off a helpless, useless individual, a perfect doubling of the process they have blindly witnessed. And yet, as with the objects of Günter Eich's famous "Inventory," the physical, literal cloth binding the eyes is not nothing; it does preserve consciousness.

In their exploration of a released and releasing language Benn and Celan press to the limits their sense of liberation from individual intentionality; Celan's "heart parts" are not only adequate, their dispersal is essential to any new version of consciousness. But when, in Enzensberger's texts, the power of interpretive narration begins to appear inadequate to its task, and the neutral, spreading sea of a moribund history submerges all perspectives that would transform it, the arbitrary oneness of the individual voice survives as a kind of residue, an enclosed point of consciousness resisting absorption. There is no question of rediscovering a totalized individual. Enzensberger's voice is that of "a haggard dog" whose self-narration tells only of frenzy and withdrawal. Yet this self-binding, self-blinded persona finds the possibilities of subversion in the sheer rigor of its skepticism. Enzensberger's radical reduction leads not to zero, but to new modes of survival—not least in the later work of Enzensberger himself. Laconic minimalism, self-indulgent improvisation, annotations of history (*Mausoleum*) or even a playful collage of symbolic events and casual private memories (*The Sinking of the Titanic*)—none of these strategies would have been adequate to the aggressive textualizing of the tradition imagined by Benn and Celan. But they mean that the poem's time needs no traditional privilege in order to remain functional as a gesture toward an alternative history. Such history, for Enzensberger, is the last imperative of consciousness, to be invoked by a voice situated at the strategic center of the machine that would nullify its very possibility.

CHAPTER FIVE

Archipelagoes of Resistance:
Becker, Meckel, Kiwus

azardous though it may be to generalize about something so recent and so multifaceted as the poetry of the 1970s, it is possible to be fairly confident about certain negative statements. The aura of the poetic narrative as a compression and reenergizing of historical materials, a vital source of power for the texts of Benn, Celan, and Enzensberger, is completely dissipated. The poem does not articulate an alternative world; there is no Archimedean point, no linguistic distillation of the Western tradition, which might serve as a vantage point for judging the repetitious banality of the present. Although Enzensberger's dog conducts his quest close to the ground, achieving neither insight nor emancipation, nevertheless the atmosphere remains apocalyptic, suggestive of radical and imminent crisis, evoking the possibility of a singular history in its very absence.

In the 1970s, not only is the apocalypse long past, the very notion of a single history, a single political landscape, has become problematic. Obviously this poetry is political in the broadest sense. But from the outset its political quality is conditioned by an intense debate about the viability of a political style, very much as Romantic litera-

175

ture could only make its universal claims on the future by privileging the concept of irony. Powerful models exist for the imagining of the world in political terms—notably Brecht, Fried, Neruda; and Enzensberger's seminal essay charts the skepticism necessary for steering the new politicized language away from the banalities of traditional political genres. A politicized poetics is both axiomatic and masked.

The argument in the late 1970s about what became known as "new subjectivity" indicates that the phrase, if used impartially, evokes the whole spectrum of linguistic problems facing a poet who attempts to say what it is possible to say in the 1970s. In the period 1920–70 the symbiosis between history and the self inaugurated by the Romantics culminated in the radical fusion of art and artist, of poetic voice and narrative temporality. The premise of the privileged artistic vision makes possible the "modernist" insistence on a wholly "constructed," decentered self. And the political voice of modernism is equally sustained by the cultural power of poetic language (a power attested to by the obsession of dictatorships of the era with censorship). The new powerlessness of the "idea" of art does not condemn poets to silence (although one of Enzensberger's last modernist gestures, in the 1960s, was a proclamation of poetic silence). But it necessitates a wholly new poetics, with two key points of continuity with the old: the political agenda of poetry moves from a secondary to a primary position; and the decentered self must be recentered, not with illusions of insight, but as a strategic base for a resistant, unprivileged aesthetic. A politicized yet detached language is nourished by a rejection of poetry's linguistic autonomy, a refusal of the role of seer.

The contemporary poet (and here the divergence from Enzensberger is clear) insists on standing nowhere, neither inside nor outside the consumer society, neither inside nor outside the structures of language. He or she does indeed speak with a new subjectivity, a quasi-biographical presence, which loosens the convention of a closed text. This presence is not singular, but dispersed; it is everywhere and nowhere. The rigorous insistence on being, yet being nowhere, is what enables the poet to speak the truth of an age without escape routes, in which language and experience are equally and casually contaminated.

Benn, Celan, and Enzensberger used spatial images to convey the paralysis of history, the silent dispersal of significant time. But whereas they could see this process as a threatening encroachment, to be combated by the narration of an alternative temporality, the poets of the

1970s accept the spatial recycling of history as fully accomplished. There is simply no kind of experience, no level of language, that has not been captured and processed by the machine of the sophisticated consumer society. The dream of the phoenix, of textually reimagined time, has become an impossibility. The tradition, the mysticisms of eros and nature, the ideal of "Bildung"—all these frameworks still exist, but their living tissue has been replaced by stuffing; they have become purely decorative, adorning a mirage of secondary experience, which is neither private nor public, neither privileged nor collective, neither living nor dead.

The individual still appears to himself as the center of experience, but this perspective now mocks him, reminding him that the unique self has become an illusion manufactured by fashion and electronic processing. For the newly "subjective" poetic voice locates itself, with insistent clarity, in a far more hazardous place: clinging to a bank at the edge of a torrent of processed language that instantly contaminates, as Peter Handke's texts demonstrate, any words the poet might utter. The self is never free of this perpetuum mobile; there is no possibility of withdrawal or self-enclosure. At the same time, the experiences offered for absorption are never personal or authentic; they are preformed elsewhere and drive all individuals without exception into the margin, a margin without any opening to the outside. Indeed, no outside can now be imagined. As Jürgen Theobaldy remarks of the poets of the 1970s: "Their material is thus, in the broadest sense, prescribed for them."[1]

To our list of negatives, then, must be added the most momentous of all, the negation of the word pair "personal experience." The individual does not generate experience; experience does not support the individual. The question of the person, the question of experience—both terms have become politicized, mutually isolated, expelled from the remembered havens of privacy. The visionary language of Benn and Celan has become a repertoire item for the new subjectivity, a wistful or ironic memory in an infinitely alien collage. A polarity between space and time structures poetry before 1970; now, however, that opposition has lost its meaning. The resilient presentness of consumerism has effaced all traces of apocalyptic stasis. What the new poetic narratives must articulate is a perpetual rushing away, an ambience of proliferating "experience," which cannot be grasped, cannot be made authentic, yet never ceases to renew itself. It mocks all proclamations of the existential void (there is never a void), and it resists all

177

efforts to translate it into a code, dichotomizing an illusory surface and somewhere a real center, a political power source.

An image that does some justice to this situation is that of the centrifuge. A passage from Novalis suggests a good allegorical starting point for sketching the temporal poetics of the 1970s: "All things have a centrifugal tendency: they become centripetal through the action of the spirit, which operates against the natural inclination of the organs and forces them into a coherent pattern of "Bildung," makes them consolidate around a single point; the spirit fashions a world out of nothing."[2] The poet of the 1970s experiences this last sentence in a radicalized, almost dialectical form. As the individual is endlessly devalued, but never to a zero point, the image of a genuine nothingness, a cancellation of process, becomes the sole locus of potential narrative. The poetic self deploys a strategy of centripetal resistance: not blind resistance—the poetic posture is one of almost fanatical alertness—but resistance without hope or goal apart from itself. The words that recur as leitmotifs in the arguments about poetics in the 1970s are "defend oneself" ("sich wehren"), "oppose" ("sich stemmen"), "resistance" ("Widerstand"). The self does not dream of authenticating or reclaiming experience; the inherited versions of the poem as a container of the world, a new thing in the world, or a linguistic alternative to the world have all lost their validity, for they involve reimagining wholeness or closure where none is possible.

On the other hand, the self does not enter the centrifugal torrent in a state of pure neutrality. Although it cannot lay claim to authenticity of experience, it remains a self; it is not nothing. The self is a consciousness equipped with language, a vessel in which the fragmented tradition is stored as well as the critical capacity to analyze and sift the fragments. Just as there is no possibility of remaking experience as personal wholeness, so there is no possibility of refashioning any kind of coherent system of values out of the wreckage of the tradition—a tradition that is endlessly being recycled and piously rediscovered as if it were somehow still a functioning entity.

But out of this double negative, indeed through the very rigor with which they enforce it, poets find themselves able to speak "something," a something that knows that it lacks autonomous power and that its own location in the category "poetry" is chiefly a disadvantage (the machine consumes poetry as avidly as anything else). But inside this landscape of continual fragmentation and reduction, one verbal gesture suddenly connects with another, produced in comparable isola-

178

tion and disillusionment; specific phrases become enabling passwords through which one resisting consciousness communicates with others. New islands of consciousness, archipelagoes, force themselves above the ocean's surface.

The three values that seem to be most usable in contemporary poetry are knowledge, freedom, and history. All three are, of course, hopelessly compromised by their public usage; they are among the words most frequently recycled in the processes of repression and consumption. Indeed, it may be the residual life still in them that makes them especially vulnerable to debasement. The poet acts both as a guerrilla fighter, wresting fragments of a remembered politics from the machinery of processed experience, and as a hermit who insists on applying value-laden words only to the things he can touch, see, and feel. The poet locks the three potent values into a mutually reinforcing circle: knowledge means freedom, which means history, which means knowledge. Of the three terms, "freedom" and "knowledge" are durable embodiments of the original Western dreams, dreams reenergized by Romanticism. History, modernity's own concept, would seem to be the most debased and exhausted. Yet it remains indispensable, background and telos for any presently imaginable contingent narrative. The term "utopian" crops up frequently in poetological discussions of the 1970s, but it is clearly being used dialectically. Contemporary poets certainly do not project utopias; but their resistant temporality, inherently political, opens their narratives toward a public dimension that cannot yet be named. The word "history" has to suffice.

The three values reinforce each other in a circle. Thus, the opening of the poem to history also points to the least metaphysical, the most tangible, and the most consciously Brechtian poetic value: empirical knowledge. Once again, Novalis provides a kind of anticipatory allegory of the significance of knowing in the contemporary poem: "We know something only insofar as we can express it, i.e., bring it into being. The more completely and variously we can produce, execute something, the better we know it. We know it perfectly when we can communicate, cause a response to it everywhere and in every way, can generate an individual expression of it in every organ."[3]

Novalis, of course, is writing with a positive, expansive version of the self in mind, aligning the process of knowing with other kinds of experience. But in the reductive context that emerges in the 1970s, the context of the peripheral self and the contamination of experience, Novalis's imagery of knowing is all the more appropriate. Knowing is now the *only* authentic activity of the self, and knowing in the new context is already enclosed within rhythms of absorption that deny the very possibility of knowing, glibly registering all knowledge as "relative." Thus Novalis's notion of knowing as making becomes all the more urgent: to know means to formulate knowledge in language that cannot be refuted or processed, to "communicate" the particular thing rather than its categorical attributes. Such knowing is engendered by the total commitment of the self to the specific knowable object. The reciprocity of the relationship is crucial: the language of the self holds that which is known in a steadiness that resists the flux, and through this steadiness the self is enabled to turn its experience of the periphery and of exclusion into a posture of resistance. In effect, to know is to exist, and to exist is to know. And this process is one of ruthless reduction, of expelling every element that blurs the clear outline of knowing and existing. Without this clarity, this refusal of all expansiveness or hope, neither knowledge nor existence is possible.

That these premises of the poetics of the 1970s are applicable to all important texts, and that they are identifiably political, is suggested by the work of Erich Fried. A poet of Celan's generation (born 1921), Fried has always sought to perpetuate Brecht's political style, fusing minimalism, proverbial textures, and bitter political immediacy. Yet whereas Brecht's poetic voice is inseparable from the linguistic virtuosity, the textual ambitions, of the post-Expressionist era, Fried's speaks with the laconic self-negation, the refusal of ambition, of his younger contemporaries. Certainly, Fried strives to nourish the enfeebled life of combative political language through modes of extreme compression. But his images of the self have none of Brecht's theatrical potency. They are drenched in the processes of consuming and being consumed, grimly involved in the struggle toward Novalis's centripetal point of resistance. Two poems entitled "Experiences" ("Erfahrungen") from a 1982 collection offer a suggestive counterpoint:

Harmlose Begegnung

Ich sehe mich im Spiegel
Ich komme mir näher und näher
Mein Mund berührt meinen Mund
aber ich kann mich
nicht in den Mund nehmen
nicht von mir abbeissen
nicht mich essen

nicht mich verschlucken
Ich bleibe also noch da

Harmless Encounter

I see myself in the mirror
I draw closer and closer to myself
My mouth touches my mouth
but I cannot
take myself into my mouth
cannot bite off part of me
cannot eat myself
cannot swallow myself
So I remain there still

Lautlos

Je länger ich trete
auf meine Einsamkeit
desto dicker wird sie

ein graublauer
staubiger Teppich
den ich nicht heben kann

in dem das sitzt
was mit der Zeit meine Zeit
zerbeisst und frisst[4]

Soundless

The longer I tread
on my solitude
the thicker it becomes

a gray-blue
dusty carpet
which I cannot lift

in which that thing sits
which as time passes is chewing up
and consuming my time

"Harmlose Begegnung" deploys the Romanic *topos* of the mirror as if to test whether or not the Romantic generative self is definitively obsolete. The speaker adopts the role of the all-consuming machine, but reaches an irreducible limit. With mouth pressed on mouth's image, the integrities of self and other are certainly superseded; there can be no "seeing," no wholeness, in such monstrous proximity. Yet even without otherness, the mechanisms of knowledge persist, and with them something identifiable as a self.

"Lautlos" moves dialectically to resist that conclusion: permitting the self its "otherness," its willed "solitude," it reexposes it to the ultimate process of consumption, mortality. Yet in arriving at this originary poetic gesture, the self has spoken authentically; in other words, it has resisted its own elimination in the very act of narrating it. The corrosive process of self-knowledge always leaves a residue: by symbolically accelerating the machine's consuming, the poem reaches a level of minimal experience, the confrontation of "I remain" with "that thing sits," which enables the narration of a singular self at a singular moment within the flux.

Fried's image of a self unflinchingly directed toward self-elimination, rejecting all longings in pursuit of inviolable knowledge, is supported by the imagery of Günter Herburger's important 1967 essay "Dogmatic Notes on Poems":

> When I write, I write basically only about myself. Everything presented is my projection. I am the main character. And already I notice how I swell, pump myself up, thighs, head, and stomach fill up; soon, unless I immediately release some air, I will take off and float away. As soon as I am in the clouds, I would be unable to see anything. Hence I must hold myself to as minimal a stature as possible, in order to be everywhere on the scene. My aim is to bore into myself, to sit in my stomach, my lungs, my mucous membranes, to ride on my shoulders and to kneel in my ears. I must be immodestly small, otherwise I learn nothing.[5]

The passage is strikingly vigorous. Clearly, the self, once it renounces the illusions of productivity, is by no means condemned to silence but, rather, emancipated into microworlds of knowing and feeling hitherto occluded by poetic convention. Moreover, Herburger's image of the consciousness joyfully exploring and infiltrating the body shows the way in which possibilities of new narration continue to emerge from the Romantic encyclopedia. Novalis's "journey inward" has traditionally been received as a psychological or mystical concept, which it certainly is; but the Romantics' fascination with biological and chemical processes suggests their interest in every kind of journey, including those of the blood and the metabolism. Herburger's quest is not so much for the new as for the forgotten; his rhetoric is entirely consonant with that of Novalis.

In a sense the involvement of poetry making with physical process has always been self-protectively censored. The "mind" operates within received structures, language chief among them. And it was a key Romantic project to give a dialectical charge to the mind's self-awareness, to propel it out of its solipsism. A. W. Schlegel derives the making of poetry from the original making of language, not in order to deny poetry's significance, but rather to underline the extreme difficulty of achieving a critical understanding, a "knowing" of everyday happenings: "For the very reason that poetry is the most omnipresent, all-pervasive thing, we have greater difficulty in grasping it, just as we pay no special attention to the air in which we live and breathe."[6]

Fried and his younger contemporaries project a poetics based simultaneously on a reduction of the status of experience—an automatic suspicion of anything presenting itself as "given"—and an expansion of the scope of analysis, a restless invasion of all those spheres, both public and intimate, hitherto deemed too vulgar for poetry. Such a poetics is dialectically inseparable from the three surviving abstractions: knowledge becomes tangible reality if all commonsense assumptions about what can be known are systematically questioned; history becomes reimaginable if the machinery fragmenting it, ceaselessly in operation, can be forced into the domain of knowledge; and even the word "freedom" regains a residual savor, a memory suggesting a future, in the fragmentary yet cumulative moments of contingent authenticity.

Skeptical voices have been raised against such a program, arguing essentially that at the end of the process of reduction there is still only arbitrary experience, and that such experience has no language available to it except that of the old self-inflation evoked by Günter Herburger. As Jörg Drews puts it: "What exactly do the poets learn now in this isolation, how 'individual' are the sensitively self-probing subjects really? I'm afraid that this individuality is not especially individual, that the inwardness is sometimes not far removed from the despised old-fashioned inwardness; we can almost begin to perceive new traditions of standard posturing."[7]

The best defense against such attacks is probably not the justification of a whole generation, such as Jürgen Theobaldy undertook.[8] For

183

of course the majority of poems of any age are reducible to "standard posturing." It would seem preferable to read closely the texts that clearly *do* speak with truth in order to obtain glimpses of the complex poetics that necessarily underpins any such truth. The circularity of such reasoning does not diminish its urgency: the increasing opaqueness of the world makes it more important than ever to know why successful poems succeed. And the successful poems of the 1970s elude the net Drews would like to throw over them: they simply refuse to permit the old antitheses of private versus public, thinking versus feeling, beautiful versus useful, to remain in force. Friedrich Schlegel already found the language for this refusal: "Very significant is the expression that freedom is a *nonthing;* it is also the only *counterthing,* resistance to things."[9]

Certainly a comparable dialectic can be seen at work in poems discussed in previous chapters. The power of a poetics derives not from its discovery of something new, but from its ability to restore to narrative potency forgotten, compromised, or exhausted values. In the 1970s, poets saw their task as accomplishing what Kafka called "the negative"; but what is released by their rigorous narrative of reduction is a tight circle, an intensification ("Potenzierung") of primary values. Freedom is both the strongest element in this circle and the most elusive. In effect it can itself only be imagined in circular terms. The making of a poem is an assertion of freedom that is manifest in a seemingly "unfree" way, as controlled, skeptical reduction of the world. But this reduction is never an end in itself; the analytical narrative remains a narrative, a temporal artifact: its sole purpose is to constitute a centripetal act of resistance to the flux, hence to make the flux, the centrifugal rush, visible to a world that prefers to repress all awareness of it.

The poem's goal, thus, can only be defined as freedom, the provocation of other acts of resistance, the narrative articulation of a time zone where subjectivity, a perceptual core, is successfully emancipated from the private or arbitrary. The private includes the public; freedom is the activation of necessity. Such equations, familiar to the Romantics, are insisted on by contemporary poets precisely because they have been forgotten, because the now empty idea of private freedom is so industriously promoted by the consumer machine as being the best narcotic of all.

A juxtaposition of fragments by Schlegel evokes the almost Puritanical rigor of this poetics: "Only the detail is necessary, the whole is free"[10]; "Freedom consists in the acknowledgment of necessity (outside ourselves) and in the *destruction of randomness* within ourselves."[11] Freedom involves the radical rupture of processed experience, an emancipatory moment—but such emancipation is reachable only through a "destructive" focusing on immediate detail. Both "acknowledgment" and "destruction" are best understood as narrative acts, perhaps even the same act. To destroy the "randomness" ("Zufall") of imprecision and illusion is simultaneously to release the "chance" (also "Zufall") of a contingent narrative, for it is only in the minimalist authenticity of such gestures (as in Fried's texts) that a "necessity" not already programmed becomes imaginable. The abstraction of seemingly technical philosophical language has acquired immediacy at a time when poets feel an urgent call to resistance, yet find all the weapons (value-bearing words) in the hands of the enemy.

There is nothing new in itself in the opening of poetry to philosophy and other disciplines; but some of Gottfried Benn's poems illustrate how easily such moves become ironic, an indulgence in lists and quotations. What is perhaps new, or at least new since the eighteenth century, is the strict subordination of images to the abstract struggle for value. No symbolist aesthetic can function any longer. Indeed the values themselves cannot be directly invoked, especially not the value of freedom. The success of these poems depends on an arduous, virtually impersonal movement toward an instant when the language suddenly justifies its skepticism and narrowness by evoking in the reader a sense that freedom, freedom in time, is after all imaginable.

Nicolas Born outlines these tensions in the postscript to his volume *The Eye of the Discoverer (Das Auge des Entdeckers,* 1972):

> The illusory system of reality must be deprived of its claim to sole representation. Its taboos, its legally enforced systems of behavior, are directed exclusively against other realities. Images of these realities, utopias, are derided by "political realists"—or indeed criminalized as dangerous utopias. But every person is a dangerous utopia when he or she rediscovers the wishes, longings, and dreams that the insistent catalogue of reality suppresses. To drive out such transcending energies is the true irrationality.[12]

The last sentence underlines the key role of knowledge in the new poetics: man's "transcending energies" are not opposed to, but are close allies of, his reason. Subordination of vague longings to intensive analysis of the world's surfaces will not reinforce the ruling reality system, but subvert it. The system offers processed knowledge, processed experience, a coherence that subtly masks the terror of the centrifugal rush toward disintegration.

Nicolas Born divides his essay into two concurrent statements, printed in parallel columns. This mirror effect becomes especially valuable at the end, when he sketches how the narration of freedom is to be imagined. In the left column we read: "The need for liberation is not itself liberation, but its precondition. . . . The imaginary worlds of literature are not to be compared with musical scores or architect's plans, which are actualized piece by piece, but, rather, they possess a relative autonomy, just as fantasy itself possesses a relative autonomy." And in the column opposite: "This fly—what is it doing in reality? It runs a few hundred times up the windowpane and, once at the top, falls back down. It is important to get up again, even though the falling always looks more beautiful than the getting up."[13] The one statement is inadequate without the other.

The concept of "relative autonomy" is a little pedantic, a little strained; certainly the reality system will have no trouble endorsing it. Yet on the level of abstraction Born probably could not have come up with a better phrase: the poem's act of resistance is autonomous, self-sustaining, yet also wholly dependent on its power to release in the reader a sense of freedom's possibilities. Had Born used a more drastically oppositional phrase than "relative autonomy" he would have made things easier for the system, which has set aside a playground for "political" poetry. His strategy thus is to make a double statement, to illuminate the value of freedom through an image, the vivid unfreedom of the fly. The one autonomous thing about the fly is its refusal to stay fallen, to accept aesthetic closure. And the contemporary consciousness finds freedom only in the refusal to declare its otherness from such unfreedom.

We are indeed like flies, convulsive and deluded, says this poetics. The machine has destroyed authentic time. But the destruction cannot be definitive. Although the ruling fictions seem all-powerful, infinitely resilient, the fragments of an alternate fiction continue to exist, like the potent but forgotten legends of Borges, inside remote pockets of apparently insignificant experience. The persistence of such discordant fictions has everything to do with the persistence of "history." The double vision necessary to perceive the present historically is, as Friedrich Schlegel emphasizes, in principle inaccessible. Yet poetry retains the power to rupture the present, to articulate its hidden "revolution" as necessary enigma:

> It is not experience as such that limits our understanding; but *within* experience there are certain limits to understanding. But the limit is not absolute, only relative. Thus, we cannot understand a condition antithetical to the one we perceive a priori; from the present tranquilly unfolding development of the earth's power we can infer virtually no analogies for the revolutionary condition of that power; thus that condition is often obscure to us, in which we ourselves, in our practical lives, are completely enmeshed.[14]

This analysis holds true for the contemporary experience, but the emphasis has shifted. The "relative" limits of experience have effectively become "absolute" in that all "opposite" structural conditions, such as those engendered by revolution, turn out to be contained by the self-perpetuating consumer machine. The antithesis between "tranquil" and "revolutionary" is superseded by the seamless appearance of historical motion. Hence Schlegel's last sentence becomes a crucial challenge to the contemporary imagination: what is "obscure" must not be allowed to remain so. The intense light of negation must be trained on it. Schlegel implies a cosmos both horizontal (with shifting "limits") and vertical (with revolutionary depths); but in the absolute spatiality of the machine of consumption, there seem to be no dimensions or limits—the darkness pervades the distance as well as the immediate view. The new poetic narratives must analyze and disrupt in a single gesture, since, in a presentness that renders all direct, spontaneous experience inconceivable, analysis and disruption are inseparable, the one unimaginable without the other.

History, then, would be constituted not by transcending limits but by installing them. The recurrent juxtaposition, in this poetics, of utopian perspectives with unadorned detail suggests a determination to liberate the faculties of knowing, observing, and feeling from that mutual alienation that is so advantageous to the system of control. Arno Reinfrank writes:

> The utopian is to be understood more broadly and deeply than any given ideology. . . . Utopias are based on cognitive insights, not on speculations. One such important insight is that human beings in the work process are *not* subordinate to technol-

ogy, and that alienation only enters the picture at the point where technology, instead of releasing people from antiutopian constraints, is reinterpreted as leading to a "positive" utopia, free of humanity's limitations. To recognize the positive and negative of these social processes is not a Kantian a priori induction. It is the aggregation of experience, cognition, and prediction. . . . . My attitude is one of negating the negative.[15]

Reinfrank calls his texts "poetry of facts," and his insistence on an epistemological vocabulary ("cognition," "experience") illustrates how the thrust toward rupture coincides with analytic intensity. Only through isolation, reduction, and penetration can "facts" be released into the narrative sequence of a contemporary poem. A poem of the 1970s can assume nothing, certainly not the value of poetry.

An introduction such as this may seem to be an oppressive burden on the sometimes informal, low-key texts to be studied. But as we have seen, limitation of scope has become a prerequisite to the poets' subversive negations. Precisely because we are so close to these poems, and because they are so often casually categorized with labels designed to keep them at a safe distance, it has been necessary to sketch the radically altered situation of poetry today, especially in contrast to its high prestige in the years 1920–70. From the outset, Romanticism programmatically dissolved limits. But it is a sign of historical creativity, not defeat, when contemporary narratives rupture the continuum by demarcating limits, focusing analysis on the microcosm of the sensory—and inspecting every emotive echo that the words of the narrative would draw in with them.

If Hans Magnus Enzensberger strives to preserve the energy and fantasy of the individual through a programmatic assault on "individualism," Jürgen Becker defends more carefully limited territory. His minimalism draws the world's images into the mind's photographic storehouse while giving as little back as possible, blocking the seepage of emotion into inauthenticity, rupturing the time structures that would offer an illusion of relationality.

Im Frühling
Jürgen Becker
Grünes, verschwindend; und mehr
verschwindet: Fachwerk, Gewissheit, Stille

in Seitenstrassen
         —was, wieder, belebt
die Wüste im Kopf
         —Kein Fragezeichen;
oder ein Fragezeichen
         auf leerem Papier.
Die Ratlosigkeit, auf wenigen Gesichtern,
nein,
    ich nehme wahr
wenige Gesichter. Und ich nehme,
verschwindend,
         weniger wahr; weniger
gibt es, Grünes, Gewissheit,
           und
es ist kein Beweis, die Nachricht
von Gestern, Krise, Hoffnungen heute.[16]
         (1974)

In the Springtime

The green, disappearing; and more
disappears: framework, certainty, stillness
in side streets
         —which, again, animates
the head's desert
         —No question mark;
or a question mark
         on blank paper.
Perplexity, on few faces,
no,
    I am aware
of few faces. And I am aware,
disappearingly,
         of less and less; there is
always less, of the green, of certainty,
           and
there is no proof, the news report
of yesterday, crisis, hopes of today.

Another poem in the same collection as this one, *Das Ende der Landschaftsmalerei* (The End of Landscape Painting), is dominated by

the verb "verschwinden." Entitled "Nach einer langen Zeit," it begins
as follows:

> Verwüstung, ein Zimmer.
> > Wo
> sich nichts ändert. Irgendetwas
> verschwunden; der langsame
> Fortschritt
> > des Verschwindens.[17]

> Desolation, a room.
> Where
> nothing changes. Something or other
> disappeared; the slow
> progression
> of disappearance.

Here Becker articulates an interior scene by a sequence of three entirely different time scales: nothing changes, something has changed definitively, change is continuous. What emerges, through repetition, is
the dominance of "disappearing." This verb *includes* the other versions of time; it is the only verb adequate to Becker's narration of the
centrifugal loss of experience, in that all appearances of stasis merely
mask the multiplicity of loss.

"In Springtime," by contrast, uses a different technique to penetrate the surface of an exterior landscape. Time is not directly invoked.
"Disappear" is repeated three times; the effect, however, is not to reinforce a single meaning, but to vary the possibilities of meaning, delicately yet radically. In the first line the echo is of impressionism; the
paradox of "disappearing green" invokes the innumerable earlier poems, such as Mörike's, with the title "Im Frühling." The second line immediately adds both the literal and the metaphysical dimensions of the
verb. And the isolation of "verschwindend" in line 13 draws together
earlier meanings into the speaker's "becoming" what he is analyzing.
He refuses an Archimedean point outside the scene, validating Novalis's precept about the total absorption of the self into the act of knowing. This transformation of the analytical posture into a presence both
linguistically calm and metaphysically threatened suggests what Becker
is aiming at in his variations on the verb "disappear."

Marianne Kesting writes of Becker, in an image precisely evocative of this text: "This isolation is no longer a sealed-off condition. . . .

The author sits at his desk, but the environment reaches into his house."[18] The author's "house" involves the entire apparatus of his language. For "disappear" is not the only word subject to repetition and variation here; in fact the vocabulary is so tightly controlled that one notes the sudden entry of "perplexity" and the eruption of new words at the end as if they were intruders. The poem is organized as a reduction, a knowing more and more about less and less; yet its verbal delicacy makes of the poem a kind of resistant butterfly, a pure linguistic fabric that narrates the withdrawal of contingent energy directly and without hope.

This doubleness of vision enables Becker to convey both the presence and the absence of the world, the intensity of the moment and the emptiness of all moments, the spontaneous and traditional significance of springtime and the blankness of surface in the urban landscape. In a 1970 interview Becker states: "That is dependence on sensory stimuli. That is the luxury of a naivete, which meanwhile is constantly put in question by the fact that cities and landscapes are the objects of a social rage to destroy; by the possibility that in a few decades everything will have disappeared; by the insight, that phenomena do not reveal what the causes of phenomena are."[19] In these sentences we can hear the Baroque *vanitas vanitatum,* as well as the quest for dispassionate, reductive knowledge. Becker wants to know everything about a scene under scrutiny, an everything best revealed by the drive toward nothingness. Becker's language, in "Im Frühling," is both complex and transparent. It is impressionistic, metaphysical, autobiographical, arbitrary, political, sociological—and yet it is none of these. Becker opens all these doors in order to show how they all open onto the single ontological problem of the centrifuge: the contamination of experience as such. And the poem, opening perspectives as it reduces the self, multiplying and canceling at the same time, becomes an act of resistance. The loss of experience cannot be stemmed; but its sequences can be charted, and the language of this temporal mapping can be rendered wholly transparent.

Becker's method might be described as precise imprecision. He narrates a sense impression, encoding the apparent spontaneity and arbitrariness of a Romantic "chance"; and the closer he comes to it, the more questions about the very process of focusing and translating the spatial moment proliferate. How to account for the moment's "disappearance" even as the observer's immediate mental apparatus is being trained on it? What is the effect of the observer's immediate mental

191

state? What forces link and divide the nominal observer and the nominally observed? Such questions recapitulate, of course, the preoccupations of earlier aesthetics. But there is no longer a space between the observing and the questioning; the poem is an open circle of sensory reception and analytical reflection wherein the words as such gradually and subtly free themselves from the developing paralysis, the self-reduction of their speaker.

A juxtaposition of remarks by Becker himself illuminates the tension involved; in one interview he offers a fairly serene, coherent version of his method: "For wherever, in my texts, my 'self' expresses itself, it is always a polyphonic, multiple self, which to a certain extent can become a medium available to everyone. And hence . . . writing on the basis of private experiences no longer has anything of the isolated monologue about it."[20] But in another interview he acknowledges that the quasi-impressionist image of the medium does not solve the problem: "The anguishing thought . . . that my apparatus of consciousness only produces illusions."[21] The high quality of a text like "Im Fruhling" derives from its incorporation of this "anguishing thought" into its structuring process.

In order to develop a resistant poem out of the process of reduction and loss of certainty, Becker deploys a double linguistic strategy. The one pole of this strategy has been noted: the repetition and variation of thematic words that seem to survive and reverberate even as they are stripped of their official content. The opposite pole is a nervous acceleration of the sequence of assertion and retraction, perception and doubt. What this double strategy achieves is the disruption of the even pace of experience as it dissolves and withdraws in a centrifugal world. Any such disruption is momentary; no act of resistance can succeed if it seeks to prolong its success. Thus to accelerate the process of change (the repetition of "disappear" is emblematic here) is entirely consonant with the central gesture ("oppose," "resist") of this poetics.

Becker introduces this acceleration through a seesaw effect: his lines open with weighted negative imagery ("disappearing . . . disappears . . . desert"), but, in the first part of the poem, they rise toward the end like delicate bubbles about to burst: "more . . . silence . . . animates." The language appears precise. But the heterogeneity of images and perspectives subtly blurs this surface clarity: it is unclear whether the "stillness" is "disappearing," as the syntax would imply, or emerging into the poem as a space of potential narration. Similarly, the "enlivening" of the mental desert works both to enhance and reduce the desert image. The observer's uncertainty puts in question what purports to be external evocation, so that the question mark, and the question about the question mark, derive logically from the opening lines and incorporate the observer's entire sensorium into a trajectory culminating in the empty sheet of paper in front of him. This seamlessness emulates the seamlessness of our daily, ceaseless loss of experience in the centrifuge. But by accelerating the process Becker impels the reader to protest, to say, "Not so fast." Why is the paper blank? Haven't the opening images been written on it? What is this loss of certainty that was slipped into a sequence of images? Why does the poem seem so alive when it speaks only of loss and sterility? Is the poet offering us a little lesson in technique, showing us how a spring poem brings dead things to life? Or is the antispring, the mental desert, at its center?

Far from answering such questions, the second half of the poem compounds them. And as distinctions between levels of perception become ever less distinct, the narrowing repertoire of key words becomes increasingly an end in itself. At the center of the poem the speaker seems to decide to draw things together, to look out of his window again and synthesize outside with inside through the word "perplexity." But this abstraction is immediately framed, ironized, given the status of a fragment in a collage. Such a word ultimately reveals nothing. Only the faces themselves count; but like the opening image of springtime green, these faces lead the speaker not outward but inward, not to multiplicity but to monotony, not to the concrete but to the abstract. A psychological abstraction like "perplexity" has become useless; but the purely numerical abstraction of "few" is now potent. The speaker becomes instantly fixed in his unfocused gaze; he can say nothing new. And the poem's move toward zero perception becomes a rush. Instead of narration it now offers mere contiguity. Every word uttered is analyzed and drawn into a repertoire. As speaker and world empty out, the sensory world they have vacated is filled by the imageless sound of analytical words, particularly the word of pure knowing, or pure unknowing—"wahrnehmen." But there is no final stage to this textual restlessness, this nervous deconstruction of perception. The abstract density of the language is not an end in itself, but part of a continuous assault on the processed language of "experience." The speaker's elimination of his own claim to knowledge is itself an act of knowledge. The void of silence has no more validity than the packaged ecstasy of springtime.

And so the language turns from pure reduction to pure assertion:

"there is/always less." The reader cannot say whether this assertion applies to the world, or whether it is still inside the category of self-description; it is certainly a negative statement, but the variations on the word "less" ("weniger") make one hesitate to attach an explicit value to the statement. Perhaps the reduction of greenness and certainty can be seen as a consolidation, a holding on to the minimal as an act of resistance against smoothly processed superfluity. It is only the self-liberating words themselves, the suppleness of language expanding through variation, that encourage such a reading. As a textual sequence the words continue to dismantle their claims to significance. But such doubleness is precisely the goal of this poetics.

It is the rigor of this sequence that makes the eruption of the final lines so powerful. Not only is the double rhythm crystallized (highly emotive words are prefaced by the pure negation of "no proof"), but the continuous refinement and recycling of a seemingly closed vocabulary also makes it possible for the final trio of abstractions to strike the reader with unexpected force. The circumscribed moment is suddenly framed by "yesterday." The effect is not to reimpose continuity, but to isolate the very concept of "yesterday." Can yesterday ever be anything but a "news report," a processed invention? The text's focus on the specificity of words both invites such a question as a necessary disruption and hints at the possibility of a yesterday that might transcend the status of a report, might generate history. The impact of "crisis" is similar. Embedded between two other abstractions, it is implicitly devalued, a news item. But has not the poem itself constituted a kind of crisis? Is not the ceaseless "disappearing" of experience itself an unacknowledged crisis? All three of these words imply the immediate living of the speaker even as they formally emanate from a news broadcast. And the final words, "hopes of today," crystallize the emergence of a "new subjectivity," an interpretive narrative encoding the desolate fusion of public and private. The emptiness of public hopes, for prosperity and the like, fuses with the self's determination to expel all words and experiences that cannot "prove" themselves. There can be no freedom without knowledge and no knowledge without proof. And no experience can be proved.

The text's analytical dismantling of self is the core of its speaking. But at the same time we are not forbidden to link beginning and end: "The green . . . hopes of today." If the negation were absolute, poetry could not speak. There has to be a turning, a redirecting of the reader's gaze. Becker will allow no turn except in the direction of the

194

words themselves. But language remembers. The reality of hope persists within the word "hope." The values of knowledge and freedom,
which underpin this poetics, do not subsist apart from language; in a
sufficiently rigorous narrative of the loss of experience, the historical
dimension begins to resound as the unspoken, indeed explicitly excluded, telos beyond the poem's end.

For the poem's texture the most significant of these closing
words are "news report" ("Nachricht"). The term shifts the reader's attention from the pure sterility of the self's reflection on a street scene to
the proliferation of indirect experience, which surrounds the modern
consciousness. This is the very element of the centrifugal machine, of
endless, processed experience. And the poet of the 1970s makes this element his own, for without it no strategy of resistance can be effective.

Like Rolf Dieter Brinkmann, Becker trained himself as a skilled
photographer. And for both poets the photograph is the very opposite
of its cliché image as capturing the moment. A photograph is a starting
point for interpretation and commentary, an avenue for knowledge,
an intervention in the flux, which makes possible unfamiliar juxtaposi-
tions and perspectives. Machines such as tape recorders and projec-
tors, by virtue of their total impersonality, enable their users to turn
secondhand experience into firsthand texts—playing back, stopping,
inverting the material of life could be seen as distortion only in the context of a presumed harmonious original. The withdrawal of all such
wholeness leaves the new technological apparatus an adjunct to the
new poetics, a tool for intervention and narration that makes the concept of resistance a little less unrealistic.

The conclusion of a poem from Becker's later collection, *Erzähl
mir nichts vom Krieg* (Don't Tell Me Anything about the War), provides a perspective on "Im Frühling":

> . . . fliessend ein Film
> aus unseren Köpfen, zurück, nach vorn, Delta
> der Bilder, im Augenblick des Verschwindens.[22]

> . . . flowing a film
> from our heads, backward, forward, delta
> of images, in the moment of disappearance.

The multiplicity of "images" is in principle no different from the difficulty, articulated in "Im Frühling," of grasping even a single one. In

both poems the poverty of experience generates the narration, driving the texts toward the "moment of disappearance." The "head's desert," in "Im Frühling," is best understood not as an emptiness but as a chaos, a multileveled *perpetuum mobile* of mental tapes and films. The opening of the consciousness (an opening that cannot be evaded) to all this secondary and tertiary experience raises the stakes for which poetry must play. If there is no such thing as primary, authentic experience, if the flux is both seamless and arbitrary, then every poem must implicitly confront "everything," even as it narrows its scope continually toward the noplace where the nonthings of resistance become imaginable.

Brinkmann concludes a poem in his last collection, *Westwärts 1 und 2* (Westward):

> Hier . . . die vergessenen Tonbänder, zurücklaufende Gespräche,
> als die Blöcke der Jahreszeiten sich verschoben über das
> zärtliche Gesicht, das durch die Gespräche ging.[23]

> Here . . . the forgotten tapes, conversations running backward,
> when the blocks of the seasons shifted onto the
> tender face, which pervaded the conversations.

Like Becker's "delta of images," Brinkmann's "blocks of the seasons" is an image compressing proliferating time (i.e., time in complicity with the centrifuge) into a narration closing in on a single point. Such a point exists neither in space nor time, but solely in a rigorous distillation of both dimensions. And the narrative of access to it constitutes an intervention against the flux, a process of knowing and liberating designed always to culminate in the "moment of disappearance." The poem is the residue of this process, the antiprocess of resistance.

Becker's minimalism is not the only version of resistance. The opposite rhetoric, that of apocalypse, becomes available again to a poetics after modernism, and here Enzensberger's snuffling dog is the transitional figure. Where the Expressionist poet sees the bourgeois catastrophe all too clearly, the contemporary witness knows much but can see little. What is known is the tedious predictability of disaster; what cannot be known is the radical self-destruction of the historical machine, of experience as such: the disaster without rebirth.

Becker, Meckel, Kiwus

Epoche
Christoph Meckel

Ein Atemzug weiter, ein Schritt
im bodenlosen Welthaus ohne Luft.

Was kann gerettet werden
von Zeit und Erde?
Ein kurzer Tag, aus dem Schutt gehoben
im erstickten Grundstrom ein Hai-Skelett
aus der Schöpfung ein Zeisig, verstummt, ein halber
Mensch, zu wund zum weinen, ein
verwüsteter Knochen—und der letzte
Götze mit Schlagring tritt aus dem Qualm
und jagt in den Schraubstock Gestein und Sonne.

Zum Grund hin stehen alle Löcher offen.
Erde, ein dröhnender Tag, vor Atemausgang.
Ein Faustschlag weiter, ein Sturz, ein Gewimmer—

Erde, unkenntlich in Schutt und Foltern.[24]

(1974)

Epoch

One breath further, one step
in the bottomless world house without air.

What can be rescued
of time and earth?
A brief day, raised from the rubble
in the strangled ocean current a shark's skeleton
from the creation a siskin bird, silenced, half
a human, too hurt to weep, a
devastated bone—and the last
idol with brass knuckles strides from the smoke
and drives stone and sun into the vice.

Downward all the holes stand open.
Earth, a roaring day, before the final breath.
One blow of the fist further, one fall, one whimpering—

Earth, unrecognizable in rubble and torment.

If the notion of the poem as residue is implicit in Becker's texts, it is thematic in the work of Christoph Meckel. Meckel reaches the poetics of the 1970s, the poetics of analysis, reduction and linguistic libera-

197

tion, by a route almost antithetical to that of Becker. Becker limits his gaze, compelling a narrative to emerge through insistent questioning of a marked-off group of images never straying far from the everyday. From the start Meckel has been the most "fantastic" of contemporary poets, using a wide range of tonalities, permitting the darkest motifs the possibility of playful metamorphosis. This playfulness is always set in tension with a world that would destroy it; and as Wulf Segebrecht points out, the sources of destruction are understood more and more broadly by Meckel as his writing develops:

> The figures of fantasy are creatures helpless in this world. . . . The author's call is a vow of solidarity with these poetic figures; not only with his own, but with all figures that inhabit the world. . . . The apologia for poetic figures is not based on their being brutally repressed or even destroyed by their enemies. . . . The integration of the poetic into the political world appears as the most subtle and successful means of its destruction; Meckel assumes a posture of resistance to this destruction.[25]

The very exuberance of Meckel's imagination heightens his awareness of the need for a resistant poetics. The most vivid fantasy is now subject to the process of interpretation, absorption, dissolution. Meckel's counternarratives emerge from a protection of the contingent, an elaboration of the interpretive narrative, which questions the very possibility of authentic language. Behind the screen of proliferating self-questioning, moments of rupture are gradually actualized.

Meckel's long-running argument with himself about the function of language is an important background to a text like "Epoche," where it is thematized only in the phrase "What can be rescued . . . ?" In "Talking about Poetry" these lines occupy the center of the text:

Welt, verschollen
in Worten tausendundein
KIRSCHBAUM! während der Kirschbaum in Blüte steht
SINTFLUT! während das Meer sich entfernt
auf den Bahnen des Mondes.

Es ist Zeit, ein Ende zu machen
und heimzuführen die Welt in Worte
bewohnbar. . . .[26]

World, dispersed
into a thousand and one words
CHERRY TREE! while the cherry tree stands in bloom
FLOOD! while the sea withdraws
on the moon's pathway.

It is time to make an end
and to lead the world home to words
inhabitable.

"Cherry tree" is an inadequate term because it denotes something overpoweringly present; "flood" is inadequate for the opposite reason, for its fundamental absence except as metaphor, metaphor that is virtually exhausted. However, a role for the poet is articulated—making the world "inhabitable" as language. But the playful "Poem on the Writing of Poems" tells a somewhat different story. Poetry is still imaginable, but human habitation therein is not. Most tenuous of all is the poet's claim to the words he uses. I quote the fifth and last stanza:

Das Wort sah mich von oben an:
Was schleppst du mir für Zeug heran
das ich mit Klang versorgen soll
ich mache dir dein Glück nicht voll
ich wiege meine eigne Last
und komme nur aus Trümmern her
die du mir zu bereiten hast,
aus Aschen, die nicht schimmern, her
und werfe alle Zweifel um:
Du machst mich laut, ich mach dich stumm.[27]

The word looked down on me:
Why do you drag along such stuff to me
that I am to provide with sound
I'm not here to make you happy
I carry my own burden
and emerge only from wreckage
which you are to prepare for me,
from ashes which do not glow
and I overturn all doubts:
You give me sound, I give you silence.

Like Jürgen Becker, and yet most unlike him, Meckel presents himself in this early poem (1962) as a kind of medium whose task is to prepare the wreckage of the world for occupation by language. For both poets, of course, the medium concept is an operational mask. The speaker here is anything but "silent"; and the programmatic text "Information" ("Auskunft") suggests an instinctive faith, almost like that of Novalis, in language's alchemical power: "Because words exist like sand by the sea and my task is to pass them through a sieve, to sort them, assemble them, and polish them into sparkling grains."[28] But Meckel avoids the potentially arbitrary aestheticism of such a goal by making a decisive turn toward the reductive poetics of the 1970s. His images still proliferate; but they are embedded in interpretive narrations of the impossibility of recuperating fantasy as experience in a centrifugal world. Meckel becomes, not sober or laconic, but even more intense and paradoxical than before. Becker inserts the dimensions of death and life into a controlled microcosm; Meckel maintains, even insists on, the language of the macrocosm because the vision of its destruction authorizes an ecstatic moment in which the immensities of experience encoded in language resound once again.

A poetological text from 1977 illuminates the passionate paradoxes of this style:

Das Gedicht und was von ihm übrig bleibt in der gesammelten Zukunft
handelt vom Gegensatz und von dem, der drin lebt
heillos, in Ermangelung eines Bessern. . . .
Auf den Tod genau vorhanden
handelt es von der Hoffnung ohne erkennbaren Anlass
und von dem, was ist und sein wird: leibhaftiges Nein,
unwiderlegbar, von keiner Antwort gewürdigt, in der
Geschichte ohne Vernunft und Freude.[29]

The poem and what remains of it in the collected future
deals with opposition and with him who lives there
without remedy, lacking anything better. . . .
Precisely prepared for death
it deals with hope without recognizable reason
and with what is and will be: embodying the negative,
irrefutable, without receiving any answer,
in history without reason and joy.

The phrase "hope without recognizable reason" epitomizes the 1970s in its refusal of all processes except the activity of knowing, "erkennen" itself; like Becker at the end of "Im Frühling," Meckel finds a stripped-down, ironized usage of the word "hope" not only possible but potent. Such potency is, however, strictly dialectical, inseparable from strategies of negation. The poet can generate fantasy and the language of fantasy ("reason and joy" are still sayable), but must rigorously narrate its defeat as a refuge, a dream of residual authenticity.

"The poem and what remains of it": what cannot be claimed for the power of fantasy is precisely actualized by the making of the text. The poem is itself the residual record of a reductive, analytical thrust into the consuming centrifuge. But the image is a double one, as a residue, a verbal memory of the poem itself, lingers in the culture, resisting absorption for a while—and making connections to all the other "residues" of past civilizational achievement, now dormant but not dead in individual human minds.

In the last poem, dated September 1978, which Meckel chose for his *Selected Poems,* he sketches the effects on other people of a poetry discussion in Australia:

> Ich weiss nicht
> was übrig blieb von den Wörtern und ihrer Lunge
> von den Sätzen und Namen, den Atemzügen, dem Erdball
> vom Flug der Eule, von Tier und Herbstnacht
> und was übrig blieb im Mund der andern vom Schlaf
> und übrig vom Sommer
> vom Staub, von Tod und Sonne, vom Salz, vom Feuer
> von Verwüstung und Freude, vom Meer, vom Atem, vom Atem
> in der atemlosen Antwort, und in der Frage.
> Und was übrig blieb von Jahrhunderten in der Haut eines jeden
> von den Sprachen und Windrosen allen, und von der Zukunft
> vom Geschäft eines jeden.[30]

> I don't know
> what remained of the words and their lung
> of the sentences, names, of breaths and the globe
> of owls' flight, of animals and autumn night
> what remained in others' mouths of sleep
> what remained of summer
> of dust, of death and sun, of salt, of fire
> of devastation and joy, of sea, of breath, of breath

in the breathless answer, and in the question.
And what remained of centuries in everyone's skin
of all the languages and compasses, and of the future
of everyone's business.

Meckel is able to maintain this dangerously elevated style, with motifs strongly reminiscent of Celan and Enzensberger ("owls' flight," "breath," "compasses"), through his almost obsessive deployment of the word "remained." The disintegration of the contingent is never complete; the processing of experience does not consume language itself, so that the analytical consciousness is never without a starting point for an interpretive narrative. Beginning on a note of linguistic elevation, Meckel's texts accelerate the momentum of loss in order to reach a residual authenticity. Such a moment of rupture is then communicable; an archipelago of resistant gestures becomes imaginable.

Although "Epoche" is on one level a vision of the landscape of nuclear catastrophe, the title invites a more complex reading. One reason we are so well versed at imagining the horrors of such a scene is that we are obscurely aware that this landscape is in fact coming gradually into existence all the time: the one experience left to us in the centrifuge is that of a continuous ending. Meckel's text accelerates the entire modern "epoch" into two cosmic moments barely distinguishable from each other: the airless, lifeless space of the contemporary machine and the culminating wreckage. In effect, the poetics of reduction reveals the one as a kind of photographic negative of the other. The poem opens with a paradoxical diagram. Both a breath and a step are taken, but there is no floor and no air. The key term is "world house" ("Welthaus"): this moment before the end is located inside a house, the constructed house of Western civilization, a building given shape and coherence by the remembered dream of the spiritually centered individual. As the centrifuge has destroyed the center, it has emptied the building. And it is through the floor that the proliferating jungle returns.

The opening lines convey a closed but horizontal world. The poem shifts the imagery to the vertical at the same time as it collapses the walls of the "Welthaus," leaving only the openness of devastation. Thus Meckel blends the idea of a reverse creation, a return to chaos, with a compression into a horribly singular moment through the rush of images into a single, vertical "vice" of universal pain. This structuring toward the vertical enables the specific images to avoid the taint of arbitrariness; they are forced into the poem's own geometry, an archaeological site at the very moment of its petrification through catastrophe. And their power is further increased by the sense that the speaker is struggling with his own vision, attempting to thematize a Rilkean rescue of the disappearing world even now when it is far too late. For the answer to the question in lines 3 and 4 is, essentially, "nothing." And the poem is forced into giving this answer; it cannot resist its own knowledge. But the actual words of the question are the words of a world still remembered: "time and earth" are the missing dimensions of the opening lines, the self-understanding of human life as movement within a supporting coherence called earth. It is these inherited points of the compass, these minimal generalities, which disappear in the chaos that follows, a chaos that (unlike the French Revolution for the Romantics) permits no imagining of fruitfulness: this chaos is the nuclear implosion, the single, time canceling moment.

"A brief day" has ceased to be a temporal concept, it is definable at all only through being "raised" from the debris. This day, while echoing biblical images of "transience," is a frightening version of the end: even as it gives nominal significance to the "Epoche" of the title, it cancels the very possibility of significance, refuting the horizontal shape of time by entering the long-accumulating debris of the world as its final, vertical concentration. The shark is already a skeleton, the sea current already choked, the bird already silent, man already half a man. These images not only mock the poetic gesture of rescuing them, they tell of a world already choked in the centrifugal rush, a world that is already a catastrophe. And they offer a vertical perspective on the paralyzed cosmos, from the depths of the ocean through the semihuman surface of earth to the unbreathable air of the bird. This world is poised for the moment of the "idol with brass knuckles." The image is of the demiurge returning creation to chaos; but it also expresses the violent precision of fascist behavior, behavior that is never far from the surface of a world in which human beings can no longer claim experience as their own.

"Brass knuckles" and "smoke" are recurring motifs in Meckel's poetry; in his "author's interpretation" of the "Ode to Powerful Teams" ("Ode an mächtige Mannschaften") he tells of the childhood experience of his home being repeatedly searched (for what was never clear), before and after the end of World War II.[31] Clearly he feels that it takes very little to trigger the human delight in power and organized violence; and once initiated, there is no limit to the human capacity for destruction. Hence the energy of these lines, the sudden dynamism of "strides" and "drives" crashing into the accumulated paralysis—and the cosmic insolence, the Prometheanism in reverse, of the elimination of the last surviving elements on the remembered earth.

The final lines recapitulate the opening images, but the "Welthaus" is no longer imaginable, the category of the horizontal, which sustained the initial paradoxes, has ceased to function. The verb "stand" embodies this last vertical moment: the earth has become synonymous with "a roaring day"; distinctions between time and space, or between different physical sensations, have become superfluous in this grisly final synaesthesia. Everything is falling through the "holes," an image fusing the continuous disintegration of the centrifuge with the final decisive thrust of the "idol." The word "further" ("weiter") no longer means what it did in line 1. To move, or rather to be driven "further" is to plunge downward. And in a final line, the earth has become unknowable, all shape and contour has left the planet.

The poem is a drastic conclusion to a process that, as the initial "further" communicates, is smoothly continuous in the contemporary world. But of course the very imagining of such a culmination means that the situation is open. If "weiter" opens the poem, "unkenntlich" concludes it. So long as there is not silence, so long as a consciousness can distinguish between what is and is not recognizable, then the narrative of resistance is at work. Meckel's poem is not science fiction, not a warning, but merely a drastic acceleration and concentration of contemporary processes. The "day" he evokes is indeed the day of judgment, but there is no god at work in bringing it about, only the "idols" emerging from the frustration of lives deprived of authentic experience. In the total spatialization of this final day, cosmic memories blend seamlessly with garbage and physical pain. This is the conjuncture that must not be.

Meckel's text is a rigorously closed interpretive narrative: the dying of history certifies the impossibility of the contingent in a world become "unkenntlich." And yet the binary tension implicit in that word suggests the rupture implicit in the very closure of this self-sealing language. As long as knowing itself continues, the catastrophe on which all knowing must focus can be accelerated into premature verbal existence; and through language—this must be the poet's final faith—the predictable can once again be rendered unpredictable: both the contingent and the historical will stir within the reader.

In its directness and compression "Epoche" is a linguistic residue without framework or commentary. But Meckel gives the appropriate

commentary in "Words," another poem from the same collection, using the same apocalyptic vocabulary:

Worte, gefesselt an Welt, und losgerissen
von Atem und Stimme, Worte, deine grundlose Hoffnung. . . .
barhäuptige Worte, die zeugen werden für den Verlust der Zeit und der
Erde.[32]

Words, bound to the world, and torn away
from breath and voice, words, your baseless hope. . . .
bare-headed words, which will testify to the loss of time and of the
earth.

If the poetics of reduction links such disparate voices as Becker
and Meckel, it has also shaped poetry to such an extent that Karin
Kiwus appears to move within its confines with ease. Her combination
of curiosity and suspicion enables her to stay very close to available,
pervasively inauthentic experience; she speaks her disgust, claims no illusory refuge, simply scrapes off the skin of surface living and compels
the scrapings to tell their story.

Nebenwirkung
Karin Kiwus

Ekel-
erregend wie die Ruhe
mir zusetzt dieser
falsch verschriebene
starr und feist wuchernde
Frieden

Atem-
beraubend wie im Hals
ein Fettkloss mich würgt
die herausdrängende Bruhe
inwendig
durch die Speiseröhre platzt
mein Blut trübt und mir
die Lungenflügel verklebt

Körper-
lösend wie ich am Tropf
hänge prall eitrige Egel und
Hohlnadeln zwischen den Rippen

205

wie die Jauche allmählich sich
absaugen lässt bis ich zuletzt
trockengelegt bin und leer
vollkommen leer

Später
     in einer zweiten Zeit
   werde ich dahocken
               wie ein Leguan
     reglos scheinbar
          versteckfarben
               hornbewehrt
   ein unbezwingbares Faltengebirge Haut
    in den Augenhöhlen nur noch
      südlich hell flackerndes
      Licht
          das sich immer
      weiter
          nach innen
              entfernt[33]
           (1979)

Side Effect

Disgust—
provoking as rest
accumulates this
wrongly prescribed
stagnating, obesely
proliferating peace

Breath—
taking as in my neck
a fat lump strangles me
the liquid pressing outward
forced back
bursts through the esophagus
clouds my blood
and pastes shut the lungs

Body—
dissolving as I cling to the
dripping richly suppurating leeches and
hollow pins between the ribs
as the waste liquid is gradually

206

sucked out until at last
I lie dried out and empty
completely empty

Later
    in a second age
I will crouch there
        like an iguana
apparently motionless
        camouflaged
            armed with horns
an unconquerable mountain of skin folds
    in the eyeballs only
    a flickering bright southern
      light
        which ever
      further
        recedes
          inward.

Central to the poetics of analytic reduction is what the Romantics would have termed its encyclopedic element, the text's ability to make its detailing representative, microcosmic. It is the main current of the centrifugal flux, not some backwater, which must be resisted. And in the encyclopedia of Becker and Meckel, inherited assumptions about the artist's role, whether as seer or as solitary, inhibit the possibilities of narration in a world where all such roles are prepackaged. For both poets the reduction of self and an elaborate probing of language are the central elements in achieving a resistant narrative.

In the poetry of Karin Kiwus, seven years younger than Meckel, the inhibiting force of the tradition seems finally to have vanished; although the self can of course never be at ease on the periphery of ever-receding "experience," it has grown accustomed to the precariousness, it can speak without aesthetic preamble. The discourse of knowing is fully established in this poetry, colonizing inconspicuous moments in the centrifuge, hardening the language of resistance. Whereas the Romantic encyclopedia is of course expansive and relational, the contemporary analogue must reduce, isolate, set limits. But the liberation of language seems comparable. The analytic tone of "Side Effect" readily accommodates such emotive words as "disgust," with which it opens. Classes of sensation, like those of language, are to be explored but not ranked.

207

The poem's theme, sickness, illuminates the dimensions of the change. Novalis's speculations on the creativity of sickness underpinned a whole tradition pitting the sickly and refined against laughable or contemptible normality. Sylvia Plath's "Fever 103" (1961) sardonically deploys a plethora of motifs developed inside this tradition:

> I am too pure for you or anyone.
> Your body
> Hurts me as the world hurts God. I am a lantern—
>
> My head a moon
> of Japanese paper, my gold beaten skin
> Infinitely delicate and infinitely expensive.
>
> Does not my heat astound you. And my light.
> All by myself I am a huge camellia
> Glowing and coming and going, flush on flush.
>
> I think I am going up,
> I think I may rise—
> The beads of hot metal fly, and I, love, I
>
> Am a pure acetylene
> Virgin
> Attended by roses.[34]

The insistence on purity, however ironic; the simultaneous attention to bodily details and to a feverish, quasi-mystical sense of disembodied elevation; the alchemical image of technology; the centering of self and the proclamation of self as light; the deft use of delicate images from both nature and culture to chart the obsession with dematerialization and death—in all this we can discern the privileging of sickness deployed within a "modernist" poetics. And in "Side Effect" there is none of it. Instead, the fascination with bodily processes seems attuned to a different emphasis in Novalis's fragments, noted at the beginning of this chapter: his concern for both the singleness of the process of knowing and the multiple levels on which that process is continually taking place. The biology of one's own body is crucial to this metaknowledge, for knowing and willing, separating and connecting, are there both reduced to their primary energies and discernibly functioning in a most complex interplay:

My body would appear to me not as specifically distinct from the whole, but only as a variation of it. My understanding of the whole would thus have the character of an analogy—which would, however, be directed in the most intimate and unmediated way toward the unqualified and absolute understanding of the bodily part. . . . I can only experience something insofar as I absorb it within me; it is thus both an alienation of my being and at the same time an appropriation or transformation of another substance into mine. . . . I can distinguish as many powers of understanding within me as there are powers of effective action there. . . . I know myself as I will myself to be, and will myself to be as I know myself. . . . In myself, then, knowing and willing are a single process.[35]

The mystification of illness and the specialization of science combined in the nineteenth century to limit this frank pursuit of epistemological speculation into the systems of the body. Thus Karin Kiwus seems to be resuming an interrupted dialogue between poetry and medicine. Significantly, she focuses on the flow of fluid out of the body rather than the absorption into it on which Novalis reflects; her poem's energies are grounded in a reduction and refocusing of the self.

The precision and unsentimental directness of the poem's medical details are in no way compromised by their structuring as interpretive narrative. The Romantics understood that without "moral" urgency, without the drive to "read" the body's codes, the intimate dynamics of such physical details could not be grasped at all. Friedrich Schlegel argued that the aesthetic prerequisites of an age are essential to the generation of science, in the integrative sense of the word articulated by the Romantics: "The epidemics of the spirit have not yet been appropriately examined from a medical perspective. The history of humanity so far includes merely the origin, end, and universality of humanity. The only way of morally analyzing the animal qualities of humans is aesthetic treatment."[36] For Schlegel, as for Karin Kiwus, the aesthetic is a way of organizing language and perception in order to focus the process of knowing; there are no a priori barriers between aesthetic and other kinds of speaking.

The liberating effect of a poem such as "Nebenwirkung" is precisely that it offers itself as useful, nonesoteric language that says what otherwise cannot be said; by linking physical sensation to both technical knowledge and the energy of fantasy, poetry fills gaps, organizes the unthought in the sense outlined by Schlegel: "Gravity is what isolates and is isolated in nature. The midpoint between light and gravity is not emptiness but the most structured kind of organization. Poetry plays this role as the midpoint between reason and unreason."[37] It is when we reach the word "empty" ("leer") at the center of "Nebenwirkung" that the poem's organization is most vivid. For the third section is loaded down with the gravitational "heaviness," the distasteful, "isolating" quality of the physical symptoms. The poem is the unity between the fullness and the emptiness, the fullness conveying the clogged liquidity of the body's disease, the emptiness pointing toward the emancipated "light" of its reptilian fantasy.

The narrative of the self within the poem is controlled by a double movement that accounts for the text's unsettling yet liberating quality. The details are registered with an observer's precision, but this observing is an intense interpretive sequence, an alienation that totalizes the self at one level while dismembering it at another. Thus the self begins more or less at one with its physical functioning, but accelerates its analytic journey to a point of extreme distance—where it is at last possible to use the phrase "inward" ("nach innen"): the polarization of outer and inner realities radically disrupts the process of seamless, meaningless healing. And this disruption is reinforced by the self's figural attributes. The first three sections narrate an intensifying vulnerability and helplessness, while the last one does not so much complete the development as transform it. The self is metamorphosed into an armored creature, "hornbewehrt." The totally perforated skin surface of the third section has become impenetrable; knowledge of the depths of human weakness has produced a moment of rupture, a text of resistance.

The poem uses the first person throughout, yet prevents us from assigning any stable location to this nominally bedridden persona; and by the same token it resists a reading of the final section as an escape from observation into fantasy. By reclaiming the Romantic quest for structural knowledge, for the interweaving of flesh and dream,[38] the poem is able to subvert the artificial hierarchies of mental and physical, which are continually reproduced as inauthentic experience. The goal of the narration is not to regain the mystical center, nor to achieve a quiescent detachment—but to reconstitute itself as a resistant text.

The isolation of nouns at the beginning of the first three sections provides a kind of poetic headline: the continuous rush of the language to follow is momentarily held back, shaped; the tension between the formal and the informal is delicately underlined. Moreover, the order of the nouns registers the shifts in the self's perspective. "Disgust" is generalized, emotional; the speaker is inside the not very precise feelings. "Breath" is intended both physically and spiritually. The double meaning of "breathtaking" is exploited; the self is both very close to and clinically detached from the profound physical malfunctioning. And with the word "body" the perspective is sufficiently detached for the body and its systematic emptying out to be evoked as an alienated whole.

The first section is controlled by the abstractions "rest" and "peace." Because they are treated with disgust, and because all abstraction immediately disappears from the poem, these terms supply a disruptive allegorical background to the "light" in the iguana's eyes at the poem's end: such light is not the light of peace. The qualifiers "obesely proliferating" establish the atmosphere to be resisted. The self's involuntary physical stasis enables her to perceive the inauthenticity of life blessed by such official felicities as "rest" and "peace." Liquidity and fatness are the textures of acceptable, regulated experience: the pouring of liquid from the self accelerates the centrifugal rush, a process of reduction toward the nothingness, the state of pure knowing allegorized as dryness and emptiness.

Not that one should insist too much on the poem's continuities. The second section communicates a sudden horror, panic, a loss of control over the body that is truly threatening. The personal pronoun is passive in the most literal sense ("strangles me . . . clouds my blood"), as the medical language pours out with frightening energy. Most of the descriptive terms are obviously secondhand, the doctor's diagnosis of what is going on inside; but by seizing on these words and organizing them, the speaker connects kinds of knowledge kept separate in the sanitized world. And the act of combining such words with the terminology of immediate sensation ("pressing . . . bursts") generates an intensification ("Potenzierung") of language in the full Romantic sense. Not only are the abstract and concrete united; their conjunction opens up the paradox of fruitful knowledge. Purity of knowing, refusal to flinch from knowing, enables a vision of radical impurity, a chaos of mutually polluting liquids that the body barely holds in check. The heresy of life in the centrifugal machine is the pretense that all is normal, that life is always balanced. The body, or rather the body's text, tells us otherwise.

The plunge into its interior makes possible the equally uncompromising withdrawal of the third section. "Body-dissolving" imposes the allegorical move. As the medical machinery empties out the body's liquids, the mind translates the dissolution, the dryness, into a kind of detachment; not a detachment from anything, not a knowledge of anything, but pure detachment, pure knowing: the still center that instigates the rupture, the hardening, the allegorical creature of resistance. Whereas the flood of images in the second section is released by a single "as," the slowing down of the third section is achieved through a deployment of self-consciously neutral verbs and the careful use of three conjunctions ("as . . . as . . . until"). The withdrawal of the perspective from the physical details is most subtly managed at the end of this section: "dried out" generalizes what medicine has achieved into a new suggestiveness, and the word "empty" is then savored, repeated, embroidered with the qualifier "completely." Without breaching the framework of physical self-description, the speaker allows her language to expand into the new space of knowledge that it has brought into existence, to exploit the binary clarity of the full and the empty, the liquid and the dry.

The isolation of "later" links it to the thematic nouns introducing the earlier sections, and it is reinforced by "in a second age." This fantasy makes temporal claims. The "side effect" of the body's travail is a rupture of presentness, a sudden, imperturbable power to narrate in the future tense. The static quality of the self in her bed is maintained: the metamorphosis she projects installs a creature equally immobile. Its folds of skin contain an absolute dryness; and its prehistoric associations reinforce the reader's sense that the breakdown of the body's fluid functioning has opened up a new perspective on history itself, which suddenly has a multiple function within this resistant stasis: as memory of a deep past, as future tense, and as the graphically visual "journey" of the words themselves, inside a present moment that is "unconquerable." The spacing out of the lines and the increased deployment of adjectives enhance the monumental effect of this new temporality. The iguana is a "mountain of skin folds," a transformation of the weakness of a dried-out body into something irresistibly strong.

The final image of the eyes is of course dangerous ground for a contemporary poet; the long mystical tradition, the familiarity of Keller's "Evening Poem" ("Abendlied"), the exhaustive use of this imagery by Celan—all this weakens the suggestiveness of eyes, especially in a concluding strategy. But the poem earns its conclusion by invoking the iguana's eyes as a final reduction. The liberation of the language from the dead tradition is expressed in the use of "southern." The reader no longer has to think of Gottfried Benn's Mediterranean; instead the text directs us farther south, to the tropical prehistory, which can instigate the imagery of a posthistory. This creature is not exotic, its strangeness is the kind that refuses associative fluency; it is absolute, monumental dryness in a context of proliferation. And its eyes withdraw into nothingness, not because life is denied to them (as is the case with Rilke's panther), but because they deny the life that proliferates. Theirs is the light of nothingness, the light of resistant knowledge.

The final journey "inward" is also explicitly a withdrawal. Once again, a Romantic *topos* is given new validity by the text of Karin Kiwus. For the poem as a whole has dismantled the very possibility of inwardness in a traditional sense. And so the journey inward must indeed be, in Novalis's famous formulation, a journey outward into the world. The withdrawing light is *not* a rehabilitation of the center but the power that maintains the armored surface in being: the journey of this alien electricity from surface to center and back again gives no privileged status to the center. This creature is a countermachine, an embodiment of extreme forces from which all illusions of balance and harmony have been expelled. The interpretive narrative has culminated in this vision; and within its resistant stasis the incipient, deliberate movements of a new, drastically autonomous contingency can be discerned.

CONCLUSION

Translating the Romantic Encyclopedia

The poets discussed in my final three chapters—
the poets of the twentieth century—view the contingent narrative,
namely the emergence of authentic meaning within a specific and singular time zone, as almost an impossibility. The collapse of "Bildung"
and the sickening of the privileged moment have resulted, in this century, in a prolonged exile from the subjectively "produced,"
structurable temporality of nineteenth-century poetics. The formalization of "history," with its associated fetishes of nationalism, progress,
and growth, has produced, ironically, the paralysis of history as
modernity's operative goal. This cultural-political crisis of the West is
describable, in Romantic terms, as the domination of presentness over
all versions of countertime, the ceaseless devaluation of past and future within spatialized, programmed structures of "experience." The
crisis is first articulated as catastrophe, in the apocalyptic tonality of
Expressionism. Expressionist poets repeatedly narrate the invisible om-
nipotence of the historical machine; through the semantic inversion of
all the world's microevents, they open to view the sickness that infects
every initiative of the imagination. Thereafter poets struggle, beyond

hope and often beyond irony, to reauthorize a contingent sphere, whether through the modernist vision of a generative textuality, a sheerly linguistic power, or through the contemporary poetics of resistant knowledge.

In order to regain a vision of history as open, changeable, human, the lyric text strives to rupture its indifferent, deathly presentness, the processing sequences of its machinery. Enzensberger's simultaneous assumption, in the early 1960s, of the roles of poet, polemicist, and anthologist articulates the new agenda. The contemporary poet must play as many cultural-linguistic roles as the original Romantics. And the indispensable new alliance of the formal and the critical, a tangible reenactment of the Romantic project, in no way dilutes the creative. The poetological declarations of Benn, Celan, and Enzensberger already read like historical self-narrations, and texts by Heissenbüttel, Kunert, Born, and others may well gain comparable privileged status.

Defining the poem's territory, claiming its time zone, is the goal of these statements. And in deploying Romantic fragments as markers of that temporality, my purpose has been, not to weaken the specificities of twentieth-century texts, but to identify their power source. For to unpack these poems in terms of their explicit social and personal reference points is to miss the urgency that drives them to become texts: their starting point, indeed, is that the seemingly contingent and personal is always in the grip of the historical machine.

Neither, on the other hand, should poetry be viewed as a purely linguistic event, a self-reflective sequence of styles, themes, motifs, bequeathed by the past. I have argued in this book that poetic narratives project and reproject the possibilities of history first glimpsed by the Romantics. The historical project, in other words, has its own history. And the story that has culminated, in our own century, in the grim struggle to regain the contingent is marked by a specific turning point: the identification, discussed in Chapter 2, of the program of "Bildung" with unique, aesthetically mediated glimpses of fulfilled time.

This mid-nineteenth-century intellectual event has turned out to possess normative significance for our thinking about literature, standardizing the new genre possibilities, isolating "lyrical" poetry. The historic moment that made such rigidities possible was presumably the precarious stabilization of the bourgeois version of the individual: a priori meaning was assigned to the categories "realistic" and "subjective," which still dominate the minds of people growing up today, so long after the effective dissolution of the hierarchical bourgeois self. Just as it is increasingly difficult to imagine a world other than the one structured by commodity capitalism, so it is hard to think of literary texts without the familiar hermeneutic alternatives of formalism and explanatory historicism. But if we can manage to continue our retrospective journey back to the ferment of Romantic thinking itself, it becomes possible to recognize and reactivate sources of energy subsequently fossilized as "art," "feeling," "reality," and the like. What *cannot* be regained is the particular synthesis achieved by the post-Romantic generation and embodied in the title of Chapter 1: " 'Bildung' and the Possibility of History." Yet Romantic thinking did not die with the failure of that synthesis; its interpretive and ironic stance is open to perpetual reinvention. Indeed, the fragments of Novalis and Schlegel treat all syntheses as momentary intellectual conjunctions, interpretive narratives pointing away from themselves toward projects both more intimate and more ambitious, toward contingent and historical narratives.

Virtually all Romantic conceptual tools, from "the marvelous" ("das Wunderbare") to irony and arabesque, are born of the need to locate the intersection of the contingent with the historical, to situate the moments of a single life within the entirety of history, which the modern condition impels us to imagine. In our century the clichéd phrase "loss of center" ("Verlust der Mitte") is deployed as an interpretation of our specific crisis. But the Romantics remind us that there never was a center or middle, a comfortable life norm; the epistemological premises of modernity preclude any such stabilization. To think historically is to think critically, to adopt a perspective in which the workings of historical forces on the consciousness are the object of a conscious quest. In this perspective casual yet suggestive details of the everyday are thrust up against the limits of the culturally imaginable. Detachment from the empirical is neither desirable nor possible: indeed the act of temporal rupture, however aggressive, signifies the most intense kind of commitment. The dialectic between the contingent and the historical is incessant; its mediating elements, its stabilized moments in which the entirety is compressed within the particular, are narratives of interpretation, simultaneities of "divination" and critical consciousness.

The Romantics themselves did not single out poetry as an especially privileged mode of interpretive narrative. But the formalization of lyrical-subjective language as the key cultural discourse of the nineteenth century endowed poetry with explicit prestige at the very moment when bourgeois hierarchies of value were losing all authenticity. As a result, poets of this century have found themselves in a realm populated by ghosts, illusions of privileged experience perpetuated and reprocessed by the consumer machine. Poetry speaks from the abandoned and decaying center of bourgeois culture, a terrain on which the contingent and the historical converge in a series of shocks. The contingent appears as its own impossibility, that is, as the poisoning or paralysis of the privileged moment; while the historical looms as a machine eluding language and, in so doing, eluding experience as such.

Thus, the retrospective critical journey to Romanticism becomes prospective in its essence. For the twentieth century poet's struggle to reclaim the contingent and confront the "deathly present" of the historical machine has produced a variety of languages securing the possibilities of counternarrative: the language of invisible apocalypse, the language of textual energy, the language of resistant analysis. These languages neither yield to the processing of experience nor seek to escape from it; they enable poetry to seize and narrate a moment in which the "epoch," Schlegel's "universe as object," is glimpsed. Analysis, subversion, reduction—the remoteness of such language from Eichendorff's should not obscure the consistency of purpose among contemporary poets: to reach back to the Romantic source of all modern temporalities, from "Bildung" to modernist countertime, in order to find new translations for the inherited, still-living language of historical narration.

NOTES

Abbreviations

S   *Kritische Friedrich Schlegel Ausgabe,* edited by Ernst Behler with the assistance of Jean-Jacques Anstett and Hans Eichner. Paderborn, Munich, Vienna: Verlag Ferdinand Schöningh; Zürich: Thomas-Verlag, 1963– . Volumes cited: I, II, XII, XVIII, XIX.

N   *Novalis Schriften,* edited by Richard Samuel with the assistance of Hans-Joachim Mähl and Gerhard Schulz. Stuttgart: W. Kohlhammer Verlag, 1960. Volumes cited: II, III (*Das Philosophische Werk* I and II).

Introduction

1. *Das Nachleben der Romantik in der modernen deutschen Literatur.* Second Amherst Colloquium, ed. by Wolfgang Paulsen (Heidelberg: Lothar Stiehm, 1969).

2. Hugo Friedrich, *Die Struktur der modernen Lyrik. Von Baudelaire bis zur Gegenwart.* (Hamburg: Rowohlt, 1956). Werner Vordtriede, *Novalis und die französischen Symbolisten: zur Entstehungsgeschichte des dichterischen Symbols.* (Stuttgart: W. Kohlhammer, 1963). "The quest for 'influences' has become an ungrateful occupation. . . . Nevertheless it would be foolish not to acknowledge that there are sometimes absolute beginnings, just as with Novalis something absolutely modern begins, which has a colossally wide impact." Vordtriede, p. 30. English translations of all German texts are my own, except where noted. German originals of the fragments by Friedrich Schlegel and Novalis, as well as of all poetry, are retained for reference.

3. "Im Roman Religion der Menschen, in Lyrik die der Menschheit. . . . Jeder Mensch hat die ganze Menschheit, die ganze Geschichte in sich; sonst könnte sie nie in ihn kommen. Die Urkunde, das Denkmal ist nur Hülfsmittel der Erfindung. . . . Gott hat die Welt hervorgebracht, um sich selbst darzustellen. . . . Das Individuum ist unendlich, weil es das Unendliche darstellen soll. . . . In der höchsten Ansicht des Menschen ist der Begriff, auf den alles bezogen werden muss, der Begriff der Bildung. . . . Encyklopädie ist identisch mit Historie und den Principien derselben. . . . Im Christentum wird Gott-Mensch; in der neuen Religion wird er durch Bildung Gott. . . . Gott ist ein durch sich selbst unendlich potencirtes Ich." S XVIII, 357, no. 439; S XVIII, 361, no. 489; S XII, 39; S XII, 57; S XVIII, 343, no. 251; S XVIII, 267, no. 872; S XVIII, 108, no. 946.

4. See Raimund Belgardt, *Romantische Poesie; Begriff und Bedeutung bei Fried-*

219

rich Schlegel (Hague: Mouton, 1969); Klaus Briegleb, *Ästhetische Sittlichkeit; Versuch über Friedrich Schlegels Systementwurf zur Begründung der Dichtungskritik* (Tübingen: Niemeyer, 1962); Hans Eichner, *Friedrich Schlegel* (New York: Twayne, 1970); Hans-Joachim Heiner, *Das Ganzheitsdenken Friedrichs Schlegels* (Stuttgart: J. B. Metzler, 1971); Roland Heine, *Transzendentalpoesie: Studien zu Friedrich Schlegel, Novalis und E.T.A. Hoffmann* (Bonn: Bouvier, 1974); Eberhard Huge, *Poesie und Reflexion in der Ästhetik des frühen Friedrich Schlegel* (Stuttgart: J. B. Metzler, 1971); F. N. Mennemeier, *Friedrich Schlegels Poesiebegriff dargestellt anhand der Literaturkritischen Schriften* (Munich: W. Fink, 1971); K. K. Polheim, *Die Arabeske. Ansichten und Ideen aus Friedrich Schlegels Poetik* (Munich, Paderborn, Vienna: Schöningh, 1966); Otto Rothermel, *Friedrich Schlegel und Fichte* (Amsterdam: Swets and Zeitlinger, 1st ed., 1934, 2nd ed., 1968); Helmut Schanze, *Romantik und Aufklärung. Untersuchungen zu Friedrich Schlegel und Novalis* (Nürnberg: Carl, 1966); Heinz-Dieter Weber, *Friedrich Schlegels Transzendentalpoesie* (Munich: W. Fink, 1973).

5. "Der Dichter betet den Zufall an," N III, 449, no. 940.

6. Particularly in his critique of Eduard von Hartmann in section 9 of "Vom Nutzen und Nachteil der Historie für das Leben" (*Unzeitgemässe Betrachtungen*, part 2).

7. "Jedes Kunstwerk, jedes Gedicht sogar ist nur ein synthetischer Bewusstseinsversuch. . . . Die Poesie ist eine unendliche Rhetorik und eine logische geistige Musik." S XVIII, 472, no. 14; S XVIII, 141, no. 232.

8. Manfred Frank, *Das Problem "Zeit" in der deutschen Romantik* (Munich: Winkler, 1972). I am indebted to this book in many ways, particularly for Frank's discussion of the etymological resonance of the term "Ek-stase," "putting out of place," in Romantic theories of time.

9. "Friedrich Schlegel seeks to found a metaphysical realism, a realism that is 'totally transcendent' and 'has to do with the one indivisible whole, the infinite.' He seeks to grasp the infinite unity, the totality, and learns that Kantian discursive thinking can never grasp totalities, but remains caught in the dualism that it is precisely Schlegel's project to overcome. Hence he develops the notions of 'divination,' the capacity for 'enthusiasm' and 'longing,' in order to posit unity as certainty, as the 'reality' which he subsequently endeavors to underpin epistemologically, tries to integrate with empirical life." Rothermel, *Friedrich Schlegel und Fichte*, pp. 34, 36.

Chapter One

1. Frank, *Das Problem "Zeit" in der deutschen Romantik*, pp. 54–55. Clearly this use of the term "Bildung" is to be distinguished sharply from the privatistic tradition described by W. H. Bruford, in *The German Tradition of Self-cultivation: "Bildung" from Humboldt to Thomas Mann* (Cambridge: Cambridge University Press, 1975). Clemens Menze shows how Schlegel's conceptualization of "Bildung" stems directly from his need to overcome the dualism he perceived in Fichte; Schlegel was himself fully aware of the purely "cultural," decorative, bourgeois connotations with which the term was already burdened:

> The definition of Bildung excludes a priori the concept of Bildung that, already in the general consciousness of Friedrich Schlegel's own time, has become a cliché term of cultural criticism, expressing nothing more than unpretentious bourgeois self-cultivation. . . . For Schlegel Bildung is 'progressive,' a ceaseless becoming, infinite unfolding and actualization of the possibilities of human nature, the ultimate goal of which is infinity itself. Therefore every human being, however 'cultivated' he may be, is according to Schlegel 'only a fragment of himself.'

'The destiny of man is to marry the infinite with the finite; complete integration is, however, eternally out of reach.'

Clemens Menze, *Der Bildungsbegriff des jungen Friedrich Schlegel* (Ratingen: A. Henn, 1964), pp. 12, 16.

2. "Eine prächtige Rakete . . . die oben in tausend bunte Sterne spurlos zerplatzte." Joseph von Eichendorff, *Werke und Schriften in vier Bänden* (Stuttgart: J. G. Cotta, n.d.), vol. 4, pp. 244, 428, 453.

3. The premise of Hegel's *Phenomenology of Spirit* (1807) is that the "Bildung of the world" (his phrase) is a central and describable reality.

4. "Entwickelung der Selbständigkeit." S XII, 48.

5. "Mystischen Absicht der Selbstvernichtung in der Bildung." S XVIII, 399, no. 947.

6. "Das Rechte ist schon da und soll nicht noch erst kommen. . . . Die Bildung ist in einer Ansicht ganz da und steht still." S XVIII, 269, no. 890.

7. "Ton, Colorit, Leben Individualität ist nur in Mythologie Physik Historie." S XVIII, 124, no. 23.

8. "Der Satz: die Welt ist unvollendet, geht aus dem Satz hervor: die Welt ist ein Individuum; Raum und Zeit sind die ersten Individua, die organisch produziert sind." S XII, 42.

9. "Streben nach einem Gesetz und Gesetz eines Strebens-BILDUNG." S XVIII, 479, no. 81.

10. "Das Wesen der Bildung besteht darin dass man etwas zur Natur (warum nicht auch zur Welt?) macht und auch zum Menschen. Bildung besteht in Verbindung von Natur und Menschheit. Dieser Begriff hat die grösste Affinität auch mit Gott." S XVIII, 269, no. 897.

11. "Constitution der Menschheit als ein Gegengewicht gegen Empirie und Ökonomie, weil durch diese eben die Menschheit immer zerstückt wird." S XVIII, 301, no. 1276.

12. "Die Menschheit muss constituirt werden; denn eben darin besteht ihr Wesen. So muss auch die Vernunft Progressen machen, sonst ist sie nicht Vernunft." S XVIII, 301, no. 1278.

13. "Das Charakterisieren ist offenbar eben so kritisch als prophetisch und allein der Approximation zum Universum angemessen." S XVIII, 303, no. 1306.

14. "Das Universum vielleicht nur ein Historischer Begriff, der Welt, Menschheit, Vernunft, Natur umfasst." S XVIII, 312, no. 1421.

15. "Das Zeitalter ist das Universum als Objekt, als Incitament und beschränkend—das wahre Universum ist im Innern." S XVIII, 293, no. 1170.

16. S II, 182–83, no. 116.

17. "Der Gipfel der göttlichen Poesie muss auch eine Darstellung des Universums seyn; diese ist aber nicht mehr Poesie noch Philosophie sondern beides." S XVIII, 213, no. 219.

18. "Völlige Gegenwart wäre Todt." S XIX, 58, no. 168.

19. "Annihilation des Jetzigen." N III, 469, no. 1095.

20. "Im Ganzen nur ist das Reelle enthalten, es muss also in einem Moment die Wahrheit des Ganzen sichtbar werden, auch wenn man durch Zusammensetzung der Theile aufs Ganze gekommen ist." S XII, 100.

21. "Nur das Ganze ist real—Nur das Ding wäre absolut real, das nicht wieder Bestandtheil ware. Das Ganze ruht ohngefähr—wie die spielenden Personen, die sich ohne Stuhl, bloss Eine auf der andern Knie kreisförmig hinsetzen." N II, 242, no. 445.

22. "Such an absolute or universal presentness is for us 'outside the realm of the sense,' an empty transcendence to which no reality corresponds. It would be the utopian (in the literal meaning of the word 'placeless') sphere of the golden age realized

through Bildung." Frank, *Das Problem "Zeit" in der deutschen Romantik,* p. 192. It should be stressed that Frank's view of Novalis's temporal thinking is not shared by Hans-Joachim Mähl, who sees Novalis as evolving toward full millenarianism, explicitly mystical transcendence:

> The idea of the golden age embraces in Novalis's work all the hopes of synthesis that originally characterized his thinking and feeling and that can be expressed equally in the concretely historical reform program of the empiricist as it can in the apocalyptic visions of futurity of the mystic and poet, without ultimately signifying anything other than the one great harmonious unity, which at the end of time and history will be revealed to eyes now in darkness as the realm of eternity.

Hans-Joachim Mähl, *Die Idee des goldenen Zeitalters im Werk des Novalis* (Heidelberg: Carl Winter, 1965), p. 328. But to my mind this easy reinsertion of Novalis's ideas into an established, Christian mode of thought is precisely what "romanticizing" ("Romantisierung," his word) precludes. For all their strong involvement with mystical language, Novalis's texts ultimately historicize it.

23. "Man denkt sich unter Thatsache, Handlung hier gewöhnlich, etwas in der Zeit Vorgehendes oder Vorgegangenes. Die Thatsache, von der hier aber die Rede ist, muss schlechterdings rein geistig gedacht werden—nicht einzeln—nicht zeitmässig—quasi als Augenblick, der das ewige Universum umfasst, in sich begreift—worinn wir leben, weben und sind—ein unendliches Factum, was in jedem Augenblick ganz geschieht—identisch ewig wirckendes Genie—Ich seyn." N II, 267, no. 556.

24. "Der Adel des Ich besteht in freyer Erhebung über sich selbst—folglich kann das Ich in gewisser Rücksicht nie absolut erhoben seyn—denn sonst würde seine Wircksamkeit, sein Genuss i.e. sein Sieg—kurz das Ich selbst würde aufhören. . . . Tugend ein ewigsteigender Genuss—position—Gefühl von Kraft—Unabhängigkeit vom Zufälligen." N II, 259, no. 508.

25. "Der Dichter betet den Zufall an." N III, 449, no. 940.

26. "Je persönlicher, localer, temporeller, eigenthümlicher ein Gedicht ist, desto näher steht es dem Centro der Poesie." N III, 664, no. 603.

27. "Der Process der Geschichte ist ein Verbrennen. Die Mathematische Natur verzehrt die Unermessliche." N III, 273, no. 184.

28. "Die Welt ist ein gebundener Gedanke. Wenn sich etwas consolidirt, werden Gedanken frey. Wenn sich etwas auflösst, werden Gedanken gebunden." N III, 595, no. 252.

29. "Einst soll keine Natur mehr seyn. In eine Geisterwelt soll sie allmählich übergehn." N III, 601, no. 291.

30. "Die Natur verändert sich sprungweise." N III, 273, no. 183.

31. "Der Mensch ist ein sich selbst gegebenes historisches Individuum. Graduelle Menschheit. Wenn die Menschheit die höchste Stufe erreicht hat, so offenbart und schliesst das Höhere von selbst sich an." N II, 648, no. 476.

32. "Schlegels übersehn, indem sie von der Absichtlichkeit und Künstlichkeit der Shakespearschen Werke reden—dass die Kunst zur Natur gehört, und gleichsam die sich selbst beschauende, sich selbst nachahmende sich selbst bildende Natur ist. Die Kunst einer gut entwickelten Natur ist freylich von der Künsteley des Verstandes, des bloss räsonnirenden Geistes himmelweit verschieden." N III, 569, no. 94.

33. "Unser Leben ist unvollkommen, weil es Perioden hat. Es sollte nur eine Periode seyn, dann wär's unendlich. Der Relationsprocess ist der Substantielle. Wo mit der Verdichtung Vermehrung verbunden ist, da ist Leben." N III, 329, no. 448.

34. "Man kann durch das künftige Leben das Vergangene Leben retten und veredeln." N III, 303, no. 349.

35. "Die wirkliche Natur ist nicht die ganze Natur. Was einmal dagewesen ist, lebt fort, nur nicht in der wircklichen Natur." N III, 419, no. 776.

36. "Alles ist von selbst ewig. Die Sterblichkeit—Wandelbarkeit ist gerade ein Vorzug höherer Naturen. Ewigkeit ist ein Zeichen geistloser Wesen. Synthesis von Ewigkeit und Zeitlichkeit." N III, 436, no. 869.

37. "Des Dichters Reich sei die Welt, in den Fokus seiner Zeit gedrängt. . . . Er kann alles brauchen, er muss es nur mit Geist amalgamiren, er muss ein Ganzes daraus machen. Das Allgemeine, wie das Besondere muss er darstellen—alle Darstellung ist im Entgegengesetzten und seine Freiheit im Verbinden macht ihn unumschränkt. Alle dichterische Natur ist Natur." N III, 693, no. 705.

38. "Das Buch ist die in Striche (wie Musik) gesezte und complettirte Natur." N III, 368, no. 582.

39. "Je mehr der Mensch seinen Sinn fürs Leben künstlerisch ausbildet, desto mehr interressirt ihn auch die Disharmonie—wegen der Auflösung." N III, 278, no. 224.

40. "Wenn der Philosoph nur alles ordnet, alles stellt, so lösste der Dichter alle Bande auf. Seine Worte sind nicht allgemeine Zeichen—Töne sind es—Zauberworte, die schöne Gruppen um sich her bewegen. . . . Dem Dichter ist die Sprache nie zu arm, aber immer zu allgemein." N II, 533, no. 32.

41. "Spielen ist experimentiren mit dem Zufall." N III, 574, no. 141.

42. Frank, *Das Problem "Zeit" in der deutschen Romantik*, p. 190.

43. "In der Bildung herscht die Natur." S XVIII, 343, no. 264.

44. "Zweck der Kunst ist Bildung zur Natur." S XVIII, 381, no. 720.

45. "Zur Bildung der Erde sind wir berufen." N II, 426, no. 32.

46. Friedrich Sengle, *Biedermeierzeit. Deutsche Literatur im Spannungsfeld zwischen Restauration und Revolution* (Stuttgart: J. B. Metzler, 1971–), 3 vols., esp. vol. 2 (*Die Formenwelt*).

47. Eichendorff, *Werke und Schriften*, vol. 1, p. 106.

48. Ibid., p. 69.

49. Theodor W. Adorno, "Zum Gedächtnis Eichendorffs," *Noten zur Literatur I* (Frankfurt: Suhrkamp, 1958), p. 126.

50. Ibid., p. 127. To see Eichendorff's language as ritually organized, directed toward "Bildung" as a series of textual "acts," is to grasp the difference between his deployment of a limited group of motifs and the concept of repertoire, discussed in Chapter 2 of this book. Thus, central images of the present poem are used in chapter two of *Aus dem Leben eines Taugenichts*: "All that plunged me into an abyss of reflection. I wrapped myself, like a hedgehog, in the quills of my own thoughts. . . . And so I sat, up there in the tree like a night owl, amid the ruins of my fortune the whole night through." The strategies of this language are quite different from those of the poem: we "know" the character, have a referent for "ruins" and respond to the explicit ironies of his perpetually exaggerated behavior.

51. "Eine Welt aus nichts." N II, 581, no. 242.

52. "Die Poësie ist die Jugend unter den Wissenschaften." N III, 321, no. 434.

53. "Die Jugend ist die Poesie des Lebens." Cited by Gerhard Möbus, *Der andere Eichendorff* (Osnabrück: A. Fromm, 1960), p. 133.

54. Eduard Mörike, *Sämtliche Werke* (Munich: Carl Hanser, 1964), pp. 29–30.

55. Renate von Heydebrand, *Eduard Mörikes Gedichtwerk* (Stuttgart: J. B. Metzler, 1972), p. 21.

56. Christiaan Hart Nibbrig, *Verlorene Unmittelbarkeit: Zeiterfahrung und Zeitgestaltung bei Eduard Mörike* (Bonn: Bouvier, 1973), p. 71.

57. Von Heydebrand, *Eduard Mörikes Gedichtwerk*, p. 22.

58. Hart Nibbrig, *Verlorene Unmittelbarkeit*, p. 72.

59. Von Heydebrand, *Eduard Mörikes Gedichtwerk*, p. 20.

60. Hart Nibbrig, *Verlorene Unmittelbarkeit*, p. 6 and passim.

61. Ibid., p. 69.
62. "Alle Erinnerung ist Gegenwart. Im reinern Element wird alle Erinnerung uns wie nothwendige Vordichtung erscheinen." N II, 559, no. 157.
63. Annette von Droste-Hülshoff, *Werke in einem Band* (Munich: Carl Hanser, n.d.), pp. 67–68.
64. Clemens Heselhaus, *Annette von Droste-Hülshoff* (Düsseldorf: August Bagel, 1971), pp. 166ff.
65. Margaret Mare, *Annette von Droste-Hülshoff* (Lincoln: University of Nebraska Press, 1965), p. 128.
66. Ibid.
67. "Der Raum ist die *Fessel* der Natur, aber eben darum die Ursache, dass sie nicht unendlich schnell abläuft. So ist Zeit die Fessel des Geistes, der Schöpfung, ohne welche sie keinen Raum erfüllen würde." S XVIII, 160–61, no. 450.

Chapter Two

1. Manfred Dick, *Die Entwicklung des Gedankens der Poesie in den Fragmenten des Novalis* (Bonn: Bouvier, 1967).
2. "In seiner Wirkung soll das lyrische Gedicht dem Leser . . . zugleich eine Offenbarung und Erlösung, oder mindestens eine Genugtuung gewähren, die er sich selbst nicht hätte geben konnen, sei es nun, dass es unsre Anschauung und Empfindung in ungeahnter Weise erweitert und in die Tiefe führt, oder, was halb bewusst in Duft und Dämmer in uns lag, in überraschender Klarheit erscheinen lässt." Theodor Storm, "Hausbuch aus deutschen Dichtern," *Werke* (Stuttgart: J. G. Cotta, n.d.), vol. 3, p. 510.
3. "Wir sind gar nicht Ich, wir können und sollen aber Ich werden. Wir sind Keime zum Ich-Werden. Wir sollen alles in ein Du, in ein zweytes Ich verwandeln; nur dadurch erheben wir uns selbst zum Grossen Ich, das Eins und Alles zugleich ist." N III, 314, no. 398.
4. Karl Pestalozzi, *Die Entstehung des lyrischen Ich* (Berlin: de Gruyter, 1970), p. 162.
5. "Über den gegenwärtigen Moment, oder den immerwährenden Erstarrungsprocess der irrdischen Zeit. Sie hat eine sonderbare Lebensflamme. Die Zeit macht auch alles, wie sie auch alles zerstört, bindet, trennt. . . . Wir springen, wie ein electrischer Funken, in die Andre Welt hinüber. Zunahme der Capacität. Tod ist Verwandlung, Verdrängung des Individual-Princips, das nun eine neue, haltbarere fähigere Verbindung eingeht." N III, 259, no. 100.
6. Thus Manfred Frank's valuable study of *Das Problem "Zeit"* confines its literary analysis to Tieck's novels.
7. "Der Raum, als Niederschlag aus der Zeit—als nothwendige Folge der Zeit." N III, 564, no. 67.
8. "Zeit ist Potenz von Raum." N III, 66.
9. "Alles ist von selbst ewig. Die Sterblichkeit—Wandelbarkeit ist gerade ein Vorzug höherer Naturen. Ewigkeit ist ein Zeichen geistloser Wesen." N III, 436, no. 869.
10. "Nicht das Wesentliche karacterisirt, nicht die Hauptmassen, sondern das Unwesentliche, Eigenthümliche." N III, 278, no. 222.
11. "Die Welt ist die Sfäre der unvollkommenen Vereinigungen des Geistes und der Natur." N III, 61.
12. "Das Fatum, das uns drückt, ist die Trägheit unsers Geistes. Durch Erweiterung und Bildung unsrer Thätigkeit werden wir uns selbst in das Fatum verwandeln." N II, 583, no. 248.
13. "Ich ist kein Naturproduct—keine Natur—kein historisches Wesen—sondern ein artistisches—eine Kunst—ein Kunstwerck." N III, 253, no. 76.

14. Theodor Storm, *Gesammelte Werke* (Zürich: Bühl-Verlag, 1945), vol. 1, p. 109.

15. Gottfried Keller, *Gesammelte Gedichte* (Bern and Leipzig: Benteli, 1931), vol. 1, p. 69.

16. "Die Gemeinschaft und Eigenthümlichkeit. Alles kann Ich seyn und ist Ich oder soll Ich seyn." N III, 430, no. 820.

17. "Instinkt oder Genie heissen wir sie, sie ist überall *vorher.* Sie ist die Fülle der Zukunft, die Zeitenfülle überhaupt—in der Zeit, was der Stein der Weisen im Raum ist: Vernunft, Fantasie, Verstand und Sinn sind nur ihre einzelnen Funktionen." N III, 462, no. 1036.

18. "Die Natur ist nichts als lauter Vergangenheit, ehemalige Freiheit, daher durchaus Boden der Geschichte." N III, 580, no. 197.

19. "Wenn unser körperliches Leben ein Verbrennen ist, so ist wol auch unser geistiges Leben eine Combustion . . . Der Tod also vielleicht eine Veränderung der Capacität." N III, 559, no. 26.

20. "Alles Leben ist ein überschwenglicher Erneuerungsprozess, der nur von der Seite den Schein eines Vernichtungsprozesses hat." N II, 556, no. 135.

21. C. F. Meyer, *Sämtliche Werke* (Bern: Benteli, 1963), vol. 1, p. 121.

22. Jürgen Fährmann, *Bildwelt und Symbolische Gestaltung in der Dichtung Conrad Ferdinand Meyers* (Diss, Freiburg, 1964), p. 71.

23. Heinrich Henel, *Gedichte Conrad Ferdinand Meyers: Wege ihrer Vollendung* (Tübingen: Niemeyer, 1962), pp. 158–59.

24. Paul de Man, "The Rhetoric of Temporality," in *Interpretation: Theory and Practice,* ed. by Charles S. Singleton (Baltimore: Johns Hopkins Press, 1969), pp. 173–209.

25. "Das Individuum wird das Vollkommenste, das rein Systematische sein, das nur durch einen einzigen absoluten Zufall individualisirt ist, z.B. durch seine Geburt. In diesem Zufall müssen alle seine übrige Zufälle . . . als seine Zufälle, seine Zustände determinirt sein. . . . Je grösser der Dichter, desto weniger Freiheit erlaubt er sich, desto philosophischer ist er. Er begnügt sich mit der willkührlichen Wahl des ersten Moments. . . . Jeder Keim ist eine Dissonanz, ein Missverhältnis, was sich nach gerade ausgleichen soll." N II, 579–81, no, 242.

26. "Unser Leben ist kein Traum, aber es soll und wird vielleicht einer werden." N III, 281, no. 237.

27. "Manches kann nur Einmal erscheinen, weil das Einmal zu seinem Wesen gehört. Unser Leben ist absolut und abhängig zugleich. Wir sterben nur gewissermaassen. Unser Leben muss also z.T. Glied eines Grössern, gemeinschaftlichen Lebens seyn." N II, 607, no. 66.

28. "Unser Geist soll sinnlich wahrnehmbare Maschine werden, nicht in uns, aber ausser uns." N III, 252, no. 69.

Chapter Three

1. Frank Kermode, *The Sense of an Ending* (New York: Oxford University Press, 1967), p. 77 and passim.

2. *Literaturrevolution,* the appropriate title of Paul Pörtner's essential anthology of Expressionist theory. (Neuwied and Berlin: Luchterhand, vol. 1, 1960; vol. 2, 1961).

3. "Die Natur ist das Bild der werdenden Gottheit." S XII, 54.

4. "Bildung ist gewissermassen Beschränkung." S XVIII, 23, no. 57.

5. "Die einzige reine Irrthumsfreie Anschauung ist die der Ichheit; das Wesen der Ichheit aber so wie es angeschaut wird, ist Erinnrung." S XIX, 62, no. 212.

6. "Die ganze Menschheit ist angelegt auf den einen Moment der Selbstzerstörung." S XVIII, 394, no. 891.

7. S XII, 479.

8. "Es gibt zweierlei Ewigkeit durch Vernichtung der Pole (der Zukunft und Vergangenheit) und durch Vernichtung der Gegenwart—als der bindenden hemmenden Indifferenz. Völlige Gegenwart wäre Todt. Ewigkeit ist unendliche Zeitfülle nicht Zeitabwesenheit." S XIX, 58, no. 169.

9. "Basis einer ewigen Revoluzion (Christus führt immer noch Krieg). Das Chaos was bisher in der modernen Welt bewusstlos und passiv war, muss activ wiederkommen; ewige Revoluzion. . . . Der Stand der Natur ist Verehrung des Chaos und Poesie ist der Stand der Natur." S XVIII, 254, nos. 730, 734.

10. "Wahrscheinlichkeit einer grossen *Revolution im Bewusstsein* im Augenblick des Todes." S XIX, 100, no. 176.

11. "Der Mensch ist *Geist und Wort* in jeder Potenz. Der Mensch ist eine Zahl. . . . Jeder Augenblick gränzt so an eine unbekannte Ewigkeit, wie der Augenblick des Todes. . . . Nicht die Dinge aber die Menschen sind Zahlen und alle Dinge sind Menschen." S XVIII, 326, nos. 16, 17, 19.

12. "Wir empfinden nichts als Tätigkeit, wir schauen nichts an als Wechselwirkung—wir stellen nur im Raume vor, wir begreifen nur in der Zeit. . . . Wahrheit bezieht sich auf Verhältnisse nicht auf die Dinge." S XVIII, 410, nos. 1075, 1076.

13. "Die letzte Revolution der Welt wird eine unendliche Geburth sein; sie selbst dann eine ewige Zeugung, in der alle ehemaligen Zeugungen wieder kommen. Tod—die letzte Geburth." S XVIII, 192, no. 785.

14. "Aus Chaos und Allegorie die Welt zu construiren." S XVIII, 422, no. 1226.

15. "Die Zeit richtig zu construiren ist eine magische Kunst." S XVIII, 169, no. 541.

16. "Im Raum umgiebt uns vielleicht das Ideal der Zeit. In dem Fantasiren könnte etwa eine formlose Form construirt werden." S XVIII, 397, no. 920.

17. "Ursprung des Chaos aus der Liebe." S XVIII, 254, no. 734.

18. Ludwig Rubiner, "Der Mensch in der Mitte" (1917), in *Literaturrevolution*, vol. 1, p. 72.

19. Hugo Ball, "Die Kunst unserer Tage, Vortrag über Kandinsky" (1916), in *Literaturrevolution*, vol. 1, p. 137.

20. Ibid., pp. 137–38.

21. Rudolf Pannwitz, "Die Kunst unserer Zukunft" (1918), in *Literaturrevolution*, vol. 2, p. 62.

22. Martin Heidegger, *Nietzsche* (Pfullingen: Neske, 1961), vol. 2, p. 62.

23. "Unmöglich bleibt absolutes Gleichgewicht zwischen Idealismus und Realismus dem Menschen. Die Harmonie muss immer dadurch entstehn, dass eins das andere verschlucke, das Verschluckende dominirt stets über das Verschluckte." S XVIII, 307, no. 1368.

24. Hugo Ball, "Die Kunst unserer Tage," pp. 138–39.

25. S XVIII, 421, no. 1226.

26. Clemens Heselhaus, *Deutsche Lyrik der Moderne von Nietzsche bis Yvan Goll* (Düsseldorf: August Bagel, 1962), pp. 146ff.

27. Heidegger, *Nietzsche*, vol. 2, p. 33: "Nihilism is the history of Being itself, through which the death of the Christian god slowly but irresistibly enters reality."

28. Heidegger, "Georg Trakl. Eine Erörterung seines Gedichtes," *Merkur* 61 (1953), pp. 226–58.

29. "Alles, was wir erfahren, ist eine Mittheilung. So ist die Welt in der That eine Mitteilung. Offenbarung des Geistes. Die Zeit ist nicht mehr, wo der Geist Gottes verständlich war. Der Sinn der Welt ist verlohren gegangen. Wir sind beim Buchstaben

stehn geblieben. . . . Die Bedeutung der Hieroglyphe fehlt. Wir leben noch von der Frucht besserer Zeiten." N II, 594, no. 316.

30. "Die wahre Hieroglyphe ist eine Analogie über das Universum, eine Approximazion zu demselben in Religiöser Form." S XVIII, 311, no. 1412.

31. "Gefühl in den Augenblicken totenähnlichen Seins: Alle Menschen sind der Liebe wert." Georg Trakl, *Dichtungen und Briefe*, ed. by Walther Killy and Hans Szklenar (Salzburg: Otto Müller, 1969), vol. 1, p. 463.

32. Rainer Maria Rilke, *Sämtliche Werke*, vol. I (Wiesbaden: Insel-Verlag, 1955), p. 461. The poem is from *Das Buch der Bilder*, book II, part 2.

33. "Leurs yeux, d'où la divine étincelle est partie,/Comme s'ils regardaient au loin, restent levés/Au ciel; on ne les voit jamais vers les pavés/Pencher rêveusement leur tête appesantie." "Il n'était pas voûté, mais cassé, son échine/Faisant avec sa jambe un parfait angle droit." Charles Baudelaire, *Les Fleurs du Mal*, with translations by Richard Howard (Boston: David R. Godine, 1983). "Les Aveugles," pp. 97, 275; "Les Sept Vieillards," pp. 92, 270.

34. Rilke, *Werke*, vol. II, p. 77.

35. Georg Heym, *Dichtungen und Schriften*, ed. by Karl Ludwig Schneider (Hamburg: Ellermann, 1964), vol. 1, pp. 511–12.

36. "Der ganze Markt schien eine einzige, dicht zusammengedrängte Volksmasse, so dass man glauben musste, ein dazwischengeworfener Apfel könne niemals zur Erde gelangen. . . . 'Dieser Markt,' sprach der Vetter, 'ist auch jetzt ein treues Abbild des ewig wechselnden Lebens. Rege Tätigkeit, das Bedürfnis des Augenblicks, trieb die Menschenmasse zusammen; in wenigen Augenblicken ist alles verödet, die Stimmen, welche im wirren Getöse durcheinanderströmten, sind verklungen, und jede verlassene Stelle spricht das schauerliche: Es war! nur zu lebhaft aus.'" E.T.A. Hoffmann, *Späte Werke* (Darmstadt: Wissenschaftliche Buchgesellschaft, 1965), pp. 599, 621.

37. Heym, *Dichtungen und Schriften*, vol. 1, p. 443.

38. Ibid., p. 349.

39. Trakl, *Dichtungen und Briefe*, vol. 1, pp. 132–33.

40. "Die Bäume hingen in dem zauberhaften Schein wie wallende Wolken auf ihren Stämmen, und die Wohnungen der Menschen waren in dunkle Felsengestalten und dämmernde Geisterpaläste verwandelt. Die Menschen, nicht mehr vom Sonnenglanze geblendet, wohnten mit ihren Blicken am Firmamente, und ihre Seelen spiegelten sich schon in dem himmlischen Scheine der Mondnacht." "Da klangen alle Sterne und dröhnten einen hellstrahlenden, himmlischen Ton durch die Lüfte, bis der Genius sich in das unendliche Firmament verlor." W. H. Wackenroder, *Werke und Briefe* (Heidelberg: Lambert Schneider, 1967), pp. 197–202.

41. "Die construierten Werke der Poesie sind in der Tat eine Bibel." S XVIII, 313, no. 1441.

42. "Ist das Potenziren und Combiniren etwa identisch? Im Potenziren combinirt man die Quantität mit sich selbst." S XVIII, 405, no. 1011.

43. "Soll der Mensch die Welt verändern wollen? Kann und darf das sein Zweck sein? Der Gegenstand des Menschen in logischer Rucksicht ist nur die Menschheit. Sie soll ein Individuum werden. *Totalität* soll er in sich, *Individualität* in der Menschheit bewirken." S XVIII, 338, no. 191.

Chapter Four

1. Walter Benjamin, "The Work of Art in the Age of Mechanical Reproduction" (1936), in *Illuminations*, trans. by Harry Zohn (New York: Schocken, 1969), p. 236.

2. "Das Bewusstsein des Unendlichen muss constituirt werden—indem wir das

Gegentheil annihiliren. Constituiren muss man sich durch einen Act, und dieser ist kein andrer als die Vernichtung jener Einbildung des Endlichen." S XVIII, 412, no. 1095. See also S XII, 11: "Der Schein des Endlichen soll vernichtet werden; und um das zu thun, muss alles Wissen in einen revoluzionären Zustand gesetzt werden." [The appearance of the finite is to be destroyed; and in order to achieve that, all knowledge must be recast into a revolutionary state.]

3. "In der Theorie der Welt nichts nöthig als Masse und Raum zu vernichten und alles auf Zeit und Thätigkeit zu reduciren." S XVIII, 404, no. 1002.

4. "Der Raum ist fixirte, gestörte verwesste, todte Zeit." S XVIII, 175, no. 594.

5. Marshall Brown, *The Shape of German Romanticism* (Ithaca, N.Y.: Cornell University Press, 1979), p. 195.

6. "Das absolute Gedicht—nein, das gibt es gewiss nicht, das kann es nicht geben!" Paul Celan, "Der Meridian," in *Ausgewählte Gedichte. Zwei Reden,* ed. by Beda Allemann (Frankfurt am Main: Suhrkamp, 1968), p. 145.

7. Hans Magnus Enzensberger, introductory essay to *Museum der modernen Poesie* (Frankfurt: Suhrkamp, 1960), p. 13.

8. Wallace Stevens, *The Palm at the End of Mind,* ed. by Holly Stevens (New York: Alfred A. Knopf, 1971), pp. 338–39.

9. Gottfried Benn, *Gesammelte Werke in acht Bänden,* ed. by Dieter Wellershoff (Wiesbaden: Limes Verlag, 1968), vol. 4, pp. 1087–88.

10. "Das Gegenwort . . . ein Akt der Freiheit." Celan, *Ausgewählte Gedichte,* p. 135.

11. Dietlind Meinecke, *Wort und Name bei Paul Celan: zur Widerruflichkeit des Gedichts* (Bad Homburg: Gehlen, 1970), p. 50.

12. "Das Gedicht wird. . . . Gespräch. . . . Erst im Raum dieses Gesprachs konstituiert sich das Angesprochene, versammelt es sich um das es ansprechende und nennende Ich. Aber in diese Gegenwart bringt das Angesprochene und durch Nennung gleichsam zum Du Gewordene auch sein Anderssein mit. Noch im Hier und Jetzt des Gedichts—das Gedicht selbst hat ja immer nur diese eine, einmalige, punktuelle Gegenwart—, noch in dieser Unmittelbarkeit und Nähe lässt es das ihm, dem Anderen, Eigenste mitsprechen: dessen Zeit." Celan, *Ausgewählte Gedichte,* pp. 144–45.

13. Enzensberger, *Museum der modernen Poesie,* pp. 11–12.

14. "Das Gedicht ist die Antiware schlechthin." Ibid., p. 15.

15. Benn, *Werke,* vol. 1, pp. 233–34.

16. "Geschichtsbildend sind nicht die Kriege, sondern die Kunst. . . . Auch die Kunst ist Entsagung, aber eine Entsagung, die alles empfängt." Ibid., vol 3, p. 953.

17. "Die Dichtung bessert nicht, aber sie tut etwas viel Entscheidenderes: sie verändert. Sie hat keine geschichtlichen Ansatzkräfte, sie wirkt anders: Sie hebt die Zeit und die Geschichte auf, ihre Wirkung geht auf die Gene, die Erbmasse, die Substanz— ein langer innerer Weg. . . . Sie bringt ins Strömen, wo es verhärtet und stumpf und müde war, in ein Strömen, das verwirrt und nicht zu verstehen ist, das aber an Wüste gewordene Ufer Keime streut, Keime des Glücks und Keime der Trauer." Ibid., vol. 4, p. 1157.

18. "In der Mystik erscheint die Welt als *Nichts.* In der Mythologie als *Spiel,* als *Poesie.* Das ist die positive und höchste Ansicht.—Diese allein ist anwendbar, aber ohne den Grund jener hält sie nicht Stich." S XVIII, 359, no. 467.

19. Celan, *Gedichte* (Frankfurt am Main: Suhrkamp, 1975), vol. 1, pp. 280–81. Originally in *Die Niemandsrose* (1963).

20. "Der Künstler ist ein geistig menschenverzehrendes Wesen. Ganze Massen von Geisterblüthen und Keimen verschlingt er in einem Augenblick. Er fühlt immer etwas Höheres als Mitgefühl." S XVIII, 318, no. 1506.

21. "Wo ewige unabänderliche Gesetze walten, da ist Alterthum, Vergangenheit.

Der Process der Geschichte ist ein Verbrennen. Die Mathematische Natur verzehrt die Unermessliche." N III, 273, no. 184.

22. Meinecke, *Wort und Name bei Paul Celan*, p. 72.

23. "Aber es sind ja zugleich auch, unter wie vielen anderen Wegen, Wege, auf denen die Sprache stimmhaft wird, es sind Begegnungen, Wege einer Stimme zu einem wahrnehmenden Du, kreatürliche Wege, Daseinsentwürfe vielleicht, ein Sichvorausschicken zu sich selbst, auf der Suche nach sich selbst.... Eine Art Heimkehr." Celan, *Ausgewählte Gedichte*, p. 147.

24. Meinecke, *Wort und Name bei Paul Celan*, p. 152.

25. "Alles aus Nichts erschaffne Reale, wie z.b. die Zahlen und die abstracten Ausdrücke—hat eine wunderbare Verwandtschaft mit Dingen einer andern Welt—mit unendlichen Reihen sonderbarer Combinationen und Verhältnissen—gleichsam mit einer mathematischen und abstracten Welt an sich—mit einer poëtischen mathematischen und abstracten Welt." N III, 440–41, no. 898.

26. "Selbstbewusstseyn im grössern Sinn ist eine Aufgabe—ein Ideal—es wäre der Zustand, worinn es keine Zeitfortschreitung gäbe, ein zeitloser—beharrlicher immer gleicher Zustand." N III, 431, no. 832.

27. Friedrich Kluge, *Etymologisches Wörterbuch* (Berlin: de Gruyter, 1967), p. 461.

28. Hans Magnus Enzensberger, *Landessprache* (Frankfurt am Main: Suhrkamp, 1960), p. 24.

29. Enzensberger, *Einzelheiten* (Frankfurt am Main: Suhrkamp, 1962), p. 272.

30. Hans Egon Holthusen, "Hans Magnus Enzensberger," in *Die Deutsche Lyrik 1945–1975*, ed. by Klaus Weissenberger (Düsseldorf: August Bagel, 1981), p. 340.

31. Enzensberger, *Brentanos Poetik* (Munich: Carl Hanser, 1961).

32. "Die Einheit des Fragments ist Individualität, Charakteristik ist Historisches Fragment. Die Charakteristik des Individuums steht im Verhältniss mit der Charakteristik des Universums; jeder Mensch ein Mikrokosmus." S XVIII, 69, no. 488.

33. "Wenn man die Geschichte der Revoluzion erst besser versteht, muss sich auch die Entstehung der Erde und Menschen historisch begreifen lassen." S XVIII, 331, no. 89.

34. Enzensberger, "An alle fernsprechteilnehmer," Selbstinterpretation, in *Doppelinterpretationen*, ed. by Hilde Domin (Frankfurt am Main: Athenaum, 1966), p. 175.

35. Holthusen, "Hans Magnus Enzensberger," p. 335.

36. Enzensberger, "Poesie und Politik," in *Einzelheiten*, p. 350.

37. Enzensberger, "Schaum," *Landessprache*, p. 35.

38. Walter Benjamin, *Illuminations*, pp. 257–58.

Chapter Five

1. Jürgen Theobaldy and Gustav Zürcher, *Veränderung der Lyrik: Über westdeutsche Gedichte seit 1965* (Munich: edition text + kritik, 1976), p. 136.

2. "Alle Dinge haben eine Centrifugaltendenz; Centripetal werden sie durch den Geist, dort wirkt der Geist gegen jene natürliche Neigung der Organe und zwingt sie, sich zu Einer Bildung zu vereinigen, um Einen Punct her zu konsolidiren; er bildet eine Welt aus nichts." N II, 581, no. 242.

3. "Wir wissen etwas nur, insofern wir es ausdrücken, i.e. machen konnen. Je fertiger und mannichfacher wir etwas produciren, ausführen können, desto besser wissen wir es. Wir wissen es vollkommen, wenn wir es überall und auf alle Art mittheilen, erregen können, einen individuellen Ausdruck desselben in jedem Organ bewircken können." N II, 589, no. 267.

4. Erich Fried, *Das Nahe Suchen* (Berlin: Verlag Klaus Wagenbach, 1982), p. 76.

5. Günter Herburger, "Dogmatisches über Gedichte," in *Was alles hat Platz in einem Gedicht?* ed. by Hans Bender and Michael Kruger (Munich: Carl Hanser, 1977), p. 76.

6. "Eben weil die Poesie das Allgegenwärtigste, das Alldurchdringendste ist, begreifen wir sie schwerer, so wie wir die Luft, in welcher wir atmen und leben, nicht insbesondere wahrnehmen." August Wilhelm Schlegel, "Poesie" (1802), in *Über Literatur, Kunst und Geist des Zeitalters,* ed. by Franz Finke (Stuttgart: Reclam, 1964), pp. 97–98.

7. Jörg Drews, "Selbsterfahrung und Neue Subjektivität in der Lyrik," in *Lyrik-Katalog Bundesrepublik,* ed. by Jan Hans, Uwe Herms, Ralf Thenior (Munich: Goldmann, 1978), p. 457.

8. Jürgen Theobaldy, "Literaturkritik, astrologisch," in *Lyrik-Katalog Bundesrepublik,* pp. 463–67.

9. "Sehr bedeutend ist der Ausdruck, die Freiheit sei ein *Unding;* sie ist auch das einzige *Nicht und Gegending.*" S XIX, 115, no. 301.

10. "Nur das Einzelne ist nothwendig das Ganze ist frey." S XVIII, 409, no. 1063.

11. "Die Freiheit besteht in der Anerkennung der Nothwendigkeit (ausser uns) und in der *Vernichtung des Zufalls* in uns." S XVIII, 565, no. 61.

12. Nicolas Born, "Nachbemerkungen zu dem Band *Das Auge des Entdeckers,*" in *Was alles hat Platz in einem Gedicht?* p. 146.

13. Ibid., pp. 147–48.

14. "Nicht die Erfahrung ist die Gränze unsrer Erkenntniss; aber *in* der Erfahrung giebt es bestimmte Gränzen der Erkenntniss. Aber Gränze ist nicht absolut, sondern nur relativ. So können wir nicht erkennen einen Zustand der dem unsrigen zunächst entgegengesezt ist; aus der jetzigen sich ruhig entwickelnden Epoche der Erdkraft reichen fast keine Analogien auf den revoluzionären Zustand derselben; so ist uns oft dasjenige dunkel, wovon wir selbst ganz (praktisch und lebendig) befangen sind." S XIX, 120, no. 348.

15. Arno Reinfrank, "Zur Poesie der Fakten," in *Lyrik-Katalog Bundesrepublik,* p. 418.

16. Jürgen Becker, "Im Frühling," in *Das Ende der Landschaftsmalerei* (Frankfurt: Suhrkamp, 1974), p. 32.

17. Ibid., p. 43.

18. Marianne Kesting, "Beckers *Umgebungen,*" in *Über Jürgen Becker,* ed. by Leo Kreutzer (Frankfurt: Suhrkamp, 1972), p. 101.

19. Jürgen Becker interview, in Kreutzer, *Über Jürgen Becker,* p. 43.

20. Ibid., p. 25.

21. Becker, 1971 interview, in Kreutzer, *Über Jürgen Becker,* p. 43.

22. Jürgen Becker, "Anderes Jahr, andere Jahre," in *Erzähl mir nichts vom Krieg* (Frankfurt am Main: Suhrkamp, 1977), p. 72.

23. Rolf Dieter Brinkmann, "Diese Blöcke der Jahreszeiten," in *Westwärts 1 und 2. Gedichte* (Hamburg: Rowohlt, 1975), p. 81.

24. Christoph Meckel, "Epoche," in *Wen es angeht* (Düsseldorf: Verlag Eremitenpresse, 1974), p. 24.

25. Wulf Segebrecht, "Nachwort" to Meckel's *Verschiedene Tätigkeiten* (Stuttgart: Reclam, 1972), pp. 80–82.

26. Christoph Meckel, "Talking about Poetry," in *Verschiedene Tätigkeiten,* p. 48.

27. Meckel, *Ausgewählte Gedichte 1955–1978* (Königstein/Ts.: Athenäum, 1979), p. 43.

28. Meckel, *Werkauswahl*, ed. by Wilhelm Unverhau (Munich: Nymphenburger Verlagshandlung, 1971), p. 6.
29. Meckel, "Gedicht in Ermangelung eines Besseren," in *Lyrik-Katalog Bundesrepublik*, pp. 409–10.
30. Meckel, *Ausgewählte Gedichte*, p. 99.
31. Meckel, "Ode an mächtige Mannschaften," self-interpretation, in *Doppelinterpretationen*, pp. 262–65.
32. Meckel, *Wen es angeht*, pp. 46–47.
33. Karin Kiwus, "Nebenwirkung," in *Angenommen Später: Gedichte* (Frankfurt am Main: Suhrkamp, 1979), pp. 24–25.
34. Sylvia Plath, *Ariel* (New York: Harper and Row, 1966), p. 54.
35. "Mein Körper würde mir nicht specifisch vom Ganzen verschieden, sondern nur als eine Variation desselben vorkommen. Meine Erkenntniss des Ganzen würde also den Character der Analogie haben—diese würde sich aber auf das innigste und unmittelbarste auf die direkte und absolute Erkenntniss des Gliedes beziehn. . . . Ich kann etwas nur erfahren, in so fern ich es in mir aufnehme; es ist also eine Alienation meiner selbst, und eine Zueignung oder Verwandlung einer andern Substanz in die meinige zugleich. . . . Ich unterscheide so viel Erkenntniss-Kräfte in mir, als es wirckende Kräfte dort gibt. . . . Ich selbst weis mich, wie ich mich will, und will mich, wie ich mich weis. . . . In mir ist also Wissen und Willen vollkommen vereinigt." N II, 551–52, no. 118.
36. "Die Epidemien des Geistes hat man noch gar nicht recht medicinisch betrachtet. Die Geschichte der Menschheit umfasst bloss den Ursprung, das Ende und die Universalität der Menschheit.—Die einzige Art, den thierischen Menschen zu moralisiren, ist die aesthetische Behandlung." S XVIII, 268, no. 879.
37. "Die Schwere ist das Isolirende und das Isolirte in der Natur. Der Mittelpunkt zwischen Licht und Schwere ist nicht ein leerer sondern die organisirteste Organisation—So auch der Mittelpunkt der Poesie zwischen Vernunft und Unvernunft." S XVIII, 163, no. 474.
38. "Der Traum ist Reaction des Korpers, der dann herscht; eben darum dürften sich im Traum die Geheimnisse der Organisation und selbst der Seele spiegeln." [The dream is a response of the body, which then takes control; for that very reason the secrets of human organization and even the soul are probably encoded in the dream.] S XVIII, 335, no. 148.

SELECTED BIBLIOGRAPHY

Note: This bibliography offers a concise guide to recent criticism on topics discussed in the present study. Primary texts are not listed. For works on Schlegel and Novalis, see note 4 of the Introduction. Each poet is listed separately, except for those discussed in Chapter 5, for whom a fuller bibliographical context seems appropriate.

German Romanticism and Poetics

Benjamin, Walter. *Illuminations.* Edited by Hannah Arendt. Translated by Harry Zohn. New York: Schocken, 1969.

Berman, Antoine. "La Bildung et l'exigence de la traduction." In *L'épreuve de l'étranger,* by Antoine Berman, pp. 72–86. Paris: Gallimard, 1984.

Brown, Marshall. *The Shape of German Romanticism.* Ithaca, N.Y.: Cornell University Press, 1979.

Bruford, W. H. *The German Tradition of Self-cultivation: "Bildung" from Humboldt to Thomas Mann.* Cambridge: Cambridge University Press, 1975.

Corngold, Stanley. "Heidegger's *Being and Time:* Implications for Poetics." In *The Fate of the Self: German Writers and French Theory,* by Stanley Corngold, pp. 197–218. New York: Columbia University Press, 1986.

Dällenbach, Lucien, and Christiaan L. Hart Nibbrig, eds. *Fragment und Totalität.* Frankfurt: Suhrkamp, 1984.

de Man, Paul. "The Rhetoric of Temporality" (1969). In *Blindness and Insight,* by Paul de Man, pp. 187–228. 2nd ed. Minneapolis: University of Minnesota Press, 1983. [Includes also "Literary History and Literary Modernity" and "Lyric and Modernity."]

Dick, Manfred. *Die Entwicklung des Gedankens der Poesie in den Fragmenten des Novalis.* Bonn: Bouvier, 1967.

Dischner, Gisela, and Richard Faber, eds. *Romantische Utopie—Utopische Romantik.* Hildescheim: Gerstenberg, 1979.

Enzensberger, Hans Magnus. *Brentanos Poetik.* Munich: Hanser, 1961.

Foucault, Michel. *The Archaeology of Knowledge.* New York: Harper and Row, 1972.

Frank, Manfred. *Das Problem "Zeit" in der deutschen Romantik.* Munich: Winkler, 1972.

Friedrich, Hugo. *The Stucture of Modern Poetry.* Translated by Joachim Neugroschel. Evanston, Ill.: Northwestern University Press, 1984.

Furst, Lilian R. *Fictions of Romantic Irony.* Cambridge, Mass.: Harvard University Press, 1984.

Gray, Ronald. *German Poetry: A Guide to Free Appreciation.* Cambridge: Cambridge University Press, 1976.

Hanke, Amala M. *Spatiotemporal Consciousness in English and German Romanticism: A Comparative Study of Novalis, Blake, Wordsworth and Eichendorff.* Bern and Frankfurt: Lang, 1981.

Heidegger, Martin. *Nietzsche.* Translated by David Farrell Krell. New York: Harper and Row, 1979.

Heselhaus, Clemens. *Deutsche Lyrik der Moderne von Nietzsche bis Yvan Goll.* Düsseldorf: Bagel, 1962.

Kermode, Frank. *The Sense of an Ending.* New York: Oxford University Press, 1967.

Mähl, Hans-Joachim. *Die Idee des goldenen Zeitalters im Werk des Novalis.* Heidelberg: Winter, 1965.

Menhennet, Alan. *The Romantic Movement.* Totowa, N.J.: Barnes and Noble, 1981.

Neubauer, John. *Symbolismus und symbolische Logik: Die Idee der Ars Combinatoria in der Entwicklung der modernen Dichtung.* Munich: Fink, 1978.

Neumann, Bernd H. *Die kleinste poetische Einheit: Semantisch-poetologische Untersuchungen an Hand der Lyrik von C. F. Meyer, Arno Holz, August Stramm und Helmut Heissenbüttel.* Cologne and Vienna: Böhlau, 1977.

Paulsen, Wolfgang, ed. *Das Nachleben der Romantik in der modernen deutschen Literatur.* Heidelberg: Stiehm, 1969.

Pestalozzi, Karl. *Die Entstehung des lyrischen Ich.* Berlin: de Gruyter, 1970.

Pörtner, Paul, ed. *Literaturrevolution.* 2 vols. Neuwied and Berlin: Luchterhand, 1960–61.

Prawer, S. S. *German Lyric Poetry.* New York: Barnes and Noble, 1965.

Rey, William H. *Poesie der Antipoesie.* Heidelberg: Stiehm, 1978.

Rolleston, James. "Nietzsche, Expressionism and Modern Poetics." *Nietzsche-Studien* 9 (1980): 285–301.

Sengle, Friedrich. *Biedermeierzeit. Deutsche Literatur im Spannungsfeld zwischen Restauration und Revolution,* 3 vols. Stuttgart: Metzler, 1971– .

Staiger, Emil. *Die Zeit als Einbildungskraft des Dichters.* Zurich: Atlantis, 1938.

Steffen, Hans, ed. *Die deutsche Romantik: Poetik, Formen und Motive.* Göttingen: Vandenhoeck und Ruprecht, 1967.

Thalmann, Marianne. *The Literary Sign Language of German Romanticism.* Translated by Harold A. Basilius. Detroit: Wayne State University Press, 1972.

Träger, Claus. "Geschichtlichkeit und Erbe der Romantik." In *Studien zur Erbetheorie und Erbeaneignung,* by Claus Träger. Frankfurt: Röderberg, 1982.

Vordtriede, Werner. *Novalis und die französischen Symbolisten.* Stuttgart: Kohlhammer, 1963.

Willson, A. Leslie, ed. *German Romantic Criticism.* New York: Continuum, 1982.

Ziolkowski, Theodore. *The Classical German Elegy, 1795–1950.* Princeton: Princeton University Press, 1980.

Contemporary German Poetry

Bekes, Peter, ed. *Deutsche Gegenwartslyrik: von Biermann bis Zahl.* Munich: Fink, 1982.

Bender, Hans, and Michael Krüger, eds. *Was alles hat Platz in einem Gedicht?* Munich: Hanser, 1977. [Includes essays by Peter Hamm, Günter Herburger, Helmut Heissenbüttel, Nicolas Born.]

Born, Nicolas. *Die Welt der Maschine.* Edited by Rolf Haufs. Hamburg: Rowohlt, 1980.

Domin, Hilde, ed. *Doppelinterpretationen*. Frankfurt: Athenäum, 1969.
――――. *Nachkrieg und Unfrieden: Gedichte als Index, 1945–1970*. Neuwied and Berlin: Luchterhand, 1970.
Durzak, Manfred, ed. *Die deutsche Literatur der Gegenwart*. 4th ed. Stuttgart: Reclam, 1981. [Includes essays by Heinrich Vormweg, Hans Dieter Schäfer, Jost Hermand.]
Griesmayer, Norbert. "Lyrik und 'reflektierende Sprachbetrachtung.' " In *Gegenwartsliteratur als Bildungswert*, edited by Alois Brandstetter, pp. 6–30. Vienna: Bundesverlag, 1982.
Gutzschhahn, Uwe-Michael. *Prosa und Lyrik Christoph Meckels*. Cologne: Braun, 1979.
Hans, Jan; Uwe Therms; and Ralf Thenior, eds. *Lyrik-Katalog Bundesrepublik*. Munich: Goldmann, 1978. [Includes essays by Jörg Drews, Jürgen Theobaldy, Arno Reinfrank.]
Heise, Hans-Jürgen. "Die vom Sachdenken vereinnahmte Phantasie." In *Neue deutsche Hefte* 27 (1980): 560–75.
Hinck, Walter, ed. *Gedichte und Interpretationen 6: Gegenwart*. Stuttgart: Reclam, 1983. [Includes readings of poems by Becker, Meckel, and Kiwus.]
Höllerer, Walter, ed. *Dokumente zur Poetik 1: Theorie der modernen Lyrik*. Hamburg: Rowohlt, 1965.
Jordan, Lothar; Axel Marquardt; and Winfried Woesler, eds. *Lyrik—von allen Seiten*. Frankfurt: Fischer, 1981. [Includes essays by Walter Höllerer, Bernhard Böschenstein, Hans Dieter Schaefer.]
――――. *Lyrik-Blick Über die Grenzen*. Frankfurt: Fischer, 1984. [Includes essays by Karl Otto Conrady, Helmut Heissenbüttel, Harald Hartung.]
Koebner, Thomas, ed. *Tendenzen der deutschen Gegenwartsliteratur*. Stuttgart: Kröner, 1984. [Includes essays by Hartmut Engelhardt, Dieter Mettler, Gerhart Pickerodt.]
Kreutzer, Leo, ed. *Über Jürgen Becker*. Frankfurt: Suhrkamp, 1972.
Krolow, Karl. "Die Lyrik in der Bundesrepublik seit 1945." In *Die Literatur Der Bundesrepublik Deutschland*, edited by Dieter Lattmann, pp. 347–533. Zurich: Kindler, 1973.
Leonhard, Kurt. *Moderne Lyrik: Monolog und Manifest*. Bremen: Schünemann, 1963.
Oelmann, Ute Maria. *Deutsche poetologische Lyrik nach 1945: Ingeborg Bachmann, Günter Eich, Paul Celan*. Stuttgart: Heinz, 1980.
Raulet, Gérard. "The Logic of Decomposition: German Poetry in the 1960's." *New German Critique* 21 (1980): 81–112.
Reich-Ranicki, Marcel, ed. *Frankfurter Anthologie 4*. Frankfurt: Insel, 1979. [Includes readings of poems by Mörike, Droste-Hülshoff, Trakl, Becker, Meckel, Kiwus.]
Rolleston, James. "Der Drang nach Synthese: Benn, Brecht und die Poetik der fünfziger Jahre." In *Die deutsche Lyrik, 1945–1975*, edited by Klaus Weissenberger. Düsseldorf: Bagel, 1981.
Schneider, Irmela. "Von der Epiphanie zur Momentaufnahme, Augenblicke in der Lyrik nach 1945." In *Augenblick und Zeitpunkt*, edited by Christian W. Thomsen and Hans Holländer, pp. 434–51. Darmstadt: Wissenschaftliche Buchgesellschaft, 1984.
Theobaldy, Jürgen, and Gustav Zürcher. *Veränderung der Lyrik: Über westdeutsche Gedichte seit 1965*. Munich: edition text + kritik, 1976.
Volckmann, Silvia. *Zeit der Kirschen? Das Naturbild in der deutschen Gegenwartslyrik: Jürgen Becker, Sarah Kirsch, Wolf Biermann, Hans Magnus Enzensberger*. Königstein: Forum Academicum, 1982.
Weissenberger, Klaus. "Die Voraussetzungen der Gegenwartslyrik." In *Die deutsche*

Lyrik, 1945–1975, edited by Klaus Weissenberger, pp. 9–22. Düsseldorf: Bagel, 1981.

Zeller, Michael. *Gedichte haben Zeit. Aufriss einer zeitgenössischen Poetik.* Stuttgart: Klett, 1982.

Gottfried Benn

Alter, Reinhard. *Gottfried Benn: The Artist and Politics.* Bern and Frankfurt: Lang, 1976.

Hillebrand, Bruno, ed. *Gottfried Benn.* Darmstadt: Wissenschaftliche Buchgesellschaft, 1979.

Hohendahl, Peter Uwe. "Gottfried Benns Poetik und die deutsche Lyriktheorie nach 1945." *Jahrbuch der Deutschen Schillergesellschaft* 24 (1980): 369–98.

Liewerscheidt, Dieter. *Gottfried Benns Lyrik.* Munich: Oldenbourg, 1980.

Lohner, Edgar. *Passion und Intellekt: die Lyrik Gottfried Benns.* Neuwied: Luchterhand, 1961.

Manyoni, Angelika. *Consistency of Phenotype: A Study of Gottfried Benn's Views on Lyric Poetry.* Bern and Frankfurt: Lang, 1983.

Meister, Ulrich. *Sprache und lyrisches Ich. Zur Phänomenologie des Dichterischen bei Gottfried Benn.* Berlin: Schmidt, 1983.

Rumold, Rainer. *Gottfried Benn und der Expressionismus: Provokation des Lesers; absolute Dichtung.* Königstein: Scriptor, 1982.

Schröder, Jürgen. *Gottfried Benn: Poesie und Sozialisation.* Stuttgart: Kohlhammer, 1978.

Willems, Gottfried. *Grossstadt-und Bewusstseinspoesie: Über Realismus in der modernen Lyrik, insbesondere im lyrischen Spätwerk Gottfried Benns und in der deutschen Lyrik seit 1965.* Tübingen: Niemeyer, 1981.

Paul Celan

Janz, Marlies. *Vom Engagement absoluter Poesie.* Königstein: Athenäum, 1984.

Krämer, Heinz M. *Eine Sprache des Leidens: Zur Lyrik von Paul Celan.* Munich: Kaiser, 1979.

Lyon, James K., ed. *Paul Celan: Studies in Twentieth Century Literature* 8 (1983).

Meinecke, Dietlind. *Wort und Name bei Paul Celan: zur Widerruflichkeit des Gedichts.* Bad Homburg: Gehlen, 1970.

———, ed. *Über Paul Celan.* Frankfurt: Suhrkamp, 1970.

Menninghaus, Winfried. *Paul Celan: Magie der Form.* Frankfurt: Suhrkamp, 1980.

Pretzer, Lielo Anne. *Geschichts- und sozialkritische Dimensionen in Paul Celans Werk.* Bonn: Bouvier, 1980.

Udoff, Alan. "On Poetic Dwelling: Situating Celan and the Holocaust." In *Argumentum E Silentio: ein internationales Paul Celan Symposium,* edited by Amy Colin. Berlin: De Gruyter, 1986.

Voswinckel, Klaus. *Paul Celan: Verweigerte Poetisierung der Welt.* Heidelberg: Stiehm, 1974.

Weissenberger, Klaus. *Zwischen Stein und Stern: Mystische Formgebung in der Dichtung von Else Lasker-Schüler, Nelly Sachs und Paul Celan.* Bern, Munich: Francke, 1976.

Selected Bibliography

Annette von Droste-Hülshoff

Brall, Arthur. *Vergangenheit und Vergänglichkeit: Zur Zeiterfahrung und Zeitdeutung im Werk Annettes von Droste-Hülshoff.* Marburg: Elwert, 1975.

Gössmann, Wilhelm. "Trunkenheit und Desillusion. Das poetische Ich der Droste." *Zeitschrift für deutsche Philologie* 101 (1982): 506–27.

Heselhaus, Clemens. *Annette von Droste-Hülshoff.* Düsseldorf: Bagel, 1971.

Mare, Margaret. *Annette von Droste-Hülshoff.* Lincoln: University of Nebraska Press, 1965.

Schneider, Ronald, *Realismus und Restauration: Untersuchungen zu Poetik und epischem Werk der Annette von Droste-Hülshoff.* Kronberg: Scriptor, 1976.

Joseph von Eichendorff

Adorno, Theodor W. "Zum Gedächtnis Eichendorffs." In *Noten zur Literatur,* 1: 105–45. Frankfurt: Suhrkamp, 1958.

Alewyn, Richard. "Eine Landschaft Eichendorffs" and "Eichendorffs Symbolismus." In *Probleme und Gestalten,* by Richard Alewyn, pp. 203–44. Frankfurt: Suhrkamp, 1982.

Möbus, Gerhard. *Der andere Eichendorff.* Osnabrück: Fromm, 1960.

Schultz, Hartwig. *Form als Inhalt: Vers- und Sinnstrukturen bei Joseph von Eichendorff und Annette von Droste-Hülshoff.* Bonn: Bouvier, 1981.

Thum, Reinhard H. "Cliché and Stereotype: An Examination of the Lyric Landscape in Eichendorff's Poetry." *Philological Quarterly* 62 (1983): 435–57.

Hans Magnus Enzensberger

Grimm, Reinhold. *Texturen: Essays und anderes zu Hans Magnus Enzensberger.* Bern and Frankfurt: Lang, 1984.

————, ed. *Hans Magnus Enzensberger.* Frankfurt: Suhrkamp, 1984.

Holthusen, Hans Egon. "Hans Magnus Enzensberger." In *Die deutsche Lyrik, 1945–1975,* edited by Klaus Weissenberger, pp. 331–43. Düsseldorf: Bagel, 1981.

————. "Utopie und Katastrophe: Der Lyriker Hans Magnus Enzensberger, 1957–78." In *Sartre in Stammheim,* by Hans Egon Holthusen, pp. 5–97. Stuttgart: Klett-Cotta, 1982.

Linder, Christian. "Der lange Sommer der Romantik: Über Hans Magnus Enzensberger." In *Die Träume der Wunschmaschine,* by Christian Linder, pp. 112–45. Hamburg: Rowohlt, 1981.

Sewell, William B. "Doppelgänger Motif and Two-voiced Poem in the Works of Hans Magnus Enzensberger." *German Quarterly* 52 (1979): 503–17.

Georg Heym

Mautz, Kurt. *Mythologie und Gesellschaft im Expressionismus: Die Dichtung Georg Heyms.* Frankfurt: Athenäum, 1961.

Rolleston, James. "The Expressionist Moment: Heym, Trakl and the Problem of the Modern." In *Studies in Twentieth Century Literature* 1 (1976): 65–90.

Salter, Ronald. *Georg Heyms Lyrik: Ein Vergleich von Wortkunst und Bildkunst.* Munich: Fink, 1972.

Selected Bibliography

Gottfried Keller

Kaiser, Gerhard. *Gottfried Keller: Das gedichtete Leben.* Frankfurt: Insel, 1981.
Neumann, Bernd. *Gottfried Keller: Eine Einführung in sein Werk.* Königstein: Athenäum, 1982.
Steinecke, Hartmut, ed. *Zu Gottfried Keller.* Stuttgart, Klett, 1984.

Conrad Ferdinand Meyer

Fährmann, Jürgen. "Bildwelt und symbolische Gestaltung in der Dichtung Conrad Ferdinand Meyers." Ph.D. diss., University of Freiburg, 1964.
Henel, Heinrich. *The Poetry of Conrad Ferdinand Meyer.* Madison: University of Wisconsin Press, 1954.
————. *Gedichte Conrad Ferdinand Meyers: Wege ihrer Vollendung.* Tübingen: Niemeyer, 1962.
Kittler, Friedrich A. *Der Traum und die Rede: Eine Analyse der Kommunikationssituation C. F. Meyers.* Bern: Francke, 1977.
Staiger, Emil. "Das Spätboot: Zu Conrad Ferdinand Meyers Lyrik." In *Die Kunst der Interpretation,* by Emil Staiger. Zurich: Atlantis, 1955.

Eduard Mörike

Barnouw, Dagmar. *Entzückte Anschauung: Sprache und Realität in der Lyrik Eduard Mörikes.* Munich: Fink, 1971.
Hart Nibbrig, Christiaan L. *Verlorene Unmittelbarkeit: Zeiterfahrung und Zeitgestaltung bei Eduard Mörike.* Bonn: Bouvier, 1973.
Rolleston, James. "Time Structures: A Reading of Poems by Mörike, Rilke and Benn." *German Quarterly* 53 (1980): 403–17.
Storz, Gerhard. *Eduard Mörike.* Stuttgart: Klett-Cotta, 1967.
Strack, Friedrich. "Wehmütige Liebeserwartung in Mörikes früher Lyrik: Eine Analyse des Gedichts "Im Frühling.' " In *Gedichte und Interpretationen* 4, edited by Günter Häntzschel, pp. 82–92. Stuttgart: Reclam, 1983.
von Graevenitz, Gerhart. *Eduard Mörike: Die Kunst der Sünde. Zur Geschichte des literarischen Individuums.* Tübingen: Niemeyer, 1978.
von Heydebrand, Renate. *Eduard Mörikes Gedichtwerk.* Stuttgart: Metzler, 1972.

Rainer Maria Rilke

Baron, Frank; Ernst S. Dick; and Warren R. Maurer, eds. *Rilke: The Alchemy of Alienation.* Lawrence: Regents Press of Kansas, 1980. [Includes essays by Hans Egon Holthusen, Stephen Spender, Walter H. Sokel.]
Fülleborn, Ulrich, and Manfred Engel, eds. *Rilkes "Duineser Elegien"* 2. Frankfurt: Suhrkamp, 1982. [Includes essays by Erich Heller, Jacob Steiner, Anthony Stephens.]
Hamburger, Käte, ed. *Rilke in neuer Sicht.* Stuttgart: Kohlhammer, 1971. [Includes essays by Käte Hamburger, Beda Allemann, Jacob Steiner.]
Schwarz, Egon, ed. *Zu Rainer Maria Rilke.* Stuttgart: Klett, 1983. [Includes essays by Ulrich Fülleborn, Richard Jayne, David Wellbery.]

Theodor Storm

Lohmeier, Dieter. "Das Erlebnisgedicht bei Theodor Storm." *Schriften der Theodor—Storm—Gesellschaft* 30 (1981): 9–26.
Müller, Harro. *Theodor Storms Lyrik.* Bonn: Bouvier, 1975.
Sengle, Friedrich. "Storms Lyrische Eigenleistung. Abgrenzung von anderen grossen

Lyrikern des 19. Jahrhunderts." *Schriften der Theodor—Storm—Gesellschaft* 28 (1979): 9–33.

Wehner, Walter. "Entpolitisierung der Lyrik. Subjektivierung: Storm, Keller, Fontane." In *Einführung in die deutsche Literatur des 19. Jahrunderts,* edited by Josef Jansen, pp. 132–52. Opladen: Westdeutscher Verlag, 1984.

Georg Trakl

Calbert, Joseph P. *Dimensions of Style and Meaning in the Language of Trakl and Rilke.* Tübingen: Niemeyer, 1974.

Detsch, Richard. *Georg Trakl's Poetry: Toward a Union of Opposites.* University Park: Pennsylvania State University Press, 1983.

Esselborn, Hans. *Georg Trakl: Die Krise der Erlebnislyrik.* Cologne, Vienna: Böhlau, 1981.

Heidegger, Martin. "Language in the Poem: A Discussion on Georg Trakl's Poetic Work." In *On the Way to Language,* translated by Peter D. Hertz, pp. 159–98. New York: Harper and Row, 1971.

Killy, Walther. *Über Georg Trakl.* Göttingen: Vandenhoeck und Ruprecht, 1960.

Sharp, Francis M. *The Poet's Madness: A Reading of Georg Trakl.* Ithaca and London: Cornell University Press, 1981.

Strelka, Joseph P., ed. *Internationales Georg Trakl—Symposium, Albany, N.Y.* Bern and Frankfurt: Lang, 1984. [Includes essays by Christoph Eykman, James K. Lyon, Ulrike Rainer, Heinz Wetzel.]

239

INDEX

Index

James Rolleston is Associate Professor of German and director of graduate studies in the Literature Program at Duke University. He has also taught at Yale University. Dr. Rolleston received the M.A. degree from the University of Minnesota (1962) and the Ph.D. from Yale University (1968). In addition to numerous articles, he has published the books Rilke in Transition *(1970) and* Kafka's Narrative Theater *(1974).*

The manuscript was edited by Lois Krieger. The book was designed by Don Ross. The typeface for the text is Sabon. The display type is Quorum Bold and Sabon.

The book is printed on 55-lb. Glatfelter natural text paper and is bound in Holliston Mills' Roxite linen over .88 binder's board.

Manufactured in the United States of America.